A HISTORY OF
SCOTLAND

MACMILLAN ESSENTIAL HISTORIES

General Editor: Jeremy Black

This series of compact, readable and informative national histories is designed to appeal to anyone wishing to gain a broad understanding of a country's history.

Published

A History of the Low Countries (3rd edn) *Paul Arblaster*
A History of Italy *Claudia Baldoli*
A History of Russia *Roger Bartlett*
A History of Spain (2nd edn) *Simon Barton*
A History of the British Isles (4th edn) *Jeremy Black*
A History of France *Joseph Bergin*
A History of Israel *Ahron Bregman*
A History of Ireland (2nd edn) *Mike Cronin & Liam O'Callaghan*
A History of Greece *Nicholas Doumanis*
A History of the Pacific Islands (2nd edn) *Steven Roger Fischer*
A History of Korea (2nd edn) *Kyung Moon Hwang*
A History of the United States (5th edn) *Philip Jenkins*
A History of Denmark (3rd edn) *Knud J. V. Jespersen*
A History of the Baltic States *Andres Kasekamp*
A History of Scotland *Allan I. Macinnes*
A History of Southern Africa *Alois S. Mlambo and Neil Parsons*
A History of Australia *Mark Peel and Christina Twomey*
A History of Poland (2nd edn) *Anita J. Prazmowska*
A History of India (2nd edn) *Peter Robb*
A History of China (3rd edn) *J. A. G. Roberts*
A History of Germany *Peter Wende*

A HISTORY OF SCOTLAND

Allan I. Macinnes

First published 2019 by
RED GLOBE PRESS

Red Globe Press in the UK is an imprint of Springer Nature Limited, registered
in England, company number 785998, of 4 Crinan Street, London, N1 9XW.

Red Globe Press® is a registered trademark in the United States, the
United Kingdom, Europe and other countries.

ISBN 978–0–333–67148–1 hardback
ISBN 978–0–333–67149–8 paperback

This book is printed on paper suitable for recycling and made from fully
managed and sustained forest sources. Logging, pulping and manufacturing
processes are expected to conform to the environmental regulations of the
country of origin.

A catalogue record for this book is available from the British Library.

A catalog record for this book is available from the Library of Congress.

Laura, Ella, Ingrid og Iselin

Contents

Acknowledgements

This book is the distillation of my continuous teaching over four decades of Scottish history in its British, European and imperial contexts. Lecturing and tutoring successively at the Universities of Glasgow, Aberdeen and Strathclyde were interspersed by visiting stints at the University of Prince Edward Island, the European University at St Petersburg, the University of Chicago and the École des Hautes Études en Sciences Sociales in Paris. Learning is very much a two-way street. I benefited immensely from the questions raised, topics presented and theories discussed by my students.

Writing a history of Scotland requires major decisions about commissions and omissions of events, concepts, people and places. I was helped greatly in this complex task, particularly for the early medieval and contemporary periods, by Sally Foster, Alasdair Ross, Frederik Pedersen, Catriona Macdonald, Ewen Cameron, Richard Finlay and George Peden. Ali Cathcart, John Young, Thomas Riis, Art Williamson, Tricia Barton, Karen Jillings, Kieran German, Kirsteen Mackenzie, Neil McIntyre and Stephen Mullan made sure I was up to speed with developments in the interim periods. All errors are my sole responsibility. I have also been helped through challenging conversations with friends and family whose views have varied from the inquisitive and the informed to the unorthodox and the quixotic: so thanks to Emsley Nimmo, Linda Fryer, Mhairi Livingstone, Liam Hamilton, Jim McEwen, Lynn Mackay, Julie Christie, Nina Ashby, Norman MacLeod and Dougie Macinnes.

I should like to thank my commissioning editor, Rachel Bridgewater, for forbearance above and beyond the call of duty, Jenny Johnston for her meticulous mapping and my wife, Tine Wanning, for preparing the final manuscript and index. My main motivation in writing this book was to explain Scotland's history to the four Danish girls to whom this work is dedicated and who call me grandfather; probably the greatest honour of my life.

Scottish districts c.1266

Strathnaver

Lewis

Caithness

Sutherland

Harris

Ross

Strathglass

Strathbogie

Strathavon

Buchan

Uist

The Aird

Strathdon

Garioch

Raasay

Skye

Strathspey

Deeside

Stratherrick

Mar

Barra

Arran

Lochaber Badenoch

Atholl

Angus

Breadalbane

Gowrie

Lorn   Strathearn

Trossachs

Fife

Lennox Menteith

Cowal

Dunbar

Knapdale

Islay

Strathgryfe

Lauderdale

Kintyre

Cunningham

Kyle

Arran

Eskdale

Carrick

Liddesdale

Nithsdale Annandale

Galloway

Isle of
Man

0   50 km

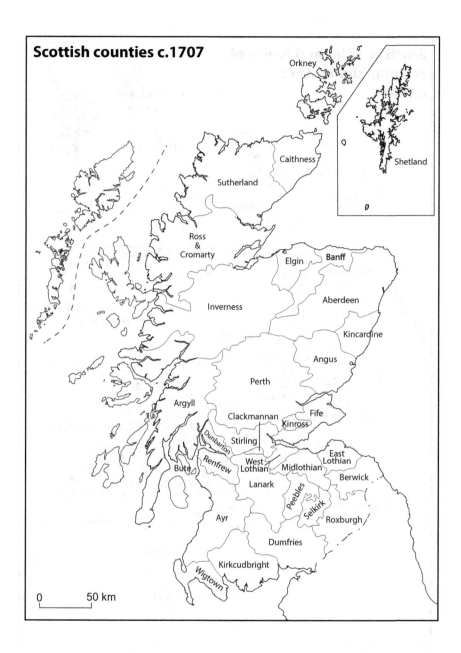

Scottish counties c.1707

Orkney

Shetland

Caithness

Sutherland

Ross & Cromarty

Elgin Banff

Inverness

Aberdeen

Kincardine

Angus

Perth

Argyll

Fife

Clackmannan
Kinross

Dunbarton

Stirling

East Lothian

Renfrew
West Lothian Midlothian

Bute

Berwick

Lanark

Peebles

Selkirk

Ayr

Roxburgh

Dumfries

Kirkcudbright

Wigtown

0   50 km

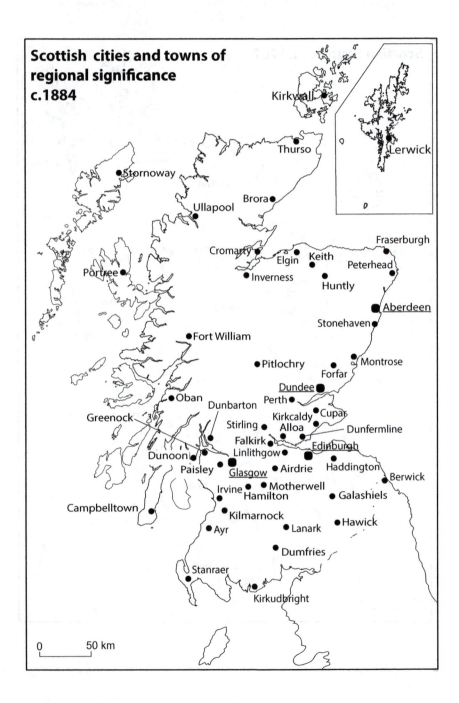

Scottish cities and towns of regional significance c.1884

Kirkwall

Lerwick

Thurso

Stornoway

Brora

Ullapool

Cromarty
Elgin
Keith
Fraserburgh
Peterhead

Portree

Inverness

Huntly

Aberdeen

Stonehaven

Fort William

Pitlochry

Montrose

Forfar

Oban
Dunbarton
Perth
Dundee

Greenock

Stirling
Kirkcaldy
Cupar
Alloa
Dunfermline

Falkirk
Dunoon
Linlithgow
Edinburgh

Paisley
Glasgow
Airdrie
Haddington

Irvine
Motherwell
Hamilton
Berwick

Campbelltown
Galashiels

Kilmarnock
Ayr
Lanark
Hawick

Dumfries

Stanraer

Kirkudbright

0   50 km

Scottish council and referendum districts 1997, 2014 and 2016

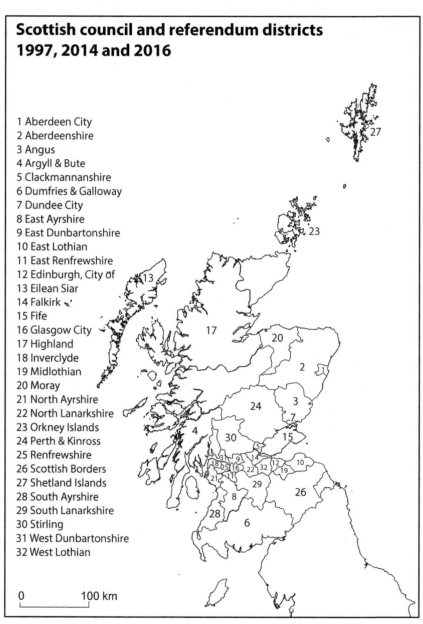

1 Aberdeen City
2 Aberdeenshire
3 Angus
4 Argyll & Bute
5 Clackmannanshire
6 Dumfries & Galloway
7 Dundee City
8 East Ayrshire
9 East Dunbartonshire
10 East Lothian
11 East Renfrewshire
12 Edinburgh, City of
13 Eilean Siar
14 Falkirk
15 Fife
16 Glasgow City
17 Highland
18 Inverclyde
19 Midlothian
20 Moray
21 North Ayrshire
22 North Lanarkshire
23 Orkney Islands
24 Perth & Kinross
25 Renfrewshire
26 Scottish Borders
27 Shetland Islands
28 South Ayrshire
29 South Lanarkshire
30 Stirling
31 West Dunbartonshire
32 West Lothian

0   100 km

Adapted from Local Authority Map of Scotland (www.gov.scot/Resource/Doc/933/0009286.pdf) and reproduced under open licence (www.nationalarchives.gov.uk/doc/open-government-licence/version/3)

1 Shaping a Mongrel Nation, 832–1214

According to legend, sometime in 832 at Athelstaneford, the Picts under their king, Aengus II, were preparing to fight a force of Angles from Northumbria, when the ominous formation of white clouds against a blue sky signified the Cross of St Andrew. With this heavenly blessing, the Picts were inspired to secure victory in the contested territories of the Lothians. Eleven years later, the Picts, who held east-central and northern districts over the Firth of Forth, were instrumental in promoting union with the Gaels of the western and central Highlands in the kingdom of Alba. This was a Celtic union of ancient migrant peoples, confederated under warlords, with more recent incomers who had established themselves in Argyll by the outset of the sixth century in the kingdom of Dalriada. Although they spoke different Celtic languages, the Picts and the Gaels shared a common Celtic Christianity that was spread by holy men from Dalriada. Christianity was also influenced by the legacy of the Roman occupation of Britain, which lasted until the outset of the fifth century but rarely advanced beyond the Firths of Forth and Clyde. The Britons, as the Celts most closely associated with the Romans, shared a similar if not the same language as the Picts that has been transmitted as Cumbric or Welsh. The Romano-British Church had already established a religious presence among the Britons through the influence of holy men in Galloway at the end of the fourth century, whose mission had reached Glasgow by the mid-sixth century. As part of the accord between the Romano-British and the Celtic Churches, some reputed relics of St Andrew, one of the original disciples of Jesus Christ who travelled great distances to spread the Christian message before his crucifixion on a cross at Paras in Greece in AD 60, had arrived in Kilrymont in Fife via Hexham in Northumbria in the mid-eighth century. Kilrymont became known as St Andrews.

St Andrew, associated with hospitality, instinctive humanity and a natural affinity to bring people together, was an apposite patron saint for shaping kindreds of migratory peoples into a mongrel nation. The Angles who had moved into Northumbria were then beginning to spread into Lothians and Borders, a migration that was checked in the eleventh century, without eradicating the

Anglo-Saxon (English) tongue. Incursions by Norse-speaking Vikings from the close of the eighth century in the Northern Isles of Orkney and Shetland and their subsequent settlement from the Hebrides to Galloway at the expense of the Picts, Gaels and Britons proved more problematic. As Alba was transformed into the kingdom of Scots in the eleventh century, the hybrid presence of the Norse-Gael on the western seaboard remained distinctive well into the thirteenth century. A new migratory element from the twelfth century was the arrival of Normans (and their French, Breton and Flemish associates) mainly through England. Brought in to consolidate and enhance the territorial influence of successive kings of Scots, the Anglo-Normans certainly facilitated the expansion of the kingdom to the north and to the west. But their continuing links to England made Scotland vulnerable to being taken over by its better resourced southern neighbour.

THE MAKING OF ALBA

The Picts have left no written record of substance. They were certainly noticed by the Romans who had penetrated the region they termed Caledonia as far north as Moray before they consolidated behind Hadrian's Wall, the fortified line between the rivers Solway and Tyne constructed in AD 121. By the time the Romans established the Antonine Wall between the Firths of Clyde and Forth in AD 139, they had named the tattooed people of both sexes whom they encountered in Caledonia as Picts. By the outset of the third century, the Romans had abandoned incursions into Caledonia though the Picts had continued to attack them until they finally withdrew from Hadrian's Wall at the end of the fourth century. The Gaels adopted the alternative name of Cruithne for the Picts who, by 600, seemed to have coalesced around an overking based north of the Mounth (the Grampian massif) in the kingdom of Fortriu. Although four of the seven reputed Pictish provinces were located south of the Mounth, that overkings were based north of the Mounth is supported by the initial missions of Columba from Iona and Moluag from Lismore to convert the Picts around Inverness and in Moray prior to 600.[1] There is also impressive archaeological evidence for Pictish centres of religious and secular power along the north-east coast from the monastery at Portmahomack in Easter Ross to the promontory fort at Burghead in Moray. Despite its coastal location, there is a notable lack of shipping either for war or for trade inscribed on monumental stones in Pictland.

Sculpted scenes of hunting on horseback, of the mobilising of hosts of fighting men and of actual battles suggest a society geared to war and a redistributive rather than a commercial economy, a situation supported by the lack of coins produced by the Picts, the Britons and the Gaels. The enigmatic symbols of abstract art represented on the monumental stones may be connected to a continuous practice of tattooing among the Picts. The social elite – from local warlords as provincial leaders to Pictish overkings – offered protection, hospitality and booty. In return, they expected allegiance, tributes and rents paid in kind (that is, livestock, grain and other consumables) and flexible military and labour services. Pictish fortifications no longer depended on the defensive round, thick-walled towers known as brochs which littered the northern and western coasts even before the arrival of the Romans. But the presence of brochs certainly added prestige to territories of warlords which continued as the Picts gave way to the Gaels in the West Highlands and Islands from the sixth century and to the Vikings in the Northern Isles from the eighth century.

A key factor in the diminishing territorial influence of the Picts was that, in a society geared to war, their succession was matrilineal; it passed through the female not the male line to the most able leader. Thus a warlord from another kindred or even migratory people, who married the sister or daughter of a Pictish warlord, made possible the succession of his male offspring through the Pictish mother. Matrilineal succession, rather than the vanquishing of the Picts by the Gaels, appears to have facilitated Kenneth MacAlpin, from the royal house of Dalriada, becoming king of the Picts in the mid-ninth century. The Gaels had first appeared on the western seaboard in the guise of pirates from Ireland who were designated as Scots for their predatory raiding on Roman Britain, activities which continued from Galloway to the Northern Isles. Gaelic settlements in Argyll were well underway during the fifth century. By AD 500, Fergus MacErc, the Gaelic king of Dalriada, transferred his kingdom from Ireland to Argyll and, in the process, laid claim to being the first king of Scots. Succession among the Gaels was patrilineal, passing through the male line usually to brothers, uncles or cousins not directly to sons. The ceremonial centre for the kingship of Dalriada was initially at Dunadd, but after the arrival of Columba in Iona, he began ordaining the kings there from 574.

Although Irish links were maintained throughout the seventh century, the Gaels of Dalriada were increasingly looking north, east and south to expand into the territories of the Picts and, to a lesser extent, the Britons. Subsequent expansion from Argyll was at the expense of the Picts to the north-west and on through Skye to the Western Isles. Raiding for booty and slaves rather than settling seemingly prevailed in the incursions of the Gaels into the Northern Isles. A Gaelic presence at the expense of the Britons was established in the Lennox around Loch Lomond, in Galloway and the Isle of Man, albeit in these latter two locations this presence was more likely the result of direct migration from Ireland rather than Argyll. Notwithstanding intermittent warfare between the Gaels, Picts and Britons, four of the six kings of Dalriada between 768 and 843 became kings of Fortriu.

A less belligerent and more pervasive incursion into Pictland was made by the Irish-inspired Celtic Church, which continuously pushed conversions from Iona and Lismore. Through the biography of St Adamnan, who served as abbot of Iona in the later seventh century, Columba appears the paramount influence as prophet and healer. Iona, in turn, became a centre of pilgrimage for Britons, Picts and Angles as well as the Gaels. Columba was the inspiration for religious works of art, such as the free-standing St Oran's and St John's Crosses, and most notably the *Book of Kells*, a work which commenced on Iona in the late eighth century. It was moved to Ireland for completion in the ninth century at Kells Abbey in County Meath, following Viking incursions in the Hebrides. Yet Moluag from Lismore had considerably more evangelising influence in the Pictish north-east. The conversion of the Picts was actually instigated by Ninian from Whithorn and Mungo from Glasgow. Later missions also came from Northumbria with Cuthbert and Boniface to the fore. No less significant in the work of conversion were inspirational women. Particularly prominent were the followers of St Brigid of Kildare in Ireland, who came to Scotland in the sixth century. Apparently 15 female saints with the name Brigid or Bride are commemorated in Scottish place names, in which context their influence was on a par with that of Columba and greater than that of Moluag.

The Celtic Church which developed in Ireland had distinctive religious observances that were spread through its evangelising missions from Dalriada into Pictland and Cumbria and on to Northumbria. The Romano-British Church had been revitalised through St Augustine's mission from Rome to the Anglo-Saxons of England in the late sixth century. Divergence over the dating of Easter, with the Celtic Church adhering to a more conservative and less scientific format, was not resolved by the Synod of Whitby in 663 that favoured the Romano-British. While this Synod can be held to have checked the expansion of the Celtic Church into the territory of the Angles, there continued to be significant interaction and co-operation in terms of illuminated works of art, carved stone monuments and pilgrimages between Gaels, Picts, Briton and Angles.

The penetration of the Celtic Church among the Britons of Strathclyde in the tenth and eleventh centuries is evident from the free-standing Christian crosses at Hamilton on the upper reaches and at Govan on the lower reaches of the River Clyde. But Govan also houses a sarcophagus or stone shrine that is derived from Pictish and Anglian sources and distinctive hogback tombstones from the same timeline that suggest a further Anglian influence. Hogbacks are also found in the Lennox at Luss on Loch Lomond, at Brechin in Angus, at Meigle in Strathmore and on the island of Inchcolm in Fife. They certainly indicate a continuing connection with Britons and Angles in the north of England at a time of Viking incursions. But it is difficult to attribute them to Scandinavian inspiration. Hogback tombstones do not feature significantly or at all in early medieval Scandinavia.

Both the Romano-British and the Celtic Churches had monasteries and administrative districts or dioceses under the control of bishops. Such bishoprics served to spread and consolidate the faith while monasteries promoted spiritual depth. Moluag had established the bishopric of Aberdeen at Mortlach in Strathbogie. Columba had also endorsed a bishopric for the Isles at Iona. Monastic practice, however, could differ between the Romano-British and the Celtic Churches. The latter had a tradition of retreats for hermits, as evident from the beehive huts on the Garvellach Islands in Argyll, a tradition based on the early Christian practice of retreat into the Egyptian and Syrian deserts. Romano-British monasteries tended to be led by abbots, which was not necessarily the case for all Celtic monasteries, albeit lay abbots served as hereditary protectors of some foundations from the outset of the ninth century, particularly after the incursions of Vikings.

The monastic foundations of the Culdees tended to be led by a spiritual elite. The Culdees were notably prominent among the Picts from St Andrews in Fife to Monymusk in the Garioch. Their spiritual elite, who abstained from worldly comforts and pleasures in pursuit of an ascetic religious life, certainly drew on the hermetic tradition which had crossed from Ireland to Scotland before Columba established himself on Iona. But the main body of Culdees, who supported the spiritual elite both piously and materially, were influenced by another early Christian practice of sustaining the faith through communal living. Culdees certainly included married clergy and may have included single women as well as single men. In all events, their religious communities afforded a spiritual dynamic to the Celtic Church that was sustained well into the eleventh century.

SCANDINAVIANS, VIKINGS AND NORSE-GAELS

Having announced their arrival by sacking the Holy Isle of Lindisfarne in 793, the Vikings went on to ravage the Hebrides. Iona, initially sacked in 795, faced further predatory raids in 802 and 806 that persuaded the majority of monks to remove to Kells in Ireland by 807. Not only for the clergy, but for all the laity, the incursions of the Vikings were greeted with shock and awe.

Viking pillaging and skirmishes with the indigenous peoples around the coasts of Scotland and into the firths of Clyde, Moray, Tay and Fife lasted until the 1030s. The Vikings were not irresistible, however, particularly where troops on horseback could be rushed to head off an invasion.

Nevertheless, the Viking terror persisted due to technologically advanced shipping, ruthless human trafficking and intensely ferocious raiding. The Vikings perfected the development of sailing ships. Clinker built with overlapping planks and with reinforced keels to carry sails that could tack against the wind, Viking ships were resilient and powerful enough to cross open and dangerous waters and shallow enough to be rowed up rivers and carried over headlands. Longships for warriors were complemented by broader bottomed boats for carrying merchandise, slaves and other market-able commodities. Human trafficking by Vikings involved taking hostages either for ransom or for selling on as slaves, usually to Arab traders in the Mediterranean. Carvings on slate by Celtic monks on Inchmarnock, an island to the west of Bute, provides graphic evidence of Viking incursions but not the manner in which the vanguard of their warriors frequently went berserk. Their consumption of vast quantities of alcohol, spiced with bog myrtle and supplemented by hallucinogenic or 'magic' mushrooms, induced a trance in which they seemed impervious to pain.

Like the Scots who had raided Roman Britain from Ireland prior to settling in Dalriada, the Vikings had initially arrived as pirates. But they operated and, indeed, disrupted on a far grander scale. As evident from the accumulation and use of coinage in commodity exchange, they were much more engaged as commercial traders than the Gaels, the Britons or the Picts. Their most dense area of settlement in Scotland was in the Northern Isles where they displaced the Picts. That this was not accomplished peaceably was evident from their sacking of St Ninians Isle in Shetland and their imposition of their longhouses over as well as alongside Pictish settlements and churches at Sumburgh (Jarlshof) on the Shetland Mainland and in Orkney at Langskaill in Westray and on the Brough of Birsay. Hordes of silver jewellery and coins mark the expansion of Viking activity from the Northern Isles to Caithness and on to Easter Ross, Tayside and the Lothians on the eastern seaboard and from the Hebrides to Argyll on into the Clyde estuary and on to the Isle of Man on the western seaboard. These hordes suggest insecurity of settlement as well as impressive Viking trading networks. The Vikings in association with the Gaels displaced the Picts in the Small Isles, Skye and the Outer Hebrides and the Britons in Galloway and Man. Jewellery, weaponry and domestic utensils found in pre-Christian or pagan graves (as far west as St Kilda) testify not only to the impressive material wealth accumulated by the Vikings from the late eighth to the early tenth century, but also to their intermingling with the indigenous local peoples, especially the Gaels on the western seaboard. Their sophisticated and highly decorative art work in metal, leather and stone featured gripping or interlocking animals that readily melded in with contemporaneous Celtic design.

In contrast to Orkney, there have been relatively few silver hoards and Viking graves found in Shetland. On the one hand, this testifies to the security of Viking settlement, but on the other to limited commercial opportunities. This latter point is particularly important in relation to the phases of permanent settlement evident from place names in Shetland. Primary settlements tended to be coastal with ready access to a beach or sheltered harbour with extensive fertile land for arable and pastoral farming. Secondary settlements developed from the primary sites in less accessible coastal areas or inland in what had originally been hill-grazing land. They had good arable land and extensive grazings for livestock but their access to beaches or sheltered harbours for fishing was restricted. The tertiary settlements were on marginal land and subsequently reverted back to shielings for the summer grazing of animals. When established as permanent settlements they were not agriculturally viable in their own right. Alternative work and subsistence were provided through the quarrying of soapstone. However, the most feasible reason for extensive tertiary settlement was for the location of labour for the primary and secondary settlements, particularly if these latter settlements were worked for a warrior class frequently absent on raids or trading with menaces.

The Vikings were not just merchants of menace. They were global adventurers. The Vikings from Scandinavia were by no means a coherent ethnic group nor did they necessarily have distinctive Norwegian, Danish or Swedish spheres of influence. Initial raids probably emanated from the Northern Isles of Orkney and Shetland which, like the Faroes, had come under Viking control in the course of the eighth century. Colonising the Northern Isles at the expense of the Picts was undoubtedly linked to seasonal and eventually permanent migration from Norway, as was settlement in the Western Isles, the Isle of Man and Ireland that followed on from a marked increase in raiding during the 830s. After their seizure of Dublin in 841, the Vikings forged a kingdom that stretched from Ireland to the eastern seaboard of England, which came under sustained pressure in 865 from Danes who came to centre their operations on York. This Viking kingdom of Dublin–York was not readily governed from either Norway or Denmark nor indeed was the subkingdom of Man and the Western Isles that later emerged in the eleventh century. The Northern Isles remained under a *jarl* or earl of Orkney appointed by and beholden to the kings of Norway.

Although Caithness, Argyll and the Western Isles were acquired in the course of the tenth century, the Vikings had no clear design to take over Scotland. By late eleventh century, the kings of Norway exercised a more assertive presence on Viking settlements in Scotland and Ireland. The autonomy of the Viking kingdom of Dublin–York was terminated by Norwegian action to the west no less than by Danish and Anglo-Saxon exertions to the east. Resurgent Irish warlords also posed a renewed threat as did the internal tensions that led to the creation of separate dependent kingdoms based on Man and the Western Isles and on Galloway. These dependent kingdoms were taking on a more distinct Norse-Gaelic identity in which Gaelic not Norse was becoming the language of the elite as well as the common people. In part, this Gaelic emphasis was actually assisted by the spread of Christianity from the centre of Scandinavian pilgrimage at Trondheim (Nidaros), which revitalised the Celtic Church Vikings in Man and the Western Isles. In marked contrast, the Northern Isles remained securely Norse. The diocese of the Isles, like that of Orkney, came under the spiritual direction of Nidaros and, indeed, remained so until the late fifteenth century.

The engagement of the Norse-Gael with the kingdom of Dublin–York as with Scandinavia had also led to the first significant out movement of peoples from Scotland as active colonisers, not just slaves, to Iceland in the late ninth century and, subsequently, in the seizure and settlement of the Cotentin peninsula which was wrested from the Celtic kingdom of Brittany by the outset of the tenth. The Cotentin peninsula and the territories around Rouen on the Atlantic coast of France duly became the duchy of Normandy, held nominally of the French Crown, from where the Norman Conquest of England was launched in 1066. In the interim, resurgent Irish warlords offered regular seasonal employment to the Norse-Gaels as mercenaries exacting booty and tributes – employment which ensured the persistence of a warrior class among the Norse-Gaels no less than the Vikings of the Northern Isles and perpetuated the use of the galley or *birlinn* throughout the Middle Ages.

A UNITED KINGDOM?

Viking association tended to enhance rather than diminish the territorial ambitions of the kings of Alba. The royal house of Fortriu was all but wiped out by the Vikings in 839. The resultant succession crisis allowed Kenneth MacAlpin to become a contender for the Pictish kingship. His triumph over three other warring factions was not complete by 843 and his kingship took another five years to consolidate. By 849, Scone in Strathtay had become his administrative centre, which not only transferred governance from Dalriada, but also moved the focus of Pictish power from north to south of the Mounth. A fortified house or palace at Scone was replicated at Forteviot in Strathearn, which marked a more open and less defensive style of kingship than that associated with the former hill or promontory forts. Kenneth, who raided Northumbria six times in the decade before he died peaceably at Forteviot in 858, also appears to have brought the Stone of Destiny, the celebrated inauguration stone for the kings of Dalriada, to Scone. The administrative centre for the Celtic Church was relocated from Iona to Dunkeld. Notwithstanding this political and religious shift away from Dalriada, the Pictish language was losing out to the pervasive penetration of Gaelic in terms of both governance and settlement and can be deemed defunct by the end of the tenth century.

Although Kenneth did not actually inaugurate the united kingdom of Alba, the accession of this Gaelic warlord to the kingship of the Picts laid its dynastic foundations. Kenneth was to be succeeded by two sons and two grandsons as king of the Picts. One son, Constantine I, commenced the reduction of Strathclyde to a client kingdom in 872 and one grandson, Donald II, appears to be the first king of Alba, being designated so at his death in 900. In the interim, the kingdom of Alba in east-central Scotland was consolidated by subsequent Viking coastal raids in the north-east, such as their assault in 890 on the Pictish fortress at Dunottar in the Mearns. Twenty years earlier, the prolonged siege of Dumbarton Rock for almost four months by a large Viking fleet from Dublin weakened the territorial influence of the British kingdom of Strathclyde from the Firth of Clyde to Galloway and the Solway Firth. Indeed, this kingdom was effectively separated with the detachment of Galloway and the land south of the Solway, leaving Strathclyde running from the Firth of Clyde to the northern shores of the Solway. At the same time, the kingdom of Alba set about absorbing the Lennox district around Loch Lomond and the Trossachs. But in shifting their political centre from Dumbarton to Govan, the Britons signified their resistance to Strathclyde becoming a satellite kingdom of Alba. Notwithstanding continuing threats from Vikings, they expanded east from Strathclyde into Annandale, Tweeddale and Teviotdale and recovered territory south of the Solway in the course of the tenth century. The territorial acquisitiveness of the Britons was reflected in their reconstitution of their kingdom of Strathclyde into that of Cumbria.

The actual merger of the kingdoms of Dalriada and Fortriu, the union of the Picts and Gaels on terms of equality in the kingdom of Alba, was the achievement of Constantine II, grandson of Kenneth and cousin of Donald II. From the outset of his reign in 900, Constantine II had fought against incursions on Alba from the Viking kingdom of Dublin–York. Both Alba and the

Viking kingdom had to contend with the expanding territorial influence of the Anglo-Saxon kings. Edward the Elder claimed and was conceded the status of overlord by the kings of Alba, Cumbria and Dublin–York in 920. This was essentially a concession of political expediency not a commitment to provide tributes or military service or to cede control of the royal succession in Alba. This concession was repeated for the benefit of Edward's son and successor Athelstan seven years later. By 934, Athelstan felt it necessary to punish Constantine's raiding in the Lothians by invading Alba by land and sea, pushing up as far as Dunottar. Three years later, Constantine in alliance with the kingdoms of Cumbria and Dublin–York mounted a counter-invasion to push the boundaries of Alba southwards and exploit the increasing vulnerability of Northumbria and Cumbria south of the Solway to Viking incursions. He was emphatically defeated by Athelstan at Brunanburh in Annandale and obliged to recognise the futility of pursuing military adventures beyond the Lothians. Constantine's reign of 43 years, which actually ensured the vitality of the kingdom of Alba, ended not with his violent death, but by his own volition. He retired to join the Culdee community in St Andrews in 943.

Two years later, his nephew, Malcolm I, secured Cumbria south of the Solway through an alliance with the Danes. Internal warfare in the Mearns and Moray respectively occasioned his death in 956. Political stability within Alba was restored by Kenneth II, a younger son of Malcolm I. Nevertheless his 24-year reign ended in internal disharmony in 995. Kenneth III was killed in battle at Monzievaird in Strathearn in 1005 by his successor Malcolm II. The new king ranks with Kenneth MacAlpin and Constantine II, as a powerful dynastic ruler. The kings of Alba did not abandon claims on the Lothians, Northumbria and Cumbria. They exploited the threat to the Anglo-Saxon kingdom as well as Dublin–York by renewed Viking invasions, mainly from Denmark in the later tenth century, by which time Edinburgh was securely annexed to Alba. It was on Malcolm II's watch that the Northumbrians were defeated at Carham on the River Tweed near Kelso in 1018.

This victory demarcated the eastern Borders between Scotland and England. Malcolm II also stepped up his endeavours to incorporate Cumbria as a client kingdom of Alba, which was becoming known by the Angles in Lothian and Northumbria as the kingdom of the Scots. The designation Scotland, originally applied to Dalriada and then to Alba by the Anglo-Saxons, was also taken up by the Vikings. The formal ceding of the Lothians to Alba after Carham was done by Cnut, then King of Denmark–Norway as well as England, who obliged Malcom to recognise him as overlord when he invaded Alba in 1031 after stirring up trouble in Cumbria, to the south of the Solway Firth and in Galloway where there was now a substantive Viking as well as

Gaelic presence. Cnut also supported the ambitious ruler of Moray, Macbeth. The Britons were not reconciled to Malcolm's installation of his grandson Duncan, his designated heir or *tainistear*, as ruler of Cumbria after the battle of Carham. The 16-year reign of Malcolm II, which was marred by feuding within the royal house, ended violently in 1034 when he was assassinated at Glamis in Angus.

In order to secure the accession of his grandson Duncan, Malcolm II had revived Pictish rules of succession, last used in 878. However, the Gaelic practice of favouring the most able candidate from within the royal line was exploited by Macbeth, whose kindred were associated with the territorial magnates from Lorn in Argyll who, as mormaers of Moray, acted as military governors and dispensed justice; a mormaer was roughly equivalent to the Anglo-Saxon earl or the Viking *jarl*. Duncan I initially sought to consolidate his rule in Cumbria and the Lothians, Gaelic penetrations south of the Forth, not getting much further than West Lothian. After an abortive raid on Northumbria which was rebuffed at Durham in 1039, Duncan marched north the following year to confront Macbeth. At Pitgarvey, near Elgin, he was killed fighting against the combined forces of Macbeth and Thorfinn, the *Jarl* of Orkney, who was also a grandson of Malcolm II.

Macbeth was duly crowned king of Alba at Scone in 1040. His 17-year reign was later turned into a historical travesty by the great English dramatist William Shakespeare. Macbeth, a purposeful and relatively successful monarch by the homicidal standards of the kingdom of Alba, was intent on consolidation north and south of the Mounth. Having accomplished this task during 1049, he departed for Rome where he celebrated Easter in the following year. On his return to Scotland, Macbeth faced renewed English aggression from the restored Anglo-Saxon monarchy of Edward the Confessor, whose forces in association with dissident Britons invaded Alba in 1054. Macbeth was purportedly routed and his influence over Cumbria and the Lothians terminated. Macbeth demitted office in favour of his stepson, Lulach, in late 1056, whose coronation at Scone was also an attempt to pre-empt a succession crisis. Malcolm Canmore, the son of Duncan I, had found a more secure refuge among the Vikings of Orkney than among the Anglo-Saxons of England in the wake of his father's killing. Married to Ingibiorg, the daughter or widow of *Jarl* Thorfinn, Malcolm mounted a successful challenge from the north. With assistance from the Northern Isles, he invaded Alba through the Moray Firth. In March 1057, Macbeth was killed at Lumphanan in Deeside. Lulach was defeated in battle at Essie in Strathbogie around Easter 1058.

After he was installed as king of Alba, Malcolm III took no offensive action against the Vikings or the Norse-Gaels in the course of his 15-year reign.

He had crushed rebellion among the kindreds associated with Macbeth and Lulach in Moray and had absorbed Cumbria into what was becoming the kingdom of Scotland by the time of his second marriage in 1070 to Margaret, a member of the outed Anglo-Saxon dynasty. Malcolm III, supported by Margaret, subjected Alba to serious political and religious disruption. Malcolm's frequent incursions into England, both in the run up to and in the wake of the Norman Conquest in 1066, manifestly overestimated his capacity to turn political instability to his territorial advantage. Indeed, his Gaelic designation as Canmore can be more accurately translated as wrong-headed rather than big-headed.

CELTIC DISCONNECTIONS

Malcolm III's initial raid into Northumbria in 1061, which affirmed his control over Cumbria south of the Solway, brought no reprisals from the last Anglo-Saxon monarch, Edward the Confessor. However, Malcolm's next raid into Northumbria in 1070 came after he had given shelter to the exiled Anglo-Saxon royal house and just before his marriage to Margaret. Two years later, William the Conqueror retaliated with an invasion by land and sea that culminated in Malcolm doing homage to the Conqueror, recognising William I as his overlord, at Abernethy on Tayside. Not only was the Anglo-Saxon royal house, with the exception of Margaret, temporarily expelled from Scotland, but Malcolm was obliged to provide hostages, including his eldest son Duncan. William the Conqueror also commenced the building of impressive Border castles to defend Northumbria. Like past kings of Alba acceding to English overlordship, Malcom treated his submission to William I as a political expedient. He again invaded Northumbria in 1079 and faced Anglo-Norman reprisals in the following year. The accord of Abernethy may have been reaffirmed but no new concessions were asked from Malcolm. Eleven years later, Malcolm attacked Northumbria in retaliation for William II Rufus, the son and heir of the Conqueror, having built a substantial castle at Carlisle. This was a clear marker that Cumbria south of the Solway was now under English control, albeit some lands on the western Borders remained debateable. Attempts to reach a diplomatic accord broke down in 1093 when Malcolm refused to accept William II as his overlord. His final invasion of Northumbria ended in an ambush in which Malcolm was killed. There followed four years of internecine conflict between his brother Donald and his sons by both Ingibiorg and Margaret. This conflict may seem as a return to a Celtic pattern of succession. But, in reality, the succession was now largely being determined by Anglo-Norman monarchs intent on subordinating if not appropriating Scotland to England.

Donald, who had shared his brother Malcolm's exile, pressed his claim to the throne with assistance from the Norse-Gaels. Donald III expelled the Anglo-Saxon royal house, but not all the sons of Margaret. They took refuge at the court of William II. However, Duncan, the former hostage and surviving son of Ingibiorg, mounted an invasion from England in 1094 with the active connivance of William II. Donald III lost his throne but not his life and the Celtic lords seemingly made Duncan II's accession conditional on his removing his Anglo-Norman auxiliaries from the kingdom. Duncan II held the throne for only a few months before he was slain by the mormaer of the Mearns. Donald III was restored, but Edmund, the second surviving son of Margaret, was now the designated heir.

Margaret's eldest surviving son, Edgar, returned with an Anglo-Norman army in 1097, having done homage to William II two years earlier in anticipation of assistance to reclaim his father's kingdom. Donald III and Edmund were captured, but not immediately killed. Sentenced to perpetual imprisonment Donald III was blinded. Edmund was exiled to a monastery in the English West Country. Edgar moved swiftly to avenge his half-brother, taking Mearns under direct royal control after he had the mormaer executed. His disregard for this Celtic office was further evident in 1104 when he made his brother Alexander his designated heir and Earl of Gowrie, notwithstanding that province still had a mormaer. He reached a diplomatic understanding with Magnus Barelegs, king of Norway, whose control over Man and the Isles Edgar now recognised. In return, Magnus Barelegs surrendered Norwegian claims over the mainland districts of Argyll, Ross and Caithness. This concession did not immediately expand the territorial boundaries of the kingdom of Scotland. But it did consolidate its control over Strathclyde, which Edgar entrusted to his youngest brother, David, who was also given the Borders as his nominal responsibility. Edgar focused his rule on the Lothians, maintaining his court at Edinburgh and thereby continuing a practice initiated by Malcolm Canmore after his marriage to Margaret. His clear intent was to look south rather than north.

While Edgar was a beneficiary of William II, his relationship with Henry I of England was more problematic. Henry took upon himself the right to marry off Edgar's sisters. Matilda the elder sister became his queen. When Edgar died in 1107, the succession of Alexander was ratified by Henry I, who was manifestly more partial to David as a brother-in-law. David attended the English court when not in Normandy exercising lordship in the Cotentin peninsula. In 1113, Henry forced Alexander to recognise David as his designated heir and convert his nominal hold over Strathclyde and the Borders into a functioning principality, which David pretentiously designated as Cumbria. In the following year, Sibylla, an illegitimate daughter of Henry, became queen to Alexander, who was obliged not only to set aside Malcolm, a son by a previous liaison, but also to undertake military service for Henry I in Wales. David was given in marriage to Maud, a rich widow who brought him the earldom of Huntingdon, extensive lands in the English Midlands and a claim on the earldom of Northumbria. David, again with the approval of Henry I, duly succeeded his brother in 1124. Nevertheless, his long reign as David I was to be marked by more sophisticated relations with England that fended off rather than acceded to the Norman Conquest of Scotland.

However, this immense task had not been facilitated by the religious reforms initiated by his mother. Queen Margaret's unstinting commitment to pilgrimage and spiritual revival, combined with her personal piety, her charitable giving and her reputed self-denial in matters material has been eulogised by her confessor and biographer Turgot. Thus Margaret laboured diligently 'to eradicate wholly the illegalities' that had sprung up in the Celtic Church 'contrary to the rule of the true faith and the holy custom of the universal church'.[2] In order to bring back the Celtic wanderers to the path of truth she held reforming councils in which she was supported by her husband Malcolm, who acted as her translator, a clear admission that she never mastered Gaelic and, indeed, sought to make their court in Edinburgh more Anglo-Saxon than Celtic. The Celtic Church, which had nine rudimentary dioceses, was certainly in need of reinvigoration. Some dioceses had no bishops; other dioceses had no cathedral churches. Most would seem to have lacked an effective body of clergy in the cathedrals to assist the bishops. Within each diocese there was an elementary system of very large parishes endowed mainly by lay patrons and containing churches with outlying chapels.

Margaret did not engage in root and branch reform. She primarily sought to identify with, as well as comfort, the poor and the destitute, being much given to intensive, emotive and exhaustive prayer in tandem with extensive fasting, even to the point of self-harm. As such, like other remarkably devout women in the Middle Ages, she was an exponent of holy anorexia, whose excessive rigour ultimately claimed her life. Margaret encouraged devotion to the saints of the Celtic Church. But she did not support deviations from the Romano-British Church as received in Anglo-Saxon England in terms of the observance of Lent, participation in regular communion, marriage with stepmothers or brothers' widows and working on Sundays. Notwithstanding her subsequent canonisation as a saint by the papacy around 1250, Margaret was not in the mainstream of the radical reform programme emanating from

Rome in the later eleventh century, a programme that involved the central-
ising of spiritual oversight and the direction of canon law. The papacy had a
particularly militant interpretation of pilgrimage and spiritual renewal when
instigating the first in a series of Crusades in 1089 to recover Jerusalem and
the Holy Land from Muslim rule.

While Margaret's commitment to institutional reform was certainly mod-
est in comparison to the papacy, she did open the door to radical initiatives
that ultimately disadvantaged both men and women who adhered to the early
Christian practices associated with the Celtic Church. Margaret favoured St
Andrews as a Scottish centre of pilgrimage and to this end provided ferries on
both sides of the Firth of Forth. She and Malcolm were generous patrons to
Culdee monasteries in Fife at St Andrews and in Kinross at St Serf's Isle in
Loch Leven, but not so to other religious communities at Abernethy in Tayside
and Brechin in Angus, which were not necessarily less vibrant. Margaret did
pave the way for more thorough papal reforms by establishing a Benedictine
monastery at Dunfermline, staffed initially by three monks from Canterbury.
The spread of the Benedictine rule had been integral to spiritual revival in
continental Europe since the tenth century. It propagated the commitment
of separate communities of men and women to contemplation that was sustained by celibacy, obedience and poverty. By 1128, Dunfermline Abbey had
planted priories at Urquhart and Dornoch in the northern Highlands and on
Iona in the Inner Hebrides.

Margaret and Malcolm were also supporters of the cult of St Cuthbert,
centred in Durham and particularly strong in the Lothians. With the permission of Henry I in 1107, Alexander I had Turgot, then prior of Durham, made
bishop of St Andrews where he attempted a reforming programme similar to
that he attributed to Queen Margaret. Around 1020, Alexander brought from
Yorkshire to Scone another continental reforming order, the Augustinians,
whose canons were permitted to preach in churches. Their prior, Robert, was
subsequently appointed bishop of St Andrews in the forlorn hope that the
Culdees would conform to Augustinian rule. Culdees at Dunkeld were no less
resistant. Alexander established an Augustinian monastery on Inchcolm in
the Firth of Forth in 1123 as part of a personal endeavour to propagate the
cult of St Columba and counter the fostering of the cult of St Cuthbert by his
parents and his elder brother, Edgar.

Prince David, while in control of the Borders, had brought in a third
reforming order, the Tironensians, who placed greater stress on craft work
and labouring in the fields than on preaching or contemplating. Their abbey
at Selkirk was generously endowed from 1113 and included a cell at Melrose.
When the abbey was re-established at Kelso in 1128, endowments were set

aside to turn Melrose into a second abbey for the order. However, this intrusion of continental orders and Anglo-Norman clergy led to boundary disputes between the archbishops of Canterbury and York for ecclesiastical supremacy over Scotland. The first round in this turf war went to York when the archbishop, after an appeal to the papacy in 1119, was confirmed as metropolitan with the right to consecrate all Scottish bishops. This claim for ecclesiastical superiority gained further momentum with a further clerical influx of monks, canons and priests in tandem with the substantive migration of Anglo-Norman traders and artisans, lords, knights and their retainers initiated by David I from 1124 and continued by his grandsons, Malcolm IV and William I (the Lion), until 1214.

The first substantial grant made by David I around 1124 was the lordship of Annandale to Robert de Brus, whose father hailed from the Cotentin peninsula in Normandy and became lord of Cleveland in Yorkshire. Major English barons were exceptional among migrants, however. Many came from David's own estates in the English Midlands and were often younger sons of English barons, most notably Walter, second son of Alan who had been steward of the archbishopric of Dol on the border of Brittany and Normandy before acquiring lands in Shropshire. Around 1136, Walter was given the lordship of Strathgryfe in Renfrewshire and the office of royal steward, an office that was confirmed heritably by Malcolm IV along with the lordship of Kyle Stewart in Ayrshire. The Stewarts secured Bute from William the Lion and gradually acquired lordship over Cowal, Arran and Knapdale in the thirteenth century before going on to establish the longest serving royal Scottish dynasty in the fourteenth. Migrants were not only attracted by the opportunities to acquire provincial lordships in Scotland. They were also pushed out by endemic civil war in England from 1135 to 1153. Other migrants came directly from Flanders. Flemish knights were hired as royal enforcers and Flemish traders were brought in to develop the towns. Initially established in Lanarkshire and West Lothian, the knights made their name securing royal control over Moray from the 1130s from where they pushed on to Strathnaver in Sutherland. At the same time, leading migrant families were acquiring Scottish earldoms, usually through marriage. The Bruces had gained Carrick and the Stewarts Menteith. Migrations from England and Flanders primarily brought in kindred groups who accrued usually small and scattered estates. Their search for lands and the patronage led to chain migration from the south to the north of Scotland. Some existing Celtic kindreds were boosted through merger with the new migrant families. But other Celtic kindreds were certainly displaced to make way for the incomers in both Highlands and Lowlands.

KINDREDS AND GOVERNANCE

Internal migration and consolidation of kindred groups within Scotland cut across ethnic divisions between Picts, Britons, Gaels, Angles, Vikings and Anglo-Normans (see Appendix). Kindred groups, in laying the basis for the communities of the realm, made a more extensive contribution to the shaping of Scotland as a mongrel nation than the kings of Alba and their successors as kings of Scots. Kindreds were bound together by ties of blood and local association. In Gaelic areas, the kindred emerged as clans; elsewhere in Scotland, they constituted powerful families supported by lesser or satellite families. In tracing the emergence of these kindreds, genealogies and heraldic representations are helpful in terms of folk memory – less so in terms of outright fabrication of kindred origins that can promote romanticised and glorified notions of clan and family back into Celtic mythology.

Only one confederation of Norse-Gaelic clans that came to prominence in Knapdale and Cowal in Argyll can trace their ancestry back to the fifth century – to Niall of the Nine Hostages, High King of Ireland. The progenitors of clans and families can rarely be authenticated further back than the eleventh century as Alba gave way to Scotland and as the Borders between England and Scotland became demarcated. The emergence of identifiable kindreds was less an issue of ethnicity as of political turmoil and social opportunity, features compounded by the arrival of Anglo-Normans in the twelfth and thirteenth centuries as the kings of Scotland faced internal discord in Moray and strove to integrate Galloway, Argyll, Man and the Hebrides, and Caithness. In most cases, continuity of lineage within clans and families cannot be detected until the thirteenth or fourteenth centuries, when rights to land as conveyed through written charters became commonplace.

The warlords who led kindreds imposed their dominance over diverse localities whose indigenous families accepted their protection either willingly or by force through the payment of tributes and taxes. Kindreds claiming descent from warrior chiefs are particularly prominent among the Gaels and Norse-Gaels. There were also kindreds in Alba and Galloway who had functional links to the Celtic Church as followers of saints. Descendants of abbots, priests and monks usually relate to a time of lay abbots and married clergy, not to breaches of celibacy. Kindreds of Alba who were probably Pictish settlers rather than Gaelic migrants from Easter Ross to Angus can be classified as Celtic. Relocation rather than displacement accounts for the movement of Celtic kindreds from the locations after which they are named in Alba into the Lothians where the Scots also feature as a more generic name for settlers from across the Firth of Forth. At the same time, families of Anglian or Northumbrian origin moved on from the locations after which they were named in Lothian into Alba, Galloway and Strathclyde. Britons moved with the expansion of Strathclyde into the Borders and also intermingled with Gaelic kindreds on from Loch Lomond into Argyll. Anglo-Norman kindreds moved into the Highlands where they established themselves as distinctive clans.

The protection afforded by kindreds provided not only the mutual assurance necessary to settle and work land productively, but also the basis for the doing of justice. Contractual elations within and between kindreds were governed according to diverse law codes that operated from the Shetlands to Galloway and from Lewis to the Merse on the Borders. These codes viewed the kindred as essential for the doing of justice, especially to seek or make reparations for crimes that led to disfigurement or loss of life, destruction of property and rustling of livestock. Rather than pursue retribution through mutilation or execution, the kindreds engaged in arbitration to attain reparations, paid in money or livestock, that were scaled to the status of the persons injured and the nature of the crime. A murderer of a king or kindred leader faced summary execution, however.

The upper ranks of the social elite prior to the arrival of the Anglo-Normans consisted of earls, mormaers, thanes and lay abbots. They were not so much kings' men as men recognised by kings as leaders of substantial kindred groups. Kings had no power over the succession of the social elite. As in the royal family of Alba, succession was determined by the kindred on the basis of personal capacity among the leaders who could be replaced by brothers, sons or nephews. Succession through women by husbands and sons was also possible, but this Pictish practice had become rare. The mormaers within Alba were provincial leaders with public responsibilities to lead out the host in time of war and the hunt in time of peace, maintain territorial security and sustain communications through the construction and repair of bridges. The mormaers were drawn from the dominant provincial kindred. The subordinate offices of thane or toiseach were shared out among the dominant and lesser kindreds of the province. These lesser officers also had public duties, as war leaders and in keeping the peace. The social elite had power to do justice, but this was largely to oversee arbitration processes, resolve boundary disputes and harmonise estate management. Professional kindreds of lawmen pronounced but did not determine judgements in each province.

Mormaers and thanes held lands as heads of kindred and lands associated with their offices. While their estates as heads of kindred varied, lands held by right of office tended to be fixed and notably less extensive. Kings likewise held estates within provinces as head of kindred groups and as monarchs.

Centralised powers were limited. Mormaers gave advice and consent to major public pronouncements at the royal court. Kings authorised the raising of the host for service by land and sea and were ultimately responsible for keeping the peace within Alba. They levied taxes to meet common burdens for the security of the kingdom. As evident from discord in Moray, the power and influence of kings, mormaers, thanes and kindred groups fluctuated. Yet there was a relative consistency in doing justice, in levying of taxes and tributes and in settling and working lands.

The basic unit for governance, assessment and productivity within Alba tended to be davochs and shires. The former predominated in northern Scotland and had a financial as well as an arable rating; the latter prevailed in central and eastern Lowlands and only rated arable capacity. The shire was also to the fore in the Lothians and the Borders. Variants of the davoch were to be found in Galloway and in the Lennox. Each davoch or shire consisted of a manor or domain and of portions. Farmers in a manor paid rents collected seasonally and regulated by custom to their kindred lords, mormaers or thanes. Farmers in portions only paid annual tributes and occasional taxes to their kindred or office-holding lords. Payments were made in kind as well as in money as the kindreds placed more emphasis on consuming than on marketing grain and livestock. Rents could also involve boon work; that is labour services at sowing, at harvesting and in conveying commodities to households and markets. The raising of specific numbers of men for hosts, hunts, guard duty and bridge building, ensured the rest of the inhabitants of the davochs and shires would continue to work land productively. The kindred or office-holding lords managed the communal working of arable and pastoral land by the peasantry. The produce of individual strips or rigs of arable were assigned to farmers, but periodically reallocated to ensure that some farmers were not privileged over others. This customary practice has been characterised as run-rig for open fields. However, marginal land was also worked within small plots formed by rocky enclosures.

As well as being tenants in manors, farmers held portions in their own right. They were itinerant when engaged in hosts, hunts or work services. Labourers aided farmers in working the land. Some received small plots for personal subsistence but they were usually bound to their settlements as unfree men, women and children. As they could substitute payments in kind for work services to farmers, holders of small plots can be viewed as serfs rather than slaves. Nonetheless, they were tradeable commodities between kindred and office-holding lords. As such their labour, which was also transferred when churches were endowed with lands from davochs and shires, was appropriated, a process extended to the Lothians in the later eleventh century.

The migration of the Anglo-Normans had a notable impact on governance as on landholding by kindreds. Davochs and shires were gradually incorporated within sheriffdoms. Sheriffdoms, administered by sheriffs usually from royal castles, were only gradually introduced and expanded in the twelfth and thirteenth centuries. The first creation of David, perhaps when he was Prince of Cumbria, was Roxburgh, followed by Berwick, Stirling and Perth. Malcolm IV created six more, but only Forfar (or Angus) was north of the Tay. The 12 creations of William the Lion provided extensive cover in west and south-west Scotland, but only in Moray, Inverness and Kincardine north of the Tay.

The sheriffs uplifted tolls and customs due to the Crown and collected the profits of justice from cases before their courts. The emphasis on these profits marked a shift from reparations to retribution in which the king and leading landlords, lay and ecclesiastical, benefited at the expense of kindred groups. A sheriff was expected to keep the king's peace and to harmonise and resolve disputes, civil and criminal between the earls, thanes and other landlords within his bounds. The most heinous crimes which became known as the king's pleas – arson, murder, rape and robbery – were tried at the royal court. The creation of sheriffdoms also required a degree of centralisation as their accounts had to be audited and approved at the royal court. Regular audits seem to have been instigated from around 1201 and were usually held in the part of the royal court designated as the exchequer. Civil servants, invariably highly educated clerics, as well as leading lords were summoned to give the king regular counsel and advice, with this counsel being enlarged for matters of war, diplomacy and the raising of taxation. The royal court was not stationary. It was necessary for the king to maintain his authority by travelling and eating his way around the country. Most royal business would appear to have been done in Edinburgh, Perth, Stirling and Roxburgh, albeit Montrose regularly hosted the court during the reign of William the Lion.

No less integral to the Anglo-Norman transformation of Scotland was the introduction of primogeniture, the transformation of mormaers into earls and the appropriation of property to enhance lordship. Although David I had succeeded his two brothers Edgar and Alexander I, he himself was succeed by two grandsons, Malcolm IV and then William I. However, the latter was succeeded by his eldest son Alexander II in 1214. Primogeniture, the succession of the eldest son or eldest surviving male, so long as they were of legitimate birth, made redundant the practice of a designated heir or *tainistear* in Alba. Primogeniture was extended from the royal house to mormaers, thanes and others claiming or exercising lordship. If there were no legitimate male heirs succession passed through legitimate daughters or even sisters who held and retained lands in their own right. If there was more than one legitimate female heir, the estates were divided equally between them and were passed on separately through their legitimate heirs.

The extension of primogeniture from the royal house to provincial governors led to the phased replacement of mormaers by earls, who owed their position to the crown not just to their standing as heads of kindred groups. The majority of the 13 earls created initially by David I and confirmed by his immediate successors were in the heartlands of the old kingdom of Alba to the north of the Firths of Clyde and Forth. There were also two earldoms in former provinces of the Britons in Lennox and Carrick and another for the Merse in the Lothians. Earls and thanes continued to exercise jurisdiction independent of the sheriffs as royal officials. But, like the sheriffs, their jurisdiction in civil and criminal cases prioritised the profits of justice accruing to them from punitive fines rather than to their kindreds from reparations. Lands ceased to be inherited on terms prescribed by oral custom. Rights over land were conveyed through charters specifying the boundaries of estates, the jurisdiction over them and the conditions of service due to the Crown, earls, lords, bishops and abbots. Charters were feudal contracts. Feudal landholding required the heads of kindreds to act as proprietors not as trustees for their clans or families. Lands were held in feu in return for homage, the swearing of allegiance and military or nominal services.

Within Celtic units of settlement, the impact of feuing was more apparent than real in the case of manorial lands, which were now held as property by the mormaers turned earls, as by the thanes and other heads of kindreds. But the portions that formerly paid occasional tributes were now appropriated as superiority. Leading kinsmen had to give specific military or monetary services that became known as feudal casualties. Succession to offices, jurisdictions and estates was no longer a matter of acclamation by kindreds but of feudal conveyancing. Charters were validated ultimately by the Crown as feudal superior and font of justice in Scotland. Rights to offices, jurisdictions and estates specified in stereotyped charters soon became heritable in order to accommodate the way in which land was held to the way in which it was settled by kindreds. Earls, thanes and other feudal landlords who held directly from the Crown were freeholders and expected to attend sheriff courts. Those feudal landlords who held their estates from earls, thanes or other freeholders were deemed feuars who were not obliged to attend sheriff courts. In the course of the thirteenth century, the acquisition of lands took priority over feudal services and swearing homage. Freeholders and feuars lacking an official title or rank became designated as lairds.

THE BUILT ENVIRONMENT OF KINGSHIP

From the reign of David I, the main persuasive agencies that allowed the monarchy to extend its influence throughout Scotland were the church and the burgh. Patronage for religious orders gained successive kings of Scots a good press from the clergy. Licensing of towns to trade as burghs encouraged prosperity through the marketing rather than the consumption of native produce.

David I expanded his foundations of monasteries from the Borders to Moray and from the Lothians to Galloway. This practice was continued by his immediate successors and was emulated by earls, other leading lords and heads of kindreds. New orders such as the Cluniacs, the Cistercians and the Trinitarians supplemented the existing orders of Benedictines, Augustinians and Tironensians. The older orders held the most prosperous priories in Scotland, respectively at Dunfermline and St Andrews in Fife and Arbroath in Angus. Orders of preaching friars, most notably the Dominicans, the Franciscans and the Carmelites, were introduced during the thirteenth century, mainly into towns in the central Lowlands and along the east coast; likewise the Knights Templars and the Knights Hospitallers, founded to aid and protect pilgrims on Crusade to the Holy Land.

Religious orders originated predominantly in France and usually spread from England to Scotland. All orders bar the Augustinians retained international links with their founding houses. They spread through Scotland by chain migration. Thus Arbroath Abbey, established by William the Lion in 1178, attracted Tironensian monks from Kelso Abbey in the Borders that was founded by David I in 1128. They also observed strict demarcation between the sexes, with the Benedictines, Cistercians and Augustinians having orders for nuns as well as monks. This was later the case with the Dominican and Franciscan friars. The days of the Celtic Church were numbered. In 1144, David I decided that the Culdees at St Andrews were to be phased out if they did not opt to join the Augustinians as canons for the cathedral. Culdees at St Serf's on Loch Leven were forced to conform.

The endowment of monasteries, friaries and nunneries with lands, serfs and revenues were not just acts of piety. The religious orders kept records which cast favourable light on their patrons and questioned the legitimacy of any Celtic or Norse-Gaelic challengers to David I and his immediate successors. Monks and friars were chroniclers for Scotland as for Western Europe. Their writing skills were also vital for issuing charters. The abbots and priors who headed religious houses acted as spiritual lords who took on secular functions as advisers and civil servants around the royal court. They ran extensive estates that shaped the prosperity of Scotland. Estates of orders that placed particular emphasis on manual labour, such as the Tironensians and the Cistercians, tended to be worked directly by monks assisted by serfs and lay workers. They were noted pastoral farmers running extensive sheep walks in the Borders. But they also grew grain, fished salmon, worked coal and panned salt. More contemplative orders leased their estates and their serfs to peasant farmers. Leases ranged from a few to 19 years or even ran for more than a generation. Although regulated by custom and often contracted orally, leases were renegotiable, which enabled the abbots and priors to increase their revenues as prices for livestock, grain and fish increased.

This dual capacity of spiritual lord and civil servant also applied to bishops who ran estates in their respective dioceses. That these estates tended to be scattered rather than concentrated encouraged their lease to peasant farmers. The bishops, no less than the abbots and priors, were adroit estate managers. David I and his immediate successors ensured a continuous supply of bishops notwithstanding ongoing controversy with the archbishops of York and Canterbury as with the papacy over issues of nomination and consecration. Before he became king, David had aligned the boundaries of the diocese of Glasgow with those of his principality of Cumbria. As king, he ensured that parishes were allocated to specific dioceses and that a tenth of the produce of each parish was assigned for spiritual purposes; this exaction of tithes common throughout Christendom became known in Scotland as teinds. The Church's financial resources were further enhanced by the founding of towns in bishoprics and close to monasteries and priories. The two most significant towns established as burghs by bishops were St Andrews and Glasgow. Monasteries and priories promoted the erection of substantial towns into ecclesiastical burghs, most notably the Cistercians at Melrose, the Tironensians at Kelso and Arbroath, and the Benedictines at Dunfermline.

In licensing burghs, David I and his immediate successors promoted existing towns and created new towns. Towns had already grown up on overland livestock routes, as at Rutherglen, Linlithgow, Peebles and Roxburgh; some were at important intersections of land and water, such as Perth, Stirling and Dumfries; and others were located by good harbours at river mouths, such as Berwick, Ayr, Montrose and Aberdeen. Burgh privileges were accorded to Edinburgh as a royal stronghold. Forres and Elgin were planted to promote royal influence in Moray. Burghs were concentrated or nucleated settlements with rarely more than a single street from which lanes ran adjacent between the small plots held by the inhabitants. As evident from William the Lion's founding charter for Inverness between 1172 and 1189, a burgh was expected to protect its inhabitants and trading privileges by erecting an earthen dyke on which a wooden enclosure or palisade was constructed. As the houses in the burgh, apart from churches, priories and friaries, tended to be of timber construction, fire was a continuous hazard.

The privileges of the burghs could be reconfirmed and expanded by monarchs as by leading ecclesiastical and lay lords. Each burgh's charter designated a precinct or area for its exclusive trade where annual fairs supplemented weekly markets. As William I's charter to Perth reiterated, sometime between 1200 and 1211, any outside merchant must trade through the burgh if he traded in the sheriffdom of Perth. This trading monopoly helped develop cloth manufacturing in Perth from spinning and weaving to fulling and dyeing. The latter task required capital to import expensive dyes. The merchants who financed the manufacture of cloth were licensed to operate through guilds which also controlled the production of cloth in the rural hinterland of burghs. Merchant guilds came to dominate the running of burghs, particularly in larger towns engaged in overseas trade. The development of burghs as self-governing corporations under provosts, bailies and other magistrates was tied to their capacity to make a meaningful contribution to royal or lordly finances.

The licensing and planting of burghs certainly increased wealth creation. Regular markets acted as an incentive to increase flocks of sheep, to plough more land, to produce more cloth and to fish coastal waters for herring as well as rivers for salmon. The proliferation of burghs led to some challenging and some overshadowing neighbouring foundations. Glasgow came to dominate the Firth of Clyde to the detriment of the king's burghs of Renfrew, Dumbarton and Rutherglen and the neighbouring ecclesiastical burgh of Paisley. The most successful non-royal or non-ecclesiastical foundation was Dundee, which challenged both the king's burghs of Perth and Forfar and the ecclesiastical burghs of St Andrews and Arbroath. Kings established mints to promote the use of money. David restricted his mints to Roxburgh, Berwick and Edinburgh. William the Lion established mints in Stirling and Perth for the commercial development of central Scotland. But it was not until the reign of Alexander II that 16 mints provided cover for the whole kingdom from 1214, with Montrose, Aberdeen and Inverness prominent in the north and Glasgow, Ayr and Lanark in the west.

Turf, timber and stone were extensively extracted to build monasteries, priories, friaries and burghs. Feudal lords also constructed fortified homes around which woods were cleared usually by compulsory peasant labour. Sophisticated castles of enclosure were created by the ramping up of earth mounds or mottes that were surrounded by ditches. Added protection was provided by barrier walls known as baileys often enclosed by a wooden stockade. Timber towers were erected on the mottes, sometimes with other timber houses for storing food supplies or conducting religious services. Incoming

Flemings in Clydesdale built relatively modest castles. Enormous motte and bailey constructions were erected in Galloway and Moray by Anglo-Norman lords and in Strathdon and Carrick by Celtic earls. The replacement of timber with stone, for outward defences, was particularly evident in castles built to enhance royal authority and feudal lordships. Such enclosures became less necessary after stone keeps were built on top of mottes.

By the outset of the thirteenth century, castles were becoming primarily lordly residences and centres of estate management. Defence remained important, but less of a priority as evident from the construction of stone hall houses and tower houses. The former were built on two floors. The upper hall was the lord's residence and the basement was used for storing provisions and for cooking, baking and brewing. The tower house, a fortified construction that was widespread throughout Europe, came into increasing prominence. The tower house was built upwards with multiple floors rather than extend outwards. The first tower houses were constructed in the twelfth century for Norse rather than Scottish lords, initially in Orkney from where they spread to Caithness.

Having become acquainted with hunting reserves while earl of Huntingdon in the English Midlands, David I imported the concept of the royal forest to Scotland. Ettrick in Selkirkshire was probably his first creation. From the 1130s, no one could hunt in a royal forest without the king's permission. David's creation of royal forests extended from the Borders to the north of Scotland. The king also granted feudal lords the right to establish their own exclusive forests, mainly in the west of Scotland as well as the Borders. Such extensive forests constricted the scope for productive arable farming. The implementation of punitive game laws furthered the appropriation of resources over which kindreds had customary claims to hunt and fish and to extract wood for housing and fuel.

CONTESTED POWER

The appropriation of lordships, lands and labour from the twelfth century was not without a significant measure of internal dissension. David I initially encountered resistance in Moray, which had less to do with Anglo-Norman migration as with contested succession to the Scottish Crown by kindreds descended from past kings of Alba. Having disputed the inauguration of David I in 1124, Malcolm, son of Alexander I, sided with Angus, the head of the kindred in Moray descended from Lulach. Angus was killed after leading a substantial force into battle at Stracathro in the Mearns in 1130. Victory

was achieved by forces loyal to David, with Anglo-Norman friends and associates to the fore. Malcolm escaped and four years later launched a seaborne
invasion with the assistance of his brother-in-law, Somerled, the leader of the
Norse-Gaels in Argyll and most of the Western Isles. Pitched battles by land
and sea were avoided when Malcolm was betrayed, captured and confined to
Roxburgh. David commenced the settlement of Flemings and Anglo-Normans
in Moray thereafter.

The accession of his grandson Malcolm IV in 1153 did not pass off without
incident. Somerled reasserted the claims of Malcolm MacAlexander, whose
sons joined him in a rebellion of the Norse-Gaels. Somerled was soon diverted
from his rebellion in 1154 by an opportunity to breach the territorial integrity
of the kingdom of Man and the Isles following the murder of his father-in-
law, Olaf the Red. Within two years, he had forced Godred the Black, Olaf's
legitimate heir and successor, to cede him the Inner Hebrides excluding Skye
and Raasay. Somerled made peace with Malcolm IV in 1160 but again rebelled
four years later. He was killed near Renfrew having sailed up the River Clyde
with a large army of Norse-Gaels; a surviving son of Malcolm MacAlexander
ended up in permanent confinement with his father in Roxburgh. The family
claim on the Scottish throne was ruthlessly extinguished at Coupar Angus in
1186 by William the Lion, when a grandson of Malcolm and around 38 of his
followers were summarily executed. In the interim, the breach with Man was
made permanent and augmented by the acquisition of the Outer Hebrides,
except Lewis and Harris, by Somerled's sons. Endemic feuding on the western seaboard was sustained by the territorial rivalry maintained by kindreds
descended of Somerled, by the ongoing difficulties faced by the Manx dynasty
in ruling a geographically segregated kingdom, by the ready opportunities for
seasonal employment in the internecine wars of the Gaelic chiefs in Ireland
and by the ambivalence in political lordship. Clans held their mainland possessions from the Scottish Crown and their island possessions from the
Norwegian. This situation led to the building of spectacular stone castles of
enclosure on rocks that projected out to sea with good anchorages for galleys
nearby.

Galloway, like Argyll, had served as a marcher lordship between Scotland
and the kingdom of Man and the Isles. Fergus of Galloway, who had worked
fairly harmoniously with David I, continued the rebellion against Malcom IV
begun by Somerled in 1160. Within two years, Malcolm IV invaded Galloway
on three occasions. Fergus retired to Edinburgh to become an Augustinian
canon at Holyrood. Galloway was divided between his two sons, Uhtred taking the eastern and Gilbert the western portion. Following the accession of
William the Lion in 1165, Gilbert submitted to Henry II of England. William

could still call on the loyalty of Uhtred's son, Lachlan, who had become so enamoured with the codes of chivalry emanating from France that he changed his name to Roland. After the death of Gilbert in 1185, Roland seized the whole of Galloway and worked with William the Lion to introduce feudal settlement. A steady trickle of Anglo-Normans came from Cumbria.

Roland proved a useful ally of William the Lion in suppressing the rising of the MacWilliams, a kindred descended from a son of Duncan II who had been a rather quiescent courtier under David I. Although Donald MacWilliam's personal claim on the throne was terminated in 1187, his kindred remained rebellious for over 20 years. Their main area of support came from Ross with sporadic backing from the shires of Inverness and Aberdeen as well as Moray. They were also aided by the *jarls* of Orkney until the Scottish Crown enforced its authority over Caithness. Other than in Sutherland, there was limited feudal penetration in the central and northern Highlands, which may in part explain Alexander II's ruthless extermination of the last MacWilliam heir, an infant girl whose brains were battered out at the market cross of Forfar in 1230.

The extinguishing of native rebellions and the expansion of the kingdom's frontiers were not achieved without compromising the independence of Scotland. The basic difficulty was not so much the overlordship claimed by successive English kings as the territorial ambitions of their Scottish counterparts in England. As earl of Huntingdon, David I had sworn in 1127 that he would support the succession of Henry I's daughter, Matilda, to the English throne. When Stephen, a grandson of William the Conqueror, moved to become king of England in 1135, David invaded and secured control of Cumbria and Northumbria. A renewed incursion into northern England in 1138 met with defeat in the battle of the Standard at Northallerton in Yorkshire. Nevertheless, Stephen in 1139 conceded not the whole of Northumbria but the earldom of Northumberland to David's son, Prince Henry, who did homage to Stephen and actually fought for him against Matilda. David I offered no homage and was actively on the side of Matilda by 1141, when he lost his earldom of Huntingdon. In return for Prince Henry retaining his earldom of Northumberland, David promised to aid Matilda's son, Henry of Anjou, to recover the English throne in 1149. But David provided no material assistance. When Prince Henry died in 1152, his second son, William, became earl of Northumberland. Malcolm, the eldest, as designated heir to David I, succeeded his grandfather as king in 1153.

Three years after he became king of England, Henry of Anjou persuaded Malcolm IV to hand back the earldom of Northumberland in return for the earldom of Huntingdon in 1157. In 1163, Henry II made further claims on Malcolm for the homage due to him as overlord of Scotland. Malcolm declined, though he did give up a younger brother, Prince David, as a hostage. When Malcolm IV died in 1165, he was succeed by his brother, William the Lion, who was obsessed about winning back the earldom of Northumberland. Baronial rebellion against Henry II in 1173 was supported by Louis VII of France and by William who twice invaded England. Captured at Alnwick in Northumberland in 1174, William was transported across to Falaise in Normandy in 1174. He was only released from captivity after doing homage to Henry II for Scotland. After William acted in Galloway as directed by Henry II, Prince David was restored the earldom of Huntingdon in 1185.

In 1189, the determination of Henry II's son, Richard the Lionheart, to play a leading role in the Third Crusade, afforded William the opportunity to be quit of homage to the English Crown. At Canterbury, Richard I freed William from his obligations at Falaise for 10,000 merks. Relations between both kingdoms were to be as they had stood between Henry II and Malcolm IV. But this was ambiguous. It still left Scotland open to demands for homage and William's claim on the earldom of Northumberland remained unrequited. When William attempted to press this claim, with the assistance of the French Crown in 1209, he was confronted with the superior resources of Richard's brother, John, now in full control of England. Following negotiations on the Borders, William was to pay John 15,000 merks for his goodwill. Any future lands acquired by Scottish kings in England were to be held by their heirs in return for homage. Although William had no holding of substance in England, his son and heir, Alexander, duly did homage to John. In return for his assistance against the MacWilliams in Ross, John secured control over the marriage of Alexander. The latter's accession as Alexander II in 1214 ushered in a prolonged phase of affirmative action against English overlordship.

Notes

1. On his way to convert King Brude around 564, Columba protected the ferryman on the River Ness from an 'aquatic beast' that had bitten and mortally wounded a man prior to the saint's arrival (*Early Sources of Scottish History, AD 500 to 1286*, A. O. Anderson ed. 2 vols (Edinburgh, 1922) ii, p.51). Was this predator the original Loch Ness monster?

2. *Early Sources of Scottish History*, ii, pp. 70–71, 75–76, 79.

2 Wars of Independence, 1214–1424

The Anglo-Norman monarchy that controlled England was intent on subjugating Celtic lordships in Ireland and Wales and on expanding its territorial influence in France. Such a territorially acquisitive power was rarely averse to enforcing overlordship on Scottish kings, nobles and kindreds prone to cross-Border raiding. Primogeniture also opened up the prospect of royal minorities, as occurred after the deaths of Alexander II in 1249, Alexander III in 1286 and Robert I in 1329, which threatened not only the integrity but the independence of the kingdom of Scotland. Independence, which was consistently supported by the Catholic Church within Scotland, if not the papacy at Rome, rested primarily on the cohesion of diverse kindreds into one community of the realm. Its concern for the 'common weal' was upheld by the estates of the nobility, clergy and burgesses assembled in the parliaments from the late thirteenth century and was given a distinctive flavour by the Declaration of Arbroath in which the magnates as leading nobles pledged conditional allegiance to Robert the Bruce as king of Scots in 1320. The common weal duly found expression as the Scottish commonwealth that was prepared to stand out against the Crown if the independence of the kingdom was compromised. However, the standards for the common weal established by the Declaration were severely undermined by subsequent political adventuring, most notably under David II and the early Stewarts prior to 1424. Threatened, compromised and subverted, Scottish independence ultimately prevailed due in no large measure to English overcommitment to war. From the mid-fourteenth century, England became embroiled in the Hundred Years War with France. The French connection through the 'auld alliance' remained pre-eminent for Scotland.

POWER STRUGGLES

The reigns of Alexander II and his son, Alexander III, between 1214 and 1286 were marked by territorial consolidation and extension. Sheriffdoms covered all of Scotland albeit those in Caithness, Sutherland, Ross and Argyll were only partially functioning. Scotland was divided for judicial purposes into two circuits, with justiciars, usually leading lords, holding courts for Scotia in the north and Lothian and occasionally Galloway in the south. Cases on these judicial circuits, the justice-ayres, were held in the sheriff courts with the sheriffs being responsible for summoning the accused, the witnesses and the jury who decided whether charges were proved. The presence of the Scottish Crown was greatly strengthened in Galloway and in the Western Isles by both kings.

In 1234, Alan son of Roland died, leaving three daughters and an illegitimate son. Galloway rose for the son, but this rebellion was savagely suppressed by Alexander II, who partitioned Galloway among the daughters. They all married Anglo-Norman lords who founded monasteries, I but few burghs, built castles and imported followers to dilute the presence of Celtic kindreds. The largest provincial lordship was built up in eastern Galloway through the marriage of Dervoguilla into the Balliol family, originally from Picardy, who had acquired English estates in the Midlands, Yorkshire and Northumbria before initially moving into the Lothians and Ayrshire. Further subdivision among heiresses led to the Comyns, whose main English base was in Northumbria, expanding their influence from Buchan, Badenoch, Lochaber and Menteith into western Galloway. Feudal penetration can be overstated, however. Kindreds remained no less significant in Galloway than in the Highlands and Islands, albeit the latter still had divided allegiances to Scotland and Norway.

Between 1244 and 1263, Alexander II and Alexander III intermittently sought to exploit the geographic remoteness of the Norwegian king in order to annex the Hebrides, through either purchase or conquest. When Ewen, chief of the MacDougalls of Argyll, accepted a commission from Haakon IV to rule all the Isles, Alexander II mounted an expedition to the western seaboard that forced Ewen into exile. However, Alexander II died from fever on the island of Kerrera in 1249. Reconciled to the Scottish Crown by 1253, Ewen persuaded clan chiefs on the western seaboard to withhold support when Haakon IV of Norway went on the offensive in 1263. Haakon led a naval expedition that was dispersed by the Scots off Largs in Ayrshire. His forces were compelled to withdraw to Orkney through lack of supplies. The futility of this expedition was compounded by Haakon's death at Kirkwall. Alexander III mounted a successful counter-attack over the next two years to enforce his sovereignty over Man and the Isles. His intended invasion of Man in 1264 was forestalled when Magnus, its Norse-Gaelic king, made an oath of submission at Dumfries. By the Treaty of Perth concluded in 1266, Norway ceded Man and the Western Isles to Scotland in return for a payment of 4,000 merks sterling, spread over the next four years, and an annual pension of 100 merks sterling in perpetuity. Alexander III and his successors were not required to do homage for Man and the Western Isles, which were only to be subject to the laws and customs of Scotland. In practice, Man was politically dissociated from the Western Isles in 1266 and governed for the next 24 years by a succession of Scottish bailies. Direct rule was imposed after the death of Magnus, when a Scottish expeditionary force crushed an insurrection on the island in 1275.

Territorial consolidation and extension within Scotland did not abate the challenges posed by English claims to overlordship. Rebellion in England in 1215 allowed Alexander II, one year after his accession, to intervene in support of the barons who signed the Magna Carta that obliged King John to rule equitably rather than greedily. Alexander's claims over Cumbria and Northumbria were supported by the rebel barons. Over the next two years, Alexander invaded England five times, secured homage from rebels in Yorkshire and pushed as far south as the Channel port of Dover, the deepest penetration ever by a hostile Scottish force. However, Alexander did not liaise effectively with the future Louis VIII of France. John mounted a counter-invasion of the Lothians in 1216. His death on returning to the English Midlands transformed the situation, with a majority of the English political elite rallying behind the new king, Henry III. After the defeat of the rebels in 1217, Alexander made peace with Henry at York. Alexander did homage for lands acquired in England, but not for Scotland. Three years later he married Joanna, sister of Henry III and daughter of John.

Alexander II's endeavours to exploit unrest in Wales and Ireland led Henry III to revive English claims to overlordship in 1236. Alexander counterclaimed the northern English counties of Cumberland, Westmorland and Northumberland. Negotiations brokered at York by the papacy in 1237 resulted in Alexander II renouncing his claims on the northern English counties in return for isolated estates in Northumberland and Cumberland. Unfounded fears that Alexander II was supporting pirates and negotiating an alliance with France brought an English army to the Borders in 1244. This led to yet another round of negotiations at Newcastle, in which Alexander II agreed not to act against Henry's enemies. His son, the future Alexander III, was promised in marriage to Henry's daughter, Margaret, an arrangement duly accomplished seven years later.

Henry III made no attempt to exploit the minority of Alexander III to enforce English overlordship. Alexander's 12-year minority following the death of his father in 1249 was marked by power plays rooted in a feud over lands and titles between two leading Anglo-Norman families, the Comyns and the Durwards. The Comyns had amassed earldoms and provincial lordships from north-east to south-west Scotland. The Durwards held estates in Angus and a substantial lordship between the rivers Dee and Don in Aberdeenshire. They owed their rise in status to royal service, first as ushers or door-wards to William the Lion and then as justiciars for Scotia under Alexander II.

On his marriage to Henry III's daughter, Margaret, at York in 1251, Alexander III, then a precocious ten-year-old, refused to do homage for Scotland. He affirmed that homage was due only for lands held of the English Crown in England. However, Henry III helped the Comyns remove Alan Durward, then acting as sole Scottish justiciar, from Alexander's household. For the next four years, the Comyns governed Scotland. They accepted the oversight of English lords sent by Henry to protect his daughter's interests. When he came to the Borders in 1255, Henry not only had the Comyns dismissed but also had them barred from the Scottish Court for seven years. Until Alexander III was aged 21, the Comyns were not to be readmitted to his presence without the consent of Henry. For two years, the Durwards held sway until the justiciar was forced to take refuge in England after the Comyns kidnapped the king in 1257. Henry III was relatively powerless to intervene as his English barons were again restless. Alexander, who had refused to become the tool of either the Durwards or the Comyns, refrained from exploiting the English king's difficulties. After he assumed full power in 1262, Alexander consistently backed Henry III's endeavours to suppress rebellion.

The issue of English overlordship did not remain dormant, however. At Westminster in 1278, Alexander III repeated to Edward I the rebuff he gave to his father Henry III in 1251. He would do homage to the English king only for the lands he held in England. 'To homage for my kingdom of Scotland, no one has right save God alone, nor do I hold it save of God alone.'[1] Alexander's confidence was bolstered by the economic growth and prosperity that marked his reign. Agricultural productivity rose as more land was brought under cultivation. Increased demand for meat and fish intensified livestock farming and coastal fishing. Growing overseas trade was channelled through the burghs, although monasteries as well as the sea-lords and clan chiefs on the western and northern seaboards continued to trade without paying customs or tolls to the Crown.

The thirteenth century was remarkable in terms of Anglo-Scottish relations for an unprecedented period of peace which lasted from 1217 to 1296. In part, this can be attributed to good personal relations between the respective royal families of both countries, relations reinforced by marriage alliances and a shared commitment to knightly brotherhood, transnational jousting tournaments and adherence to a chivalric code which had gained considerable traction throughout Europe. The status of knight was changing from the mounted mercenary who aided the Anglo-Norman penetration of Scotland to the man of honour who, in an age of arranged marriages, upheld courtly rather than romantic love and preferred to engage in just wars against Muslims and pagans rather than fellow Christians. Nevertheless, few Scots actually went on the Crusades first initiated by the papacy in 1095 and resumed in 1145 and 1187 against Muslims in the Middle East before being extended in the thirteenth century against the Orthodox Church in Constantinople, heretics in southern France and in Bosnia, pagans in the eastern Baltic and Muslims in Spain.

Notwithstanding the spread of royal government throughout Scotland, Anglo-Norman families tended to promote their English over their Scottish estates, especially where the latter were more extensive and more remunerative. It was neither the monarchy nor the landed elite that made the kingdom distinctive and separate. Essentially this was the achievement of the Church, especially the bishops who propagated in each and every diocese the independence of Scotland to the kindreds of Lowland families and Highland clans. The bishops were usually highly educated civil servants or occasionally monks who came from landed families and were frequently supported in their dioceses by kinsmen strategically placed into key livings. In their promotion of an autonomous Church and state, they could draw on some support from abbots and priors, albeit as members of transnational orders they were at best lukewarm and at other times hostile to Scottish aspirations.

The number of bishoprics had increased from nine to thirteen. In the north-east, Moray became a separate diocese in the reign of William the Lion, but its seat was not settled until 1224, when Elgin was raised to the status of a burgh after the decline of neighbouring burgh of Spynie due to coastal erosion. At the same time, relocation of the bishopric at Mortlach to Aberdeen led to the creation of a bishop's burgh at Old Aberdeen on the Don. This was soon surpassed by the king's burgh of Aberdeen on the Dee. Alexander II also had the seat of Ross moved from Rosemarkie to Cromartie and that of Caithness from Halkirk to Dornoch. He also promoted the absorption of the diocese of Argyll into Scotland to be followed up by that of the Isles under his son, Alexander III.

Diocesan reorganisation was also marked by the great age of cathedral building in which Scotland largely conformed to the Romanesque or Norman styles prevalent throughout Europe. Skilled masons came not only from France and England, but also from Ireland, Norway, Flanders and the Rhineland. St Andrews, begun in 1160 and eventually consecrated in 1318, was one of the largest churches ever built in the British Isles. Probably the most elegant in Scotland was that at Elgin, begun around 1224 and completed by the end of the thirteenth century despite serious fire damage in 1270. The most complex was that at Glasgow, constructed between the thirteenth and fifteenth centuries as a double church on two levels, without the external support of transepts or flying buttresses. Although the work in most cases took centuries rather than decades to complete, the construction of cathedrals, as of abbeys and priories, testified to the burgeoning wealth of the Church. Papal demands for an ecclesiastical income tax, initially but not consistently to support Crusades in 1201, 1267 and again in 1291, confirmed the role of the parish as the basic ecclesiastical unit for finance. Parishes were usually provided with relatively small stone churches, but elaborate stone churches were to be found in growing towns such as Perth where there was no episcopal see.

The spiritual mission of the Church was not facilitated by the appropriation of parochial resources and manpower. By 1286, there were around 936 parishes in Scotland, of which 527 or 56% were appropriated to endow bishoprics and religious houses. Less than half the parishes were supplied by a parson or rector funded by teinds. The majority of the parishes were reliant on underfunded vicars or chaplains supplied by a monastery, friary or cathedral chapter. Appropriation of teinds, unchecked by the Crown, became a growing trend. To suit the interests of ecclesiastical kindreds, requirements for clerical celibacy, poverty and obedience were set aside.

In the Church, as in the state, there was a long-standing problem of English claims to overlordship. In 1174, William the Lion had promised ambiguously at Falaise that the Scottish Church would make such subjection to the English Church as it was accustomed to make in the reigns of former English kings. Two years later, a council of English and Scottish bishops was held at Northampton. Bishop Jocelyn of Glasgow unexpectedly produced a papal directive, *Super anxietatibus*, stating that his see was under the protection of the papacy as a special daughter of the Roman Church. Other Scottish bishops asserted that they owed no obedience to the archbishops of Canterbury and York. Later, in 1176, Pope Alexander III forbade York to exercise any right in Scotland that he could not prove at the papal court. This directive favoured the Scots, as York was only accepted as metropolitan by Whithorn. York could stop the Scots getting their own archbishop, but could not prevent special daughter arrangements being extended from Glasgow to other dioceses in Scotland. William the Lion became embroiled in a decade-long controversy over the bishopric of St Andrews from 1178. Adamant that he had the right both to nominate and have elected all bishops in Scotland, William alienated the papacy which was particularly wary of lay interference in clerical affairs. William was excommunicated in 1181, when all religious services in Scotland were proscribed for a year. Around 1192, Celestine III issued *Cum universi*, a directive that made the Scottish bishops the real winners in the dispute between king and papacy. All the existing Scottish bishoprics were declared to be special daughters of the Church and subject only to the papal court at Rome.

The Scots continued to lack an archbishop. The bishops had no powers to concert clerical reform until another papal directive of 1225, *Quidam vestrum*, partly rectified this by allowing the Scots to have provincial synods with a bishop elected to act as conservator of the privileges of the Scottish Church. While the primary aim of the provincial synods was to promote clerical and moral reform, they also upheld the independence of the Church and of the nation, an issue that became critical when Alexander III fatally fell from his horse at Kinghorn in Fife in 1286. Scotland was plunged into a succession crisis that ultimately compromised its very existence not just its independence.

OVERLORDSHIP IMPOSED

On the king's untimely death in 1286, his designated heir was his granddaughter, Margaret the Maid of Norway. Her father was Eric II of Norway who had married Margaret, daughter of Alexander III. As the Maid was in her infancy, the government of the kingdom was passed to guardians appointed by a parliament at Scone. General councils, as expanded versions of the king's councils, had been in place under Alexander II since 1235 and had become increasingly frequent in the last two decades of Alexander III's reign, being called to reaffirm succession by primogeniture in 1281 and to lay down the actual succession of the Maid of Norway in 1284. Such representative assemblies in the thirteenth century had dealt with judicial resolutions as with issues of war, taxation and diplomacy at the behest of the monarchy. They were attended by leading churchmen, as well as earls and lords who were also heads of the foremost kindreds. The assembly of 1286, the first parliament to represent the community of the realm in the absence of a king, chose as the six guardians two clerics – William Fraser, bishop of St Andrews; and Robert Wishart, bishop of Glasgow – together with four magnates – Alexander Comyn, the aged Earl of Buchan; Duncan, the Celtic Earl of Fife; John Comyn, Lord of Badenoch; and James Stewart, now the hereditary royal steward. The two clerics, who both represented strong ecclesiastical kindreds, effectively maintained the balance of power in a governing body which, from 1286 until 1292, attempted to keep the wheels of government turning.

In 1289, commissioners for Eric II of Norway, Edward I of England and the Scottish guardians engaged in tripartite negotiations at Salisbury.

Eric II consented that Margaret was to come to Scotland or England by November 1290. Unknown to the Scots, Edward had already applied successfully to the papacy for a dispensation for the marriage of the Maid to his son Edward. As cousins, they were within the forbidden degrees of canon law. The guardians did not object to Edward I's actions, which were endorsed by a Scottish Parliament in March 1290. Four months later, the Treaty of Birgham was concluded between English and Scottish commissioners for the marriage of Edward and Margaret that ambiguously preserved the rights, laws and liberties of Scotland. Edward I demanded that the guardians defer to any lieutenant he should appoint to oversee the interests of the married couple and castles were to be handed over as surety. These conditions were refused. After the treaty was ratified by Edward I at Northampton in August, the guardians undertook to hand over castles to the couple, once they swore to observe the customs of Scotland. The issue of homage to Edward I was neither claimed nor conceded. The proposed marriage meant a dynastic not an incorporating union. If there were no heirs from the marriage Scotland was to return to the rightful heir of the kingdom. But who was this heir? This question became critical in September when the Maid of Norway died at Orkney on her way to Scotland.

Robert Bruce, the fifth lord of Annandale of that name, moved to seize the throne. But the claim of John Balliol, his long-standing rival, was supported by two guardians – John Comyn and Bishop Fraser of St Andrews. In October 1290, the latter invited Edward I to march to the Borders to ensure the tranquillity of Scotland. Bishop Fraser also indicated that if Balliol became king, he would follow Edward's counsel. An anonymous response to the pro-Balliol guardians informed Edward I that the choice of the king of Scots belonged to the community of the realm. Neither party invited Edward to choose between Balliol and Bruce. Nevertheless, Edward I legalistically exploited the succession crisis to impose his overlordship on Scotland. The Isle of Man afforded a precedent. In June 1290, Edward had taken the Manx community into his protection. However, the petition of the islanders, which unanimously affirmed they needed protection, was made after not before the English king had reached the same conclusion and several months before the death of the Maid of Norway. His designs on Scotland were implemented from May 1291, when he presided over the court tasked by the guardians to decide not only between Balliol and Bruce but 11 other claimants.

The Great Cause, that is the judicial process that should determine who should become king of Scots, took over 18 months to resolve. Edward was intent on exploiting the disputed succession. By August, he had established a court of 104 auditors to hear and judge the 13 claims to the Scottish throne at

Berwick. The Court consisted of 24 members of his council and 40 assessors each for the two principal claimants, Balliol and Bruce. Prior to the formal submission of claims, Edward made a military incursion into Scotland pushing up to Perth, taking submissions of homage from magnates and leading clerics. Edward demanded that all competitors in the Great Cause acknowledge him as overlord of Scotland as well as sole arbiter of the judicial proceedings. Seven of the 13 complied, including Balliol and Bruce. Because of the complexity of the claims, the court was prorogued in November 1291 and again in June 1292 while Edward sought legal advice from the universities of Oxford, Cambridge and Paris. Albeit this advice proved conflicting, Edward gave his judgement in November 1292. Scotland, like any other true kingdom should not be divided up even though the main claimants were descended from the co-heiresses of Prince David, the younger brother of Malcolm IV and William the Lion. Of the two principal claimants, Balliol was the grandson of Prince David's daughter, Margaret, while Bruce was the son of Prince David's second daughter, Isabella. By the strict application of primogeniture, John Balliol was declared king.

Prior to his inauguration as king of Scots on St Andrew's Day (30 November), Balliol did homage to Edward I. He thereby accepted the status of client-king. Only Bruce among the leading clerics and magnates in Scotland withheld homage to King John, whose reign of less than four years was not without accomplishment. He held parliaments, administered justice and took steps to recover royal lands alienated during the guardianship. But he was bedevilled by appeals, often encouraged by Edward I, which required his attendance as a client-king at the English court. Edward's rebuttal of Scottish protests against judicial cases being taken out of Scotland was accepted by John. The Scottish magnates and bishops took collective action against John in July 1295, depriving him of power in favour of a council of 12. Three months later, the council concluded a defensive and offensive alliance with France, which was duly approved by John in a parliament attended by representatives from the leading burghs in February 1296. Although this was the genesis of 'the auld alliance', the French reneged on providing armed assistance when some magnates rebelled against Edward I. Robert Bruce, the son of the competitor of 1291–2, who had acquired the Celtic earldom of Carrick two decades earlier, was among Edward's supporters.

In March 1296, after Edward I laid waste to the town of Berwick, John renounced his allegiance. In April, a sizeable Scottish army was routed at Dunbar. Three months later, resistance gave way to submission as magnates and leading clerics did homage to Edward I. In July, Balliol surrendered himself, his kingdom and his people at Stracathro in Angus. He was stripped of his status as a client-king. Edward I summarily rejected the claim to the Scottish throne of Bruce the younger. John de Warenne, Earl of Surrey, the victorious commander at Dunbar was made sole Guardian of Scotland. Berwick, which was resettled with English merchants and craftsmen, became the centre of Edward's Scottish administration. The records and regalia of the Scottish crown were removed to England, as was a piece of cut rock that Edward I believed to be the Stone of Destiny, on which the kings of Scots had been inaugurated at Scone since the ninth century.

THE WARS OF WALLACE AND BRUCE

Although the nobility was defeated and John Balliol was exiled in France, a new rising against Edward I was led by William Wallace, the younger son of a Renfrewshire laird. His first act of resistance had been to murder William Hazelrigg, the sheriff of Lanark appointed by Edward I. Based on an extant sword of around 1.63 metres in length, Wallace cut an imposing figure as an exceedingly tall man close to 2 metres in height. Establishing himself as the leader of an outlaw band in Ettrick Forest in the Borders, he attracted the support of lairds of French and Flemish stock whose loyalties were not compromised by landholdings in England. Further support was gathered from Scottish kindreds of diverse origins facing forfeiture for refusing to pay taxes or do military service overseas.

Rebellion did not become a national endeavour until Wallace, from a British kindred, linked up with Sir Andrew Moray from Flemish stock, who was leading resistance in the north-east. At the same time, Robert Bruce, the grandson of the competitor in the Great Cause and now Earl of Carrick, with backing from James the Steward and Bishop Wishart of Glasgow, initiated a rising in Ayrshire that soon crumbled after a skirmish with English forces at Irvine. Wallace and Moray combined to smash an English army of far superior numbers at Stirling Bridge on 11 September 1297. The defeat of the celebrated English cavalry by well-drilled Scottish infantry was unexpected. The losses on the English side were compounded by drowning of English infantrymen in the River Forth once their cavalry stampeded. One of the English commanders, Hugh Cressingham, was killed and skinned by the rampaging Scots. Moray was severely wounded and died three months later.

Largely with the support of the Church and the Scottish kindreds who had mobilised to join him and Moray, Wallace assumed the guardianship of Scotland in the name of John Balliol and was knighted at Selkirk. Apart from pursuing guerrilla warfare, Wallace issued writs for government, mustered the army and appointed bishops – most notably, William Lamberton to St Andrews. Wallace was intent on promoting Scotland not just as a land or dependent, but as an independent kingdom. He worked through councils and diplomatically pushed the claims of Balliol at the French court and with the papacy. He promoted trading relations as evident from his one extant letter, written with the ailing Moray, to the Hanseatic towns of Lubeck and Hamburg in northern Germany. Although he continued to rally the kindreds and stepped up their training as infantry, he was soundly defeated at Falkirk on 22 July 1298 by superior English forces commanded on this occasion by Edward I, a warrior king not noted for his mercy. The desultory cavalry provided by the Scottish nobility held back from the fray and indeed withdrew before the final slaughter commenced.

Although he escaped the carnage, Wallace surrendered his guardianship and returned to guerrilla resistance before leaving in 1299 on a four-year mission to pursue the case for John Balliol at Paris and Rome. In Wallace's absence abroad, those Scots pursuing patriotic resistance elected a series of guardians of whom John Comyn, Lord of Badenoch and nephew of John Balliol, and Robert Bruce, Earl of Carrick, were the most prominent. Bishop Lamberton became the principal Scottish diplomat to France. When the possibility of a French-backed restoration of Balliol was mooted, Carrick made his peace with Edward I. The English king campaigned personally in Scotland in 1300 and again in 1301. He achieved little apart from the capture of Border castles and the dispersal of Scottish forces. He mounted a more substantial invasion in 1303. Despite Wallace and Lamberton's best endeavours, there was little prospect of support from France or the papacy. Nevertheless Comyn, acting in concert with Wallace's close ally Sir Simon Fraser, defeated an English advance vanguard at Roslin in Mid-Lothian in February 1304. Although the main English force penetrated as far north as Moray, Edward concentrated on besieging castles held by the Scots. After the fall of Stirling Castle, there was a general surrender of the leaders of the Scottish resistance in July 1304.

Edward I summoned a Scottish Parliament in May 1305 to elect commissioners to attend at Westminster where they were to treat with English commissioners on how the land of Scotland was to be governed. Although greatly outnumbered, the Scottish commissioners were not prepared to abandon their allegiance to the community of the realm which held Scotland to be a kingdom. Edward had granted relatively generous terms to those of the nobility and leading clergy who surrendered and accepted him as overlord. But this was certainly not the case for Wallace who had returned to pursue guerrilla warfare in 1303 with little encouragement from those who had assumed the guardianship. Wallace was captured in August 1305 by the English forces after he was betrayed at Dumbarton Castle by Sir John Stewart of Menteith.

The brutal vengeance inflicted on Sir William Wallace by Edward I more than hints at psychopathic behaviour. Taken to London in chains, Wallace was humiliatingly bound to a horse and dragged through the city with a crown of laurel leaves placed on his head. At a show trial in Westminster, he faced trumped-up charges that he desired to be a king, not just a king-maker. Both aspirations were well beyond his social status in the eyes of Edward I who denied Wallace the chance to speak in his own defence. He was sentenced to a barbaric execution at Smithfield on 23 August 1305. He was first hanged then taken down barely alive from the gallows to be drawn out, effectively disembowelled. Prior to having his head cut off and his body quartered, he cried out that he had no cause to be deemed a traitor to Edward I as he had never sworn allegiance to the English king. His head was affixed to London Bridge and the four body parts were despatched back to Newcastle, Berwick, Perth and Stirling as a warning to rebellious Scots.

Wallace has an enduring legacy in Scottish history, not just for epic heroism in leading the Scottish resistance or for his execution as a martyr for liberty. His patriotism has proved enduring and transcending of social, ethnic and religious divisions. He galvanised the community of the realm in pursuit of independence, a cause that could not be left to political, religious or commercial elites.

Wallace's execution was followed up by that of other prominent rebels in the eyes of Edward I at London, Newcastle and Carlisle in 1306. Robert Bruce, Earl of Carrick, with support from Bishop Lamberton of St Andrews, put forward a claim to the throne. In furtherance of this claim, Bruce had actually murdered his rival John Comyn after negotiations between them in Greyfriars Kirk, Dumfries, took a violent turn. Notwithstanding his automatic excommunication once the deed was reported to the papacy, Bruce proceeded to have himself inaugurated as king of Scots at Scone in March. Bruce enjoyed qualified backing from important leaders of the Church in Scotland, the hesitant support of several nobles and the ready acclaim of an impressive list of lairds and heads of kindreds. Backing from the community of the realm transformed his cause from that of a dynastic claimant to that of a national leader. However, his killing of Comyn plunged Scotland into civil war.

Initially, the new king had limited success in besieging castles in the southwest, Fife and Aberdeenshire. Bruce was overwhelmed by English forces at Methven near Perth in June 1306. As he made his way west in July he was routed at Strathfillan on Loch Earn by the MacDougalls of Argyll, close allies of the murdered Comyn. Three of his brothers had been captured and executed. His wife Elizabeth was kept under house arrest, his sister Christian was despatched to a nunnery, and another sister Mary was secured in a cage within Roxburgh Castle. His daughter Marjory was threatened with the same humiliation in the Tower of London. Isabel, Countess of Buchan, who had installed Bruce as king at Scone, was placed in solitary confinement in a cage within Berwick Castle. Deprived of his family by the vindictive Edward I and reduced to a handful of followers, Bruce took strength from adversity. While resting in a cave on the Isle of Rathlin in the North Channel, reputedly watching a spider strive to spin a web, Bruce discovered the fortitude necessary to win both the civil and the patriotic war.[2] He returned to Scotland at the outset of 1307 determined not only to follow Wallace's pursuit of guerrilla warfare to grind down his enemies, but also to besiege and destroy castles held by or for the English. In this strategy, which utilised surprise attacks at night, he was ably assisted by his brother Edward, by Sir James Douglas, whose father William had been an associate of Wallace, and by Sir Thomas Randolph, a nephew of Bruce who had been an adherent of Balliol.

Bruce first pursued his guerrilla strategy in Carrick and Galloway. He even engaged successfully in an encounter with English forces at Loudon Hill in Ayrshire in May 1307. An added bonus was the death of Edward I at Burgh on Sands on the Solway Firth two months later as he prepared for another Scottish campaign. His son and successor, Edward II, lacked his military capacity and the bloody-minded determination. Repeated campaigning in Scotland was ruinously expensive and logistically difficult to provision given the scorched earth policy pursued by the Scottish guerrillas. An expeditionary force sent by Edward II in late 1310 did little to shore up the English position in Scotland. Bruce came to dominate the Comyn faction by successfully besieging castles, defeating them in battle at Inverurie in the Garrioch in May 1308 and harrying their territories in Buchan, Moray and Ross. He moved on to Argyll where, in August, he avenged his past defeat by the MacDougalls with a resounding victory in the Pass of Brander between Ben Cruachan and Loch Awe. Bruce was also magnanimous in welcoming former opponents into his ranks as evident from his winning over of Sir James Stewart of Menteith, the betrayer of Wallace.

Bruce still faced formidable opposition in central and south-eastern Scotland when he determined to carry the war to England. His forces attacked Durham in the summer of 1312. He began to levy blackmail or protection money which weakened the capacity of the northern counties to contribute financially to the English war effort and compounded the problems Edward II was having in securing the support of his northern nobility. By October 1313, Bruce switched to a high-risk strategy. In a general council at Dundee, he announced that the estates of any landowner not swearing allegiance to him within the next 12 months were to be forfeited. By March 1314, all the leading

Scottish castles except for Stirling and Roxburgh had fallen to Bruce. Edward Bruce when laying siege to Stirling Castle in May made an agreement with its Scottish commander, Sir Philip Mowbray. If Edward II had not raised the siege by mid-summer's day, the castle would be surrendered. This was not a fool-hardy gesture, but a calculated manoeuvre to test the mettle of Edward II and allow Bruce to choose the ground for a decisive pitched battle.

Edward II, who had conspicuously failed to support Bruce's opponents during the civil war, duly responded as King Robert wished. Fortified by a substantial loan from the papacy and taxation from his nobles, Edward II had already proclaimed that the English army was to muster at Berwick by midsummer 1314, a date subsequently advanced to 10 June. Edward Bruce made his agreement with Mowbray after the Scots were apprised of this shift. Having reached Berwick at the end of May, Edward II ordered his troops to march for Stirling. But Bruce had gained valuable time to lay out his battle plans and prepare the ground for a pitched battle against superior numbers.

The battle of Bannockburn lasted two days on 23 and 24 June. Bruce's tactics at Bannockburn were reminiscent of Wallace's at Stirling Bridge. He chose the heights for the Scottish troops, primarily infantrymen organised in three brigades under Edward Bruce, Sir James Douglas and Sir Thomas Randolph, now Earl of Moray; with a fourth in reserve com-manded by himself. On the first day of battle, a heavily armed English knight on horseback spotted the Scottish king giving instructions from a pony. Henry de Bohun charged the relatively unprotected king who had his pony sidestep the horse. Bruce then skewered the English knight with a battle-axe. Suitably inspired, the Scottish forces repelled the English vanguard. Randolph's brigade prevented a flanking movement by English cavalry. However, some faint hearts among the Scottish nobility did desert on both evenings of battle, but not in the numbers or with the impact that befell Wallace at Falkirk. When battle was fully engaged, the intervention of mem-bers of the baggage train kept at nearby Cambuskenneth Abbey confounded the English. The River Forth again claimed numerous English lives with as many lost in the chaos of battle as in actual combat. Edward II fled the field.

Bannockburn had not secured the independence of Scotland which Edward II, safely back in England, refused to concede. Accordingly Bruce went on the offensive to stretch English resources and ratchet up the tensions between Edward II and his nobility. Over the next four years, he increased the cross-Border raids and levied blackmail systematically. His raids were carefully planned, usually proceeding through Northumberland to Durham and occa-sionally to Yorkshire before returning through Westmorland and Cumberland. Having ratified the Treaty of Perth with the Norwegian crown in 1312, Bruce authorised a six-week siege of Rushen Castle on Man in the following year, but it was not until 1317 that Randolph, Earl of Moray, made a successful reconquest of the island. The raids on Man were greatly facilitated by Hebridean sea-power, with the MacDonalds being the principal providers of galleys for Robert I. Thereafter he deployed the seafaring tradition of Man and the Isles to harass the west coast of England and supplement the destructive but remunerative impact of his cross-Border raiding.

Success on Man, however, was not replicated in Ireland. Edward Bruce had invaded in 1315 to support the Gaelic lords against the Anglo-Irish allies of Edward II. From the mid-thirteenth century, the English monarchy had utilised Ulster as a base for raiding across the North Channel, particularly in Galloway and the Isles. In 1286, Bruce's father and grandfather had allied themselves with Richard de Burgh, Earl of Ulster and an immensely powerful Anglo-Irish lord. His estates stretched from Ulster to Connacht. Around 1302, while he was still collaborating with Edward I, the future King Robert had married the Earl of Ulster's daughter, Elizabeth. The expedition to Ireland in 1315 had two specific objectives, to wrest Ulster from Richard de Burgh and to have Edward Bruce made high-king of Ireland with Gaelic backing. Edward Bruce's initial campaigning in 1315 and again in 1316 was relatively successful. He routed the Earl of Ulster. After threatening the centre of English control in Dublin, he was duly inaugurated as high-king. However, Edward could not be sure of consistent support from the Gaelic lords or of regular reinforcements from Scotland.

King Robert joined his brother for the spring campaign in 1317, bringing reinforcements which again imperilled the English government in Dublin. The Bruce brothers favoured a scorched earth policy to lay waste to Anglo-Irish lordships in Leinster and Munster. By the time they pushed west into Connacht, Irish Gaelic support was diminishing and reinforcements were arriving from England. Famine forced their retreat north. King Robert departed Ulster by the end of April. The Scottish conquest of Ireland was no longer feasible. When Edward Bruce rashly moved out of Ulster he was defeated and killed at Fochart near Dundalk in October 1318. The crushing victory of the Anglo-Irish forces was facilitated by significant desertions of his Gaelic allies.

NATION BUILDING

Despite his chequered record as a patriot before he seized the throne in 1306, Bruce proved himself a more accomplished military commander than Wallace. He had the further advantage that he could use the full powers of monarchy to secure Scottish independence. Wallace's legacy to Bruce was more than the successful tactics of Stirling Bridge being repeated at Bannockburn. Wallace had empowered the community of the realm which Bruce deployed for nation building. The regular summoning of parliaments and general councils to institutionalise the community's voice was a key element in winning support for the cause of independence at home and abroad. At his first parliament held at St Andrews in March 1309, the magnates issued a letter to Philip IV of France that Robert I was recognised as king of Scots not only by earls, lords and their followers, but by all the inhabitants of Scotland. A declaration from leading clergy to the papacy followed. Robert I was not only the rightful king but the liberator who was delivering Scotland from bondage.

In November 1314, a parliament at Cambuskenneth Abbey approved Bruce's forfeiture of those who had fought against him at Bannockburn and also those that had failed to swear allegiance to him in the past 12 months, as required by the general council at Dundee. The disinherited became a disgruntled grouping in exile in England, ready and willing to serve Edward II against the Bruce, particularly after Edward Balliol returned from France in 1318, five years after his father John died in Picardy. Balliol's return compounded the problems of the succession. At a parliament in Scone in December 1318, Robert, the son of Bruce's daughter Marjory from her marriage to Walter the Steward, became the designated successor at the age of 12. As King Robert had refused to observe a directive from the papacy that he should agree a peace or truce with Edward II, he had been duly excommunicated in June. After Edward II failed in his attempt to regain Berwick, Bruce agreed to a two-year truce. But Pope John XXII insisted in November 1319 that Lambert of St Andrews and three other Scottish bishops should attend the papal court. They declined to attend. With the backing of the king, leading clergy, nobles and lairds, they collectively issued a letter of defence on 6 April 1320 that became celebrated as the Declaration of Arbroath.

Written by Bruce's chancellor, Bernard de Linton, abbot of Arbroath, the Declaration was signed by eight earls and 31 barons on behalf of the rest of barons and freeholders 'and the whole community of the realm of Scotland'. The signatories, who included a Norse element in the person of Magnus, Earl of Caithness and Orkney, were also speaking on behalf of the foremost kindreds engaged in the War of Independence. The Declaration had three main components. Firstly, the origins of the Scots as a migrant people were traced to Greater Scythia around the Black Sea from where they travelled through the Mediterranean before settling in Spain and then proceeding to Scotland where they expelled the Britons, destroyed the Picts and fought off repeated incursions by Norsemen, Danes and Angles. They had been kept free from servitude by 113 kings of native royal stock. They were among the first Christian kingdoms and Andrew the first of the apostles – who had preached in Scythia – was their patron saint. This distinctive Gaelic identity for Scotland, which drew heavily on the mythical origins of the Irish Gaels, had been utilised when King Robert and his brother Edward had intervened in Ireland. The concept of a free kingdom and a free people had been formulated by clerical theorists in the mid-thirteenth century and, indeed, endorsed by the papacy when refusing the request of Henry III to collect ecclesiastical taxation in Scotland during the minority of Alexander III. Secondly, King Robert was the liberator of his people and ruled with their consent. However, the commitment of the community of the realm was not unconditional. Should he chose to subject Scotland to the English king or the English people, 'we would strive to thrust him out forthwith as our enemy and the subverter of right, his own and ours, and take for our king another who would suffice for our defence'. This defence of elective kingship was further affirmed 'for so long as an hundred remain alive we are minded never a whit to bow beneath the yoke of English domination'. Thirdly, beneath this resounding rhetoric was an admission from the political elite that they were to be judged by their commitment to the community of the realm:

It is not for glory, riches or honours that we fight: it is for liberty alone, the liberty which no good man relinquishes but with his life.[3]

Any member of the elite falling below the expected standards for the common weal could expect to be prosecuted as a traitor. This was soon borne out by the failure of an assassination plot against King Robert contrived in the aftermath of the Declaration of Arbroath by one of its signatories, William Soules, Lord of Liddesdale, a relative of the Comyns, who had come into the allegiance of Bruce after Bannockburn, where he had fought for Edward II. Soules and his accomplices were supportive of Edward Balliol, whose claim to the throne carried the threat of English overlordship. Forewarned of the plot, Bruce apprehended the conspirators and brought them for trial before parliament at Scone in August 1320. On confessing his guilt, Soules was given life imprisonment. Four of his accomplices, who had not escaped with other plotters to England, were hanged then beheaded after being dragged behind horses through the streets of Perth.

The governance of King Robert was more concerned with promoting stability than ruling with severity. To this end, he was prepared to innovate, as was evident by his use of the Scots not the Gaelic language or the usual Latin for parliamentary enactments in 1318. His most extensive innovation was the creation of baronies that authorised local government by lords and lairds. As a heritable jurisdiction, the barony was also institutional recognition of the personal authority exercised by heads of kindreds, not all of whom became barons. Thanages held by officials appointed by the kings or earls were now superseded. The principal concern of barony courts was estate management. The barony court could order the mutilation of thieves and the execution of murderers if caught red-handed. Royal government through the sheriff courts was now essentially about harmonising differences between barons and other freeholders.

Baronies proliferated under Robert I, who used them to reward the leading kindreds who had consistently supported him, by expanding their landed power into several sheriffdoms that were not always contiguous. The Bruce also permitted less established kindreds to consolidate their landed presence in the sheriffdoms in which they principally resided. Latecomers into his allegiance were also given baronies. The main beneficiaries of the disinheritance promulgated in the wake of Bannockburn in 1314 and the plot of 1320 were his closest allies, the Douglases in the south-west and the Borders and the Randolphs in the north. The Stewarts consolidated in the west and made moderate acquisitions in the east. The MacDougalls lost out to the MacDonalds of the Isles.

King Robert also began the process of awarding heritable jurisdictions known as regalities which were first granted to Thomas Randolph for his earldom of Moray and his lordship of Man in 1324. Regalities involved extensive civil and criminal powers, apart from trials for treason, and excluded all royal officials from their bounds. Lords of regality were permitted to repledge, that is transfer, cases involving their kinsmen and followers from sheriff or justiciar courts. Lordships of regality were subsequently awarded to the Douglases and the Stewarts and effectively implemented by the MacDonalds as Lords of the Isles. That Scotland was becoming a patchwork quilt of heritable jurisdictions was confirmed when Robert I, starting with Aberdeen in 1319, permitted the leading burghs to pay their annual duties to the Crown as a feu-ferme fixed in perpetuity rather than as a lease that was negotiated periodically. This concession allowed the burghs to pool surplus revenue into a common good fund that could be used for community projects such as the repair of public buildings, the extension of streets and the acquisition of pastoral land. The growing importance of the burghs in helping finance war and diplomacy led to burgesses attending the parliament of 1326 at Cambuskenneth Abbey that awarded Robert I an annual tenth of all rents for life and that of 1328 at Edinburgh which accorded a further tenth for three years to pay for war damages.

The pursuit of stability became particularly important after the birth of a son, David, in 1324, who was confirmed as Robert I's heir in the parliament of 1326. The prospect of a minority was now likely, particularly as the king had not enjoyed the best of health since his island-hopping, cave-dwelling sojourn in the North Channel in 1306. The 'auld alliance', reaffirmed by the Treaty of Corbeuil in April 1326, helped sway the papacy, now removed to Avignon in southern France, to look more favourably on Scottish independence. The turmoil between the king and his nobility in England culminated in the palace coup of 1327 that deposed and cruelly despatched Edward II. The regency government for his son, the new king Edward III, was highly vulnerable to the ongoing Scottish military offensive in the northern counties. The Irish dimension was again brought into play by Robert I when he crossed to Ulster at Easter 1327 to claim the earldom of his recently deceased father-in-law. Challenged by the king's four-month stay, the regency government for Edward III raised forces for an invasion of Scotland. But, three battalions under Moray, Douglas and the king's nephew Donald, Earl of Mar, crossed the Border and ran the English troops ragged. King Robert, on his return from Ulster, led reinforcements into England, threatened to annex Northumberland and by October 1327 was ready to dictate the terms for peace with the regency government.

A peace treaty negotiated in Edinburgh and ratified by the Scottish Parliament in March 1328 was subsequently approved by the English Parliament at Northampton in May. Scotland was recognised as a distinct and free kingdom, quit of all subjection to England. The Bruce's son, David, was to marry Joan, the sister of Edward III. This was duly accomplished at Berwick in July, but Robert I was incapacitated and Edward refused to attend. By October, the papacy had lifted its interdict on Scotland. King Robert and his close associates were no longer excommunicated. A papal directive on 13 June conferred the privilege of a full coronation, with enthronement and anointing to future kings of Scots. Robert I had died at Cardross in Dunbartonshire six days earlier. This privilege was first exercised at the coronation of his son, as David II, at Scone in November 1331.

WARFARE AND BRINKMANSHIP

The War of Independence entered its second phase following the death of Robert the Bruce. Sir James Douglas died In Spain taking the Bruce's heart on Crusade in 1330. Randolph, Earl of Moray, who had assumed the guardianship, died in 1331. His successor, Donald, Earl of Mar, was killed in the defeat at Dupplin in Perthshire in August 1332, when Edward Balliol and the disinherited returned in force from England. Balliol went on to be crowned at Scone where he was acclaimed as king of Scots in September by not only the disinherited but also dissident Scottish nobles, lairds and clergy. However, he was chased out of Scotland in December after he was defeated at Annan in Dumfriesshire by forces led by Sir Archibald Douglas, brother of Sir James; Robert the Steward; and John Randolph, son and successor to the late Earl of Moray. Edward III formally repudiated the Treaty of Edinburgh–Northampton and invaded Scotland, crushing forces loyal to David II at Halidon Hill on the Borders in May 1333. The next year, David II, then ten years of age, was despatched to France. In a vain attempt to rally the community of the realm behind him, Edward Balliol held a parliament in Edinburgh in February 1334. Balliol ceded the Lothians, the Borders and Dumfriesshire to Edward III. Scotland was to be governed under English direction from Berwick.

During the six years of David II's exile in France, central government in Scotland remained contested between Edward Balliol and a succession of guardians for the young Bruce. Although they had moderate success in skirmishes, the guardians had a tendency to be killed in battle or captured. Edward Balliol proved a far from effective ruler. Desertions from his forces aided the Scots to regroup north of the Forth and recover lands to the south under English occupation. Although John Randolph's lordship of Man was annexed by Edward III in 1333, English control over the island was not secured until 1344. Balliol's tenuous position was shored up by an English invasion in the summer of 1335 which penetrated as far as Perth. However, his Scottish allies were defeated in November at Culblean in Aberdeenshire by forces commanded by Sir Andrew Moray of Bothwell, the son of Wallace's colleague at the outset of the Wars of Independence. While the throne was disputed, local government continued to operate through regalities and baronies. Once Robert the Steward, David II's much older nephew, became guardian in 1339, the customs from the burghs and other royal revenues were regularised. The young king returned from exile in France in 1341.

Edward Balliol's rapid loss of support was not helped by Edward III's attempts to claim the French crown and, in the process, instigate what became known as the Hundred Years War in 1336. In serving France by invading England, David II was defeated and captured at Neville's Cross in County Durham in March 1346. John Randolph, 2nd Earl of Moray, was killed and Robert the Steward fled the field. David II was to remain captive in England for 13 years. Robert the Steward and the Douglases eventually recovered most of the land ceded by Edward Balliol apart from the lands in Annandale and around Berwick and Roxburgh. Although Scotland had been battered by six decades of warfare, it was only marginally afflicted by the bubonic plague or Black Death which afflicted much of continental Europe, Scandinavia and England in the late 1340s. The regency government reinvigorated Scottish trade to the Low Countries when a staple port was established in Flanders at Middleburg in 1347, but soon shifted back to Bruges where the staple seemingly originated in the 1320s. Staple ports acted as funnels whereby basic Scottish commodities (fish, wool, cheap cloth, animal skins and pelts) were distributed wholesale in Northern Europe in exchange for goods processed on the continent and luxury items collated from the Mediterranean and the Middle East.

Although Edward Balliol had made a brief foray from Carlisle into Scotland reaching as far as Falkirk in 1347, he retained only a token presence in Galloway and by 1354 was a spent force, albeit he enjoyed a relatively generous pension from Edward III until his death in 1364. Hard-pressed financially by his French wars, Edward III decided to release David II in 1357 for a ransom of 100,000 merks (£66,667) which was to be paid off in instalments of 10,000 merks over ten years. However, Edward III had declined to recognise David II as king of Scots. For his part, David, who had no legitimate male heirs, was prepared to gamble on the Scottish succession. At the outset of 1352, in an attempt to engineer his release from captivity, he proposed that one of the English king's younger sons could succeed in preference to Robert the Steward who had abandoned David II at Neville's Cross. He returned to Scotland on parole for five months to have this arrangement formalised, but a parliament at Scone would not accept English overlordship. In an attempt to moderate the terms for the ransom payments, David renewed his succession proposal in 1363, which was also emphatically rejected in the Scottish Parliament at Scone in 1364 where Robert the Steward could count on the support of Lord William Douglas and John MacDonald, Lord of the Isles, who had become his son-in-law. Not only were the nobility resistant to this brinkmanship. They had wholehearted support from the clergy and the burgesses who had effectively become the third estate in parliament from 1357, when their commercial acumen was deemed vital to meeting regular payments for the ransom.

Parliament, like the king, was anxious to reduce the ransom. But the estates would not alter the succession nor recognise English overlordship. Edward III duly agreed to a modification of the ransom in 1365; the annual instalments were reduced to 6,000 merks (£4,000) annually, yet the total to be paid was raised to £100,000. Edward III had long been concerned that the Scottish government, even before the return of David II in 1357, were debasing the coinage by reducing its silver content, a step made necessary by the limited supplies of silver (and gold) from overseas trade. A general devaluation, implemented by David II in 1367 to clear off his domestic debts, failed to stimulate exports, made imports more expensive and augmented his international debts. Two years later, with a new French campaign beckoning, Edward III ratified the original ransom of 100,000 merks. As 44,000 merks had been paid off, the remainder was to be paid in annual instalments of 4,000 merks. A projected ten-year ransom still had fourteen years to run.

David II was not only given to brinkmanship, he was also a financial opportunist. He insisted on his right to revoke grants of lands and heritable jurisdictions make in his minority and in his absence by regency governments. The revocation of charters detrimental to his interests was duly approved in parliaments in 1357 and 1367 as were his acts creating earldoms most notably that of Strathearn for Robert the Steward and of Douglas for Lord William Douglas. Earldoms usually, but not routinely, were accorded regality powers. On his return from England, David II was allowed a 20% share on all sales of wools and skins. Customs were doubled and then trebled in the first two years after his return and then quadrupled in 1368. Renewed taxes benefited from a revaluation of lands, rents and trading stock in 1357 and again in 1365. The parliament of 1358 had agreed to additional land and property taxes for three years to pay off the ransom and relieve the king's debts. Yet by 1360, David had defaulted on the ransom after paying two instalments. Despite renegotiation in 1365 and 1369, payments remained irregular and incomplete. Another tax, on the twentieth of all rents in 1370, was expended on diplomatic embassies. David II's chief critic in parliament and general councils was consistently Robert the Steward, supported usually by the new earl of Douglas and occasionally by the Lord of the Isles. David II, who viewed parliament as a tool of political patronage and as insurance for his own imprudence, threatened to remove the Steward from the succession in 1363 and had him marginalised in the running of central government by 1369.

In addition to parliamentary tensions over the ransom, there was persistent criticism over the partiality of royal officials in the administration of justice specifically and in governance generally, which was increasingly centralised on Edinburgh. David II sold remissions or pardons for homicide as an income stream for the Crown rather than as reparations for wronged kindreds. Although he was a relatively efficient manager of parliament, the three estates remained wary of any moves by David II to diminish the 'auld alliance'. Defaulting on the ransom was preferable to peace with England. When David died in 1371, he was succeeded by Robert the Steward. As his coronation and anointment as Robert II was contested neither within Scotland nor by Edward

III, the wars for independence were seemingly brought to a successful conclusion. However, the new Stewart dynasty was promptly reminded that the Scotland's independence was not to be compromised by any backsliding on the 'auld alliance' in favour of an accommodation with the untrustworthy English. In 1373, the archdeacon of Aberdeen, John Barbour, published his enduring work of epic heroism triumphing over adversity, *The Bruce* – the stirring antidote to brinkmanship.

PARTIAL GOVERNMENT

Robert II succeeded in 1371, aged about 55. His son, Robert III, succeeded at the same age in 1390. Although the early Stewart kings came relatively late to the throne, their main problem was not that of geriatric kingship, but of an enlarged and assertive royal family. The royal Stewards came to hold eight of the fifteen Scottish earldoms. John, Earl of Carrick, the future Robert III and the eldest son of Robert II, effectively removed his father from power in 1384, albeit the sidelined king did retain oversight of war and peace. Four years later, Carrick was ousted by his brother Robert, Earl of Fife. After Robert III ascended the throne, both brothers worked in tandem. Robert III created the new Scottish title of duke for his eldest son, David, and his brother Robert, who became respectively Duke of Rothesay and Duke of Albany in 1398. In the following year, Robert III effectively handed over the reins of power to Rothesay. Albany, with the assistance of Archibald, 4th Earl of Douglas, imprisoned Rothesay in Falklands Castle in Fife, a captivity that proved fatal. When Robert III died in 1406, Albany, then aged 65, became guardian of Scotland. His grip over Scotland was effectively strengthened by the capture of Rothesay's younger brother, James, when a ship carrying him to France in 1406 was seized by English pirates. James, now heir to Robert II, had been sent to France to remove him from Albany's control. He was to spend the first 18 years of his reign in captivity in England, eventually being released for a ransom of 60,000 merks (£40,000) in 1424 that was negotiated by Albany's eldest son, Murdoch, who had succeeded to the guardianship in 1420.

Albany had co-operated with Robert III to discipline their unruly brother, Alexander, Lord of Badenoch and for a time Earl of Buchan and of Ross. Alexander, whose lawlessness was condemned in parliament in 1384, mounted predatory raids from the Aberdeenshire in the east to Argyllshire in the west. His sacking of Elgin Cathedral in 1390 confirmed his notoriety as the 'Wolf of Badenoch'. Notwithstanding his bad press from clerical chroniclers, Alexander complied with Albany's directive to make reparations to the bishop of Moray.

Albany was less than even-handed in his treatment of the Wolf of Badenoch's son, also called Alexander who, after acquiring the earldom of Mar, pressed his claim on the earldom of Ross. Donald, Lord of the Isles, had as secure a claim through his marriage to Margaret, heiress to the earldom. In pursuit of this inheritance, Donald marched eastwards into Aberdeenshire where he was met by the forces of Alexander, Earl of Mar, at Harlaw in August 1411. The ensuing bloody conflict resulted in no outright victory, but Donald withdrew to the west. His claim on Ross was rejected by Albany to whom Donald submitted in 1412. Rather than favour the earl of Mar, Albany intruded his second son, John, then earl of Buchan, into the earldom of Ross. But the claim of Donald's wife on Ross was duly passed on to their son, Alexander, who was granted the earldom following Donald's death in 1423. Notwithstanding their expansion into Skye and across the North Channel to Antrim and their consolidation in Lochaber, Harlaw was actually the last major concerted action of the Clan Donald under the Lords of the Isles.

The main military theatre in Scotland was actually the Borders. In keeping with the practice of magnates taking the lead in defending Scottish interests during the second phase of the Wars of the Independence, Albany was to the fore in recovering lands in southern Scotland still under English control. Notwithstanding his own record as a guardian, Robert II was notably reluctant to engage in further military conflict with Edward III as David II's ransom had still to be paid off. But both Robert III and Albany decisively favoured France. They were strongly supported in their implementation of the 'auld alliance' by the Douglases in the Lothians and the Borders. By 1384, English-occupied territories were being overrun. English retaliation was largely ineffectual as the Scots, with French assistance, carried their scorched earth strategy of devastation into the northern counties. Only the strongholds of Jedburgh, Roxburgh and Berwick remained in English hands.

Following the death of Edward III in 1387, his son and successor, Richard II, was intent on confrontation with the Scots. After the burning of Melrose Abbey, his invasion was countered in 1388. Albany mounted a raid on the northern counties to exploit the rivalry between the powerful families of the Percies and the Nevilles and force a peace treaty that would recognise the independence of the Scottish kingdom, as Robert I had successfully accomplished 60 years earlier. Notwithstanding Richard II's ongoing difficulties with his English nobility, Albany did not secure the desired diplomatic recognition. However, Scottish independence was effectively secured overnight on 5 August when vastly superior English numbers were defeated at Otterburn in Redesdale. The victorious Scots earned considerable sums for ransoming the many English nobles that were taken prisoner.

Largely on account of Scottish adventuring, Border warfare resumed after Henry IV seized the English throne with the murder of Richard II in 1399. English troops defeated a Scottish expeditionary force at Homildon Hill in Northumberland. Henry IV was more intent on crushing rebellion at home and pursuing war against France. He made no serious effort to impose English overlordship on Scotland. By 1409, Jedburgh had been recovered though Roxburgh and Berwick remained in English hands. After he succeeded his father in 1413, Henry V was intent on keeping Scotland peaceful during his nine-year rule while he attempted to conquer France. Predatory raiding rather than full-scale invasion became the norm. Families of reivers with scant respect for demarcated Borders came to prominence from Annandale in the west to the Merse in the east.

Robert II and, to a lesser extent, Robert III were more generous and even-handed than David II with grants of lands, offices and privileges. Notwithstanding repeated criticisms about their laxity in upholding law and order, they sought to work co-operatively with parliaments and general councils, a policy facilitated by their reluctance to ask for taxation. Sheriffdoms were reinvigorated under Albany. But the office of sheriff was becoming hereditary, a practice that favoured the dominant kindreds in sheriffdoms and led to the exercise of partial justice. Grants of regalities also rewarded dominant kindreds. Nevertheless, lords of regalities developed sophisticated administrations as their power extended over baronies as well as freeholds and burghs. Yet kinship was no longer sufficient to hold together powerful families or clans. Loyalty within the extended royal family was sustained by bonds of retainer or of retinue which kept Albany in office.

In 1372, William, 1st Earl of Douglas, retained Sir James Douglas of Dalkeith, granting him 600 merks (£400) over three years for the provision of 8 knights and 16 archers. This was not a major fighting retinue but was a clear indication that Douglas kinship, which became particularly strained after the creation of the separate earldom of Angus for William's illegitimate son George in 1389, was no guarantee of loyalty. These bonds, which were often financed by the pilfering of royal revenues, had become commonplace by 1399. Kinship was enhanced by other bonds. The bond of manrent or maintenance extended political clientage, bringing one family under the protection of another in the running of local government or in building up parliamentary support. Further down the social scale, manrent also reaffirmed local association. Manrent brought satellite families of tenant farmers who held their lands from an isolated laird or from a distant or remote landlord, such as a monastery or priory, under protection of a local lord who headed a large kindred. These tenants continued to pay their rents to their landlords, but they also paid a death duty of their best beast to their protector. These bonds could run for generations. Often they are first recorded not when created but when renewed after a breach in local association. As a counter to partial government, bonds of friendship were also implemented in order to maintain amicable relations between clans and leading families or to ensure arbitration panels for the payment of reparations. Unlike the less formal manrent, these bonds had the force of law as they were registered in sheriff or burgh courts.

Other codes of conduct also ensured a measure of order. International tournaments engaged Scots as far afield as Prussia and regularly in England despite ongoing tensions over Scottish independence. Sir David Lindsay of Glenesk who was created earl of Crawfurd in 1398, achieved international renown when he unhorsed and humiliated the English champion of Richard II at a tourney at London Bridge in 1390. Tournaments were also developing a judicial element in resolving contentious issues through duels and other trials by combat, particularly on the Borders where it was a cheaper and usually more decisive alternative to predatory raiding or invasion. Robert III presided over an unusual if not exotic duel on the North Inch of Perth in September 1396. Two clans, probably the Clan Chattan and the Camerons, who disputed territory on the boundaries between Lochaber and Badenoch, were represented by 30 combatants on each side. Only 12 survived.

Another exotic happening occurred five years later. Henry Sinclair of Roslyn's claim on the earldom of Orkney through marriage was upheld by the Norwegian Crown in 1379 after a protracted legal dispute. In 1391, while imposing his authority of the Faroes, he met up with two shipwrecked Venetian brothers, Nicolo and Antonio Zeno. He made Nicolo captain of his fleet which crushed a revolt in the Shetlands. The earl of Orkney and the Zeno brothers proceeded to explore the western Atlantic. They investigated the east coast of Greenland and possibly landed in North America.

Maritime adventuring was not complemented by a thriving overseas trade. The late fourteenth and early fifteenth centuries saw a marked decline in woollen manufacturing in Flanders. The resultant sharp fall in exports of wool and hides from Scotland was not adequately compensated by native manufacturing and led to a drop in sea fishing for herring, mackerel and cod, although salmon catches from the rivers remained buoyant. Alternative markets for Scottish commodities opened up in the Baltic, but expansion here was checked by endemic piracy promoted by nobles with coastal estates. Indeed, leading Scottish towns such as Aberdeen were not averse to piracy to secure funding for legitimate trading ventures. The acquisition of the port of Leith on the Firth of Forth secured the commercial prominence of Edinburgh. The most significant urban development was not the renaming of king's burghs as royal burghs after the foundation of Rothesay on Bute in 1401, but the increasing dominance of the merchant over the craft guilds. Only members of the merchant guild were usually admitted to the status of burgess, a status unattainable for craftsmen unless they renounced labour in favour of trade. As evident from the earliest records for a Scottish burgh, that of Aberdeen which commenced in 1398, town councils consisted of elected burgesses drawn predominantly from the merchant guild. They appointed the magistrates – provosts and bailies – controlled the common good funds and monopolised the external representation of the burghs in parliaments, conventions of estates and general councils.

A further draw on the Scottish economy was barratry, that is, money or bullion sent out to Avignon and Rome by ambitious clergy to secure their appointment as bishops, abbots and priors. Even if nominated by the Crown or leading nobles, confirmation at the papal court was necessary for protection against rival candidates. Appointments made by papal provision led to a significant portion of the first year's income from bishoprics and other major benefices – from a half to a third – being despatched to Avignon or Rome. Although the popes had shifted to Avignon at the outset of the fourteenth century, the Church was profoundly affected by a schism from 1378 when rival popes were elected. France and Scotland continued to recognise popes elected at Avignon, but England recognised those elected at Rome. This led to the diocese of Whithorn being severed from the province of York. Scots found it increasingly difficult to gain access to the universities of Oxford and Cambridge but not to those of Paris and Orleans. Attempts to resolve the schism through councils of the Church, though ultimately successful in 1418, led to challenges to papal authority that stimulated heretical thinking in Bohemia and England. Scotland remained largely unaffected by such protest movements as Hussites and Lollards who faced being burnt at the stake if apprehended.

Scotland benefited from its loyalty to Avignon. In 1383, Clement VIII made Walter Wardlaw, bishop of Glasgow, the first Scottish cardinal. In 1410, his successor as pope, Boniface XXII, authorised the cardinal's nephew, Bishop Henry Wardlaw, to establish the country's first university, at St Andrews. But St Andrews, like the University of Paris on which it was modelled, argued that the ending of schism was necessary for the well-being of Christendom. The election of Martin V as a compromise candidate based in Rome was part of a package of reforms in 1414 that were designed to curb papal government and income. Scotland was the last country to abandon the Avignon papacy in 1418. The shift in allegiance invalidated all past papal provisions from Avignon. This let loose a welter of litigation. Barratry was to peak in the next decade until curbed by James I, who had returned to Scotland in 1424 to promote an independent and distinctive Renaissance monarchy.

The Renaissance in Scotland was not the preserve of the Crown or the Church. The Scottish scholar who initially attracted favourable notice from leading Italian exponents of the rebirth of learning in the thirteenth century was Michael Scott from the Borders. Known as 'the Wizard' for his dabbling in alchemy – the forlorn pursuit of turning lead into gold – Scott was an astronomer, physician and translator. After studying at Oxford, Paris and Bologna, he secured employment as an astronomer in Sicily at the court of Frederick II, the Holy Roman Emperor. From 1209, with the help of Jewish assistants, Scott spent eleven years at the Moorish library of Toledo in Spain consulting and translating back into Latin the classical Greek and Roman works of antiquity that had been preserved through Arabic. Prior to his death in 1234, he returned to Scotland with much of this foundation work, particularly valuable for the study of medicine. There is no convincing link yet established between Scott and families of Highland medicinars, such as the Beatons who came to prominence as physicians to Robert I and his son David II, but primarily consolidated their reputation as hereditary medicinars under the Lords of the Isles. Beaton medicinars still preserved classical medical texts translated from Arabic well into the seventeenth century.

Notes

1. *Acts of the Parliament of Scotland* [APS], T. Thomson & C. Innes eds, 12 vols (Edinburgh, 1814–72), i, p. 116.
2. The legend of Bruce and the spider has some contemporary provenance and was not just a romantic fabrication by the great historical novelist Sir Walter Scott in the nineteenth century.
3. *A Source Book of Scottish History*, W.C. Dickinson, G. Donaldson & I.A. Milne eds, 3 vols (Edinburgh, 1952–61), i, pp. 131–35.

3 Renaissance and Reformation, 1424–1625

Renaissance influences were particularly evident at the Scottish court in the fifteenth and sixteenth centuries as monarchy became more acquisitive and demonstrative. While the great age of building monasteries and cathedrals was coming to a close, there was a proliferation of collegiate Kirks that was matched by the growth and embellishment of tower houses as prosperity accompanied growing civility. However, minorities in Scotland, which afflicted all monarchs from James I to James VI, were invariably polarised by English and French interests that were sustained by pensions to leading politicians, but also by ideological differences on the future direction of the kingdom, a direction further complicated by the rise of Protestantism. The rule of Queen Mary from 1561 raised prospects of a Roman Catholic revival that were dashed by her deposition in 1567. James VI, like his mother, became fixated on succeeding to the English throne, which was duly accomplished in 1603. As James VI & I promoted British monarchy through religious uniformity, war and diplomacy, colonies and plantations, the influx of gold and silver from Spanish colonies in America brought price instability and inflation to Europe. Urban growth and rural transformation along with the recurrence of territorial and religious disputes created opportunities for Scots as merchants and mercenaries.

ACQUISITIVE KINGSHIP

James I returned to Scotland in 1424 determined to end the era of partial government and establish the monarchy on a new footing at home and abroad. He set the template that was followed by his four successors until 1542. James I distanced the monarchy from the nobility by the ruthless application of force directed principally against the extended royal family. In his first parliament of 1424, James I had his cousin, Murdoch Stewart, now Duke of Albany and some of his close associates arrested. Tried at Stirling in May 1425, Murdoch and two of his sons were convicted of treason, beheaded and had their estates forfeited. When Murdoch's brother, John, died in French service, James I claimed the earldom of Buchan. Although he defaulted on his ransom after two payments, James exploited the English Crown's demand for hostages. Despatched south in 1424, David Stewart, heir to the earldom of Atholl, languished in custody until his death ten years later.

James I's acquisitiveness was first checked then terminated by violence. After being arrested and threatened with summary execution, Alexander MacDonald, Lord of the Isles, escaped from imprisonment in Perth and burned the burgh of Inverness. When James I mounted an expedition to Lochaber in June 1429, MacDonald's forces did not wish to fight against the king in person. After a show of penitent humiliation at Holyrood Abbey, MacDonald was confined to Tantallon Castle in East Lothian. Another punitive expedition to Lochaber in the summer of 1431 was soundly beaten by the Clan Donald. Rather than mount expensive naval expeditions, James I later released Alexander MacDonald who was confirmed as both Lord of the Isles and Earl of Ross. In 1436, Sir Robert Graham, a lawyer trained in Paris, claimed in parliament that James I had failed to uphold and defend the community of the realm. Graham subsequently conspired with the master of the royal household, Sir Robert Stewart, son of David the hostage, to gain access to the king's lodgings at the Dominican friary at Perth on 21 February 1437. James I died from multiple stab wounds after being chased into an underground sewer by Graham and six other assassins.

The 12-year minority of James II, was notable for a nefarious dinner in Edinburgh Castle arranged in November 1440 by Sir William Crichton and Sir Alexander Livingston. William, 6th Earl of Douglas, and his younger brother, David, were seized, given a show trial and beheaded. The impressionable young James II, who was obliged to observe proceedings, moved against the Douglases with another after-dinner atrocity in 1452. James II was determined to diminish their extensive estates and influence over large swathes of Scotland from the Borders, along the east coast and into the Highlands. After a quarrel ensued over potential threats to royal authority James II attacked William, 8th Earl of Douglas, with a knife. Courtiers inflicted another 26 murderous wounds. A parliament in Edinburgh in June was judiciously managed to clear the king's name. In March 1455, James II launched a renewed attack on James, 9th Earl of Douglas, using artillery recently acquired from Flanders to besiege their castles and other strongholds. On being forfeited by a parliament, Earl James fled to England. In his absence, an act of revocation allowed James II to reclaim all properties alienated from the Crown through the partial actions of regency governments during his minority. Nevertheless, James

II's use of artillery backfired on him five years later. He was killed by shrapnel when one of his canons exploded as he was retaking Roxburgh Castle.

The minority of his son and successor James III was relatively short, but eventful. In July 1466, a baronial faction headed by the Boyds from Ayrshire abducted the young king from Linlithgow and lodged him in Edinburgh Castle. James III asserted his independence by negotiating his marriage to Princess Margaret of Denmark in 1468 and having Sir Alexander Boyd, his principal abductor, executed. However, he had also faced a potentially serious challenge from John MacDonald, Lord of the Isles and the exiled Earl of Douglas that also involved Edward IV of England. Their compact of 1462, which was reputedly negotiated at Ardtornish in Morvern and confirmed at Westminster, would have partitioned Scotland between the MacDonalds and the Douglases and removed the Stewart dynasty. Although the compact may not have been authentic, the Lordship of the Isles was now compromised. James III was apprised of the purported treaty of Ardtornish-Westminster in 1475. A parliament at Edinburgh duly stripped MacDonald of his earldom of Ross. John was allowed to retain Skye, but was obliged to surrender Knapdale and Kintyre in Argyll when confirmed as Lord of the Isles the next year. The Clan Donald was no longer a cohesive interest. John was defeated in a ferocious naval engagement in Bloody Bay off the north coast of Mull by his son Angus Og.

James III's relationship with the nobility was particularly problematic. As he centralised his court on Edinburgh, his leading familiars were cultured lairds, such as Thomas Cochrane, from a client family to the Stewarts in Ayrshire. Cochrane's main contribution to life at court was as an architectural adviser. But he attracted infamy for reputedly persuading the king to issue a debased copper coinage at a time of scarcity, which pushed up the price of food and other essentials. James III's approach to justice was distinctly mercenary. He liberally granted remissions even for capital crimes in return for financial compositions to the Crown rather than reparations to aggrieved kindreds. By 1479, his seeming partiality towards England over France in the 1470s had already been admonished by the minstrel known as Blind Harry in his epic poem *The Wallace*, which endured as the patriotic template that favoured the 'auld alliance' over the 'auld enemy' south of the Border. In July 1482, James III mobilised the country to defend Berwick, which had been restored to Scotland in 1461. Instead of engaging in battle against English invaders, the king was humiliated at Lauder Bridge when leading nobles led by Archibald Douglas, 5th Earl of Angus, withdrew their support. Cochrane and two other royal familiars were hanged. Berwick fell to the English. James III was incarcerated in Edinburgh Castle. However, the dissidents did not regard his brother, Alexander, duke of Albany as a credible candidate to be king. His allegiance to England or France was open to the highest bidder. James III and Albany were temporarily reconciled in December, when the king was released from custody and the duke was given a role in government as lieutenant-general. Albany, who continued to intrigue with England, was forfeited and banished in 1484.

James III continued to alienate powerful families, especially in the Borders and the Highlands. By 1488, they had secured possession of Prince James, heir to the throne. The king was suspected of seeking external assistance from Henry VII of England. At Sauchieburn in central Scotland, he faced a relatively small rebellion led by Archibald, Earl of Angus and Colin Campbell, 1st Earl of Argyll. The future James IV fought against his father who was killed more by chance than design as he attempted to leave the field on 11 June. The parliament that met in Edinburgh four months later exonerated the new king and his supporters of any involvement in the death of James III, which was attributed to a mishap. Although supporters of James III were stripped of their public offices, no attempt was made to confiscate their lands for the Crown. James IV demonstrated that he was his own master when he commenced operations against the Lordship of the Isles in 1493.

The endeavours of Angus Og to consolidate his usurpation of the Lordship and regain control over Ross were terminated in 1490 with his murder at Inverness by an Irish harper. Internal divisions with the Clan Donald were compounded by feuding with the MacKenzies in Kintail and with the Clan Chattan in Lochaber. In May 1493, John, Lord of the Isles was forfeited. James IV, the last Scottish monarch to have a command of Gaelic, then sent five naval expeditions to the Isles between 1493 and 1498. The purpose of these expeditions was essentially acquisitive though propagated as the daunting of clan chiefs to bring order to the Isles. Chiefs were obliged to pay compositions for the renewal of charters to their estates or face forfeiture. Oversight of the Highlands and Islands was entrusted to royal lieutenants, usually Colin Campbell, Earl of Argyll for the southern and western districts and Alexander Gordon, 3rd Earl of Huntly for the central and northern districts. In 1501, however, Donald Dubh, the son of Angus Og, escaped from the custody of the Campbells on Loch Awe. His efforts to resurrect the Lordship of the Isles met with some initial success and provoked another royal expedition in 1504. Daunting again took second place to the acquisitive exaction of compositions. Rebellion petered out. Donald Dubh was confined to Stirling Castle in August 1507.

It was not so much through his acquisitiveness as his reckless foreign policy that James IV inflicted immense damage on the Scottish nobility and kindreds. His marriage to Margaret Tudor, the daughter of Henry VII, was supposed to usher in an era of peace and tranquillity in cross-border relations in 1503. However, the succession of his brother-in-law Henry VIII, who more than matched his own delusions of grandeur on the international stage, drew James IV into a cross-Border raid in 1513. His campaign, a counter to an English invasion of France, ended calamitously at Flodden Field in Northumberland on 9 September. Superior numbers of Scottish forces, drawn from the length and breadth of his kingdom, were emphatically defeated by a smaller but more mobile and tactically astute English army that was also better drilled and equipped. Of the 40,000 Scots on the campaign, 12,000 never returned to Scotland. Among their number was James IV.

James V had a minority of 19 years. His first regency government was dominated by the overbearing queen mother, Margaret Tudor. Despite reinforcing her position by a second marriage to Archibald Douglas, 6th Earl of Angus, she was outmanoeuvred in 1515 by John Stewart, Duke of Albany, the son of James III's troublesome brother, whose main estates were in France. For much of the next nine years he was an absentee governor and a French client. When the Scottish nobility refused to stage another raid into England, control over the regency government passed to Angus in 1523. Now estranged from Margaret Tudor, Angus was an English client. He kept the young king confined in Stirling Castle. James V escaped in 1528. Angus was forfeited after he fled to England. James V marked the outset of his personal rule by disciplining Border reiving families in 1529 and again in 1530. He made no major assaults on magnates; but he was more subtly acquisitive.

Having attained the age of 25 in 1537, James V laid claim to a revocation. Parliament duly conceded his right to revoke all grants made through evil or false counsel since 1513. He proceeded to exact large sums of money as compositions for ratification of landed titles granted from the outset of his minority in all parts of Scotland. James V commanded naval expeditions to the Western Isles in 1539 and again via the Northern Isles in 1540. In appearance, yet another daunting of the clan chiefs, but in practice, compositions for the renewal of charters were enforced. Like his father before him he marched against England in the interest of France. Scottish forces disintegrated without fully engaging at Solway Moss in November 1542. Incandescent with rage, James V died from a stroke on 14 December, within a week of the birth of his daughter, Mary, Queen of Scots.

DEMONSTRATIVE KINGSHIP

Stewart monarchy was demonstrative as well as acquisitive. Public performance incurred lavish expenditure for coronations, for the opening of parliament and especially for the welcoming of new queens to Scotland. James I spared no expense to introduce Joanne Beaufort to Scotland in 1424 and to marry off his four daughters into other European royal and ducal houses, not to Scottish nobles, as was the case with the early Stewarts. In 1449, James II grasped the occasion of his marriage to Mary of Guelders to project his authority at home and abroad, albeit the gifts of artillery she brought from Flanders proved fatal for her husband. Through his marriage to Margaret of Denmark in 1468, James III acquired the Northern Isles. Orkney was mortgaged for £50,000 pending payment of his queen's dowry. Shetland followed suit for another £9,000 in the following year. Once William, the third Sinclair earl of Orkney, resigned his claim on the Northern Isles in 1470, they were administered by the bishops of Orkney. James IV celebrated his marriage to Margaret Tudor in 1503 with elaborate masques and balls. James V faced double expenditure on wedding celebrations. In 1536, he married Madeline, the daughter of Francis I of France, but she died within the year. Mary of Guise, from the ducal family of Lorraine, became his second wife in 1537.

Demonstrative kingship carried further costs. James III was the first to introduce Renaissance-style portraiture on his gold and silver coin. However, his issuing of inferior copper coin for domestic exchange led to shortage of silver coin that was drawn away to pay for foreign commodities. Although James IV did strive to restrain debasement and the loss of coin, his desire to outperform his brother-in-law, Henry VIII, had led him to establish a new naval dockyard at Newhaven on the Firth of Forth by 1511. With the assistance of shipwrights brought over from France, the immense *Great Michael* and other purpose-built warships were constructed to replace the practice of hiring armed ships from merchants and privateers for offensive and defensive naval ventures.

Although James I was an accomplished poet, the royal court opened up to Renaissance influences under James II, particularly as patron to Flemish painters. While James III continued this patronage, the presence of Scottish poets of the calibre of Robert Henryson increased at his court. James IV was an astute as well as a generous patron. The Scots makars – Henryson joined with William Dunbar, Gavin Douglas, who became bishop of Dunkeld, and James Kennedy, abbot of Crossraguel – created a classical structure for poetry written in the vernacular that made Scots a language of the Renaissance.

James IV sponsored Scotland's first printing press, established in Edinburgh in 1507. Its initial bestseller was Blind Harry's *The Wallace*. James V incurred considerable expenditure by his conversion of royal castles at Linlithgow, Edinburgh, Holyrood, Falklands, Dunfermline and Stirling into Renaissance palaces. James I had been content to customise these castles to enhance their capacity as royal courts, likewise James II, who was particularly concerned to proof them against artillery assaults. Whereas James III and, to a greater extent, James IV were inspired by Italian architectural styles, James V favoured French influences, particularly at Linlithgow.

Renaissance monarchs from James I to James V were reluctant to call parliaments to secure taxation. There was a persistent aversion among the nobles, higher clergy and burgess to sustain demonstrative kingship. Nevertheless, parliaments remained vital for Renaissance monarchs, not only in condoning their acquisitive behaviour, but also by giving them a platform to promote themselves as reformers for the common weal. James I initiated a legislative programme that was more show than substance. He passed laws against playing football rather than practising archery and against conspicuous consumption not geared to social status.[1] That this legislation was to be repeated and extended to golf (from 1457) by his successors was a clear recognition that such prohibitive measures were honoured more by their breach than by their implementation. James IV's education act of 1496 sought to improve the quality of and access to justice through a programme of teaching and learning from grammar schools in the burghs to the law faculties in universities. But again, this was primarily a pious exhortation not a directive to the Church which effectively ran schooling in town and country. His act of 1493, for the compulsory deployment of able-bodied poor into the fishing fleet, was an aspiration for social welfare and public order. The leading burghs could not readily build, equip and man more ships for inshore fishing and also larger busses for deep-sea.

James I had attempted to broaden the basis of representation in 1428 by enacting that two lairds from each shire should attend as commissioners; but this was an idea ahead of its time. Regular attendance was not helped by his innovation of a committee of articles in 1424, ostensibly to oversee and expedite business while the majority of parliamentarians were allowed to return home. James II broadened the basis of representation and improved his managerial control by creating lords of parliament from 1450. These heritable titles were bestowed on nobles who had neither earldoms nor lordships of regality, but like the holders of these honours they and their successors were now summoned individually to parliament. To relieve the judicial business on parliaments, James I had promoted an itinerant Court of Session mainly to deal with civil litigation in 1426. This initiative was revived by James III in 1469. However, the Session only gained substance as a court centralised on Edinburgh when James V created the College of Justice in 1532 by demanding and receiving from the Church a lump sum of £72,000 with an additional £1,400 a year for running costs. The Crown, with the compliance of the papacy, could now tap into the wealth of the Church.

The Scottish Church had been continuously criticised by Stewart kings. James I admonished the abbacies and priories in 1425 for the decline in monasticism, 'everywhere defamed and reduced to contempt', which he attributed to lax leadership by the clerical hierarchy.[2] He sought a general reform in religious observance by abbots and priors being accountable to general chapters for their clergy and in particular by the establishment at Perth of a Charterhouse in 1429, the first and only foundation for Carthusians in Scotland. James II won recognition from the bishops in 1450 that the Crown not the papacy had the right to control patronage in episcopal sees during vacancies.

James III in 1469 secured a parliamentary ban on the purchase of abbacies and any other ecclesiastical posts that hitherto had been filled by election. Patrick Graham, bishop of St Andrews, a notable purchaser at Rome, became an archbishop with papal backing. St Andrews became the metropolitan diocese for Scotland in 1472. This grant of the archbishopric, which brought the bishoprics of Orkney and the Isles as well as Galloway firmly under Scottish control, was not universally accepted by bishoprics that had enjoyed the 'special daughter' status with Rome since the thirteenth century. James III petitioned Rome in 1485 that filling vacancies should be delayed for six months to allow him to advise on promotions to bishoprics. Sympathetic to the king's domestic political difficulties, Pope Innocent VIII presented James III with a golden rose along with a directive to the nobility and prelates to obey their king. The accompanying indult conceded that James III had the right to have his recommendations to bishoprics seriously considered at Rome.

While the papacy may have regarded the indult as a personal concession, it was treated as a perpetual privilege by James IV and James V. The shifting political balance in favour of the Crown was signalled in 1489, when Robert Blackadder, bishop of Glasgow and a prominent supporter of James IV, was elevated to archbishop by parliament. Papal recognition that Scotland now had two archbishoprics followed three years later, albeit St Andrews retained pre-eminence. James IV secured parliamentary backing in 1496 to prohibit Scottish bishops going to Rome to resign their position in favour of a named successor, a practice which eliminated vacancies and diminished royal patronage. In 1504, James IV demonstrated that the indult was a means of exploiting the resources of the Church to the Crown's advantage when he had an 11-year-old, illegitimate son made archbishop of St Andrews. Adamant that he had the right to nominate all bishops as well as heads of religious houses, James V successfully petitioned the papacy for four illegitimate sons to become commendators of abbacies and priories whose revenues flowed into the Crown's coffers from 1533.

In his dealings with the papacy, James V exploited the spread of Lutheranism from Germany no less than the advent of the Protestant Reformation in England. Protestantism was merely a fringe activity in the reign of James IV. In 1494, Archbishop Blackadder of Glasgow had summoned about 30 men and women of some substance to face a catalogue of charges for being anti-papal and anti-clerical before the king and the general council. Having defended themselves with considerable wit at the expense of their accuser and his materialistic clergy, these Lollards of Kyle faced no more than mild censure. However, in 1517, the German theologian Martin Luther posted at Wittenberg fundamental challenges to papal authority. These ranged from denying the validity of purchasing indulgences to secure remission from sins, to emphasising that salvation was justified by faith not by good works and only secured by living gracefully and by relying solely on scripture. Accordingly, bibles should be written in the vernacular not in Latin. Prayers for the intercession of saints were made redundant as was the role of priests as intermediaries between God and man when administering communion. Lutheranism soon developed into the most serious threat to papal control over the Church in Northern Europe. The regency government of the 6th Earl of Angus took a firm stand against the spread of Lutheranism in 1525. The prohibition on importing books or other publications favouring Lutheranism by strangers was extended in 1527 to Scots who abetted the spread of this Protestant heresy. In 1528, Patrick Hamilton, commendator of Fearn Abbey in Easter Ross, was burnt at the stake in St Andrews for his commitment to Lutheranism.

Henry VIII had backed up his expedient support for a Protestant Reformation with the wholesale dissolution of the monasteries in England. James V preferred instead to promote the piecemeal appropriation of the Church's estates, a process known as the secularisation of the kirklands. This was achieved by intruding leading nobles and their cadet families as protectors or lay commendators for the monasteries, priories and friaries. Although the lay commendators held their office for life, they were able to dispose of the kirklands permanently by granting them in perpetuity to their kinsmen and local associates. As the Church owned around half of Scotland at the outset of the sixteenth century, secularisation brought about a major change in landownership.

The practice of cursing exemplified clerical venality. For a small fee, bishops allowed priests to deny access to religious services and threaten the pains of hell fire for relatively minor transgressions. Cursing was only relieved by purchasing indulgences from the clergy. The spread of anti-clericalism was given a full airing through *Ane Satyre of the Thrie Estatitis* in 1540, first played before the royal court in Linlithgow. Sir David Lyndsay of the Mount, the youthful companion of James V, was the foremost Scottish playwright of the Renaissance. John of the Common Weal was his principal spokesman for the public good. Lyndsay offered a notably forceful critique of a grasping and corrupt body politic dominated by kings, nobles and clergy. His play was instrumental in James V promoting an act for reforming of Kirks and Kirkmen in 1541. The bishops were to take the lead in repairing buildings, ensuring the proper administration of the sacraments, invoking the intercession of saints, improving the education of the clergy and replacing avarice with honesty. This was an agenda for reform, but not for a Protestant Reformation. The Church, whose spiritual message was not irredeemably lost to material concerns, was still a mainstay of civility. Catholicism, like the Renaissance, had continuing vitality in Scotland in the first half of the sixteenth century.

CIVILITY AND PROSPERITY

The Church expanded the number of universities in Scotland from one to three in the course of the fifteenth century. In 1451, Bishop William Turnbull with backing from the papacy and James II established the University of Glasgow, modelled mainly on Bologna in Italy with an emphasis on law, as well as the arts and theology taught at St Andrews. Teaching was organised through a college to give greater cohesion to courses delivered to students progressing through the arts to advance studies in theology or law. Glasgow was following on from St Andrews where Bishop James Kennedy had founded St Salvator's College in 1450, which proved so attractive for endowments that his successors promoted St Leonard's College in 1512 and St Mary's College from 1538. In the interim, learning and civility were further reinforced by Bishop William Elphinstone establishing a university at Aberdeen in 1495. Like St Andrews, Aberdeen was influenced by Paris, but also by Orleans. For the first time in the British Isles, emphasis was placed on medicine in addition to arts, law and theology. Teaching was co-ordinated through King's College, which honoured the political pretensions of James IV by imposing a large stone replica of an imperial crown on top of the university chapel. Scotland under the Stewarts was now an empire subjected to no other secular power.

Bishop Elphinstone, who was a strong supporter or the relatively new technology of printing, had the first Scottish press produce the *Aberdeen Breviary* in 1509–10. This devotional work served as a national liturgy that brought the saints of the Celtic Church into the mainstream worship of the Roman Catholic Church in Scotland. It stimulated plays, pageants and processions in urban areas and encouraged pilgrimages to rural districts. His endeavours to reinvigorate worship were complemented by the sophisticated choral arrangement of Robert Carver, an Augustinian canon at Scone Abbey. His musical accompaniments to the mass and other liturgical service required a well-trained and substantial choir, which was usually the preserve of cathedrals, universities and collegiate Kirks with song-schools. The collegiate Kirk, whose foundation by lay patrons in the country and by merchant and craft guilds in the towns can be traced back to the mid-fourteenth century, was the most notable growth point in ecclesiastical foundations in Scotland well into the sixteenth century. Usually a more elaborate foundation than the parish church, the collegiate Kirk placed emphasis on praying and liturgical devotion rather than preaching. A body of secular (non-monastic) clergy performed daily prayers for their ecclesiastical founders and their lay patrons who continued to provide endowments. However, such endowments further appropriated teinds from neighbouring parishes, thereby decreasing the parsons who provided a full range of religious services and increasing the impoverished vicars whose grasping conversion of free-will offerings into compulsory fees fuelled anti-clericalism. Nevertheless, the collegiate Kirk was a mark both of sustained commitment to Roman Catholicism and of the mortal fears aroused by rare and usually localised outbreaks of plague and famine. The most substantive collegiate kirks were usually found in the royal burghs. No collegiate Kirk, urban or rural, can rival the artistic sophistication, complexity and depth of Rosslyn Chapel in Midlothian, established by Henry Sinclair, 3rd Earl of Orkney in 1470.

Civility was not free of ethnic stereotyping. From the close of the fourteenth century, clerical commentators and chroniclers made facile distinctions that were repeated by travellers to Scotland between the barbarous, Gaelic-speaking Highlands and the civilised Scots-speaking Lowlands. Yet the Lords of the Isles maintained cultural contacts with Ireland that promoted both classical and vernacular developments in the arts and medicine throughout the fifteenth century and that were continued by leading clan chiefs after the forfeiture of the Lordship in 1493. The common culture of Scottish and Irish Gaeldom was sustained by hereditary families of bards, genealogists, harpers, pipers and sculptors. The cultural outreach from the Highlands to the Lowlands is particularly evident in the *Book of the Dean of Lismore*, compiled over 14 years from 1512 by James MacGregor, who also served as vicar of Fortingall in Breadalbane. The manuscript is a multilingual compilation of bardic verse in common classical Gaelic, vernacular poetry in Scottish Gaelic and in Scots, Latin commentaries and English memoranda. Poetry ranges from religious to bawdy verse; themes of courtly love compete against lascivious and fantastica imagery. A literate social elite, both men and women, drawn from diverse clans, were contributors as well as patrons.

The one artistic tradition that would appear to be exclusive to Scottish Gaeldom was that of commemorative sculpture on slabs for tombstones and free-standing crosses undertaken by itinerant craftsmen. Their work is to be found throughout the West Highlands and Islands based on commissions from religious and lay patrons that commenced in Iona in the fourteenth century and produced its most concentrated work on the island of Oronsay in the early sixteenth century. Religious patrons featured priests who were father and son, notwithstanding clerical strictures on celibacy. Lay patrons included women as well as men from the social elite of the clans. Christian imagery was supplemented by military representations of warriors, swords and galleys, with elaborate floral patterns engraved on both sides of crosses and tombstones.

Notwithstanding devotional expressions of power and status, the impact of the Renaissance on the built environment was limited. The stone castles that proliferated throughout Scotland were based mainly on the ubiquitous tower house, though the Crown and leading nobles preferred great castles of enclosure. The monarchy had an exemplary role in erecting, modifying and embellishing such castles in which stone replaced timber other than for roofing and panelling. By the later fifteenth century, bishops as well as powerful noble families were following the Crown in turning castles of enclosure into palaces dominated by halls and with enhanced domestic quarters. Smaller scale, stone castles of enclosure featured prominently in the Highlands and Islands. Ongoing engagement as mercenaries (*buannachan* or redshanks) in Ireland provided seasonal opportunities to repatriate capital, while the break-up of the Lordship of the Isles ensured that defensive fortifications took priority over enhanced domesticated space. An emphasis on defence did not deter the embellishment of tower houses, which continued to occupy space from rarely less than three to occasionally more than five storeys. Buildings were expanded horizontally as well as vertically, with separate towers linked by halls and domesticated quarters. The tower house was a power statement marking local dominance of clans and families; its embellishment enhanced their prestige. The tower house continued to offer protection from feuding occasioned by territorial disputes: it was expected to withstand sieges not only from hostile neighbours but also from marauding armies. A tower house was rarely taken by direct assault or by arson. Where accomplished, this was usually the result of a subterfuge carried out at night.

The tower house was indicative of a vernacular style of domesticated architecture, more baronial than Renaissance, throughout the Central Lowlands and the Borders. Sir James Hamilton of Finnart, Master of Works for James V, was exceptional for his Italian embellishments and artillery placements when constructing his country retreat at Craignethan in the Clyde Valley in the 1540s. Tower houses were subsequently reconfigured and remodelled as Renaissance castles, especially in the north-east of Scotland. The great age of tower-house construction, like that for collegiate Kirks, was a material indicator of stability and prosperity. The better administration of justice, centrally and locally, by Crown and nobility was supplemented by bands of association, manrent and friendship between clans and families. The spread of the more commercialised feu-ferme tenure, in vogue on Crown lands from 1503 as in the secularisation of kirklands, occasioned more intensive arable and livestock farming that led to rising rents and greater incomes for lords and lairds to invest in building projects. Nonetheless, customary ties of kindness restricted the capacity of the landed elite to bring about enclosures and other improved farming practices. Tenant-farmers who leased their lands for at least 19 years and usually for over a generation were entitled to the customary status of kindly tenant, which inhibited their removal and limited increases in rent.

Landlords diversified their revenue streams by exploiting fishing, quarrying and timber supplies. Their tenants and labourers engaged seasonally in spinning and weaving of textiles. Edinburgh was by far the foremost exporter of textiles, untreated skins and tanned hides which were sent on by neighbouring towns to make up cargoes. In terms of manufacturing and processing, Edinburgh continued to dominate the trade of the Lothians and Borders, where it had no serious rivals with the demise of Roxburgh and the English annexation of Berwick. This dominance did not extend across the Forth where ports directly exported coal and salt. St Andrews and neighbouring towns in northern Fife as well as the Tayside towns of Dundee and Perth profited from the rise of the pelagic fisheries (primarily herring rather than mackerel) from the 1470s. The revival of fishing advantaged Glasgow and Ayr on the Firth of Clyde and, in a less pronounced manner, Dumfries and Kirkcudbright on the Solway Firth, and Inverness and Elgin on the Moray Firth. In the north-east, Montrose joined Aberdeen as a centre for white fisheries (mainly cod and haddock).

Scottish prosperity cannot be measured comprehensively through customs records. Scottish ships earned income, invisible in custom returns, from their carrying trade between continental and Scandinavian ports. Instead of exchanging commodities directly to and from overseas ports, Scottish ships moved from one overseas port to another, carrying diverse commodities before returning laden to Scotland. Such tramp-trading became a particular feature of the expansion of Scottish shipping into the Baltic from the outset of the sixteenth century. Scottish adventurers also earned illicitly from piracy and legitimately from privateering under licence from the Crown. The upsurge in overseas trade led to distinctive Scottish mercantile communities emerging at Dieppe in Normandy, at Campvere in Zeeland, which came to replace Bruges as the staple for the Low Countries by 1508, at Elsinore in Denmark on the entrance to the Sound and at Danzig in East Prussia. Ongoing civil wars between Yorkist and Lancastrians made the Scottish presence in London insecure during the fifteenth century, but it did prosper with the stability brought by the Tudors after 1485.

REFORMATION AND DEFORMATION

Tudor monarchs were key players in shaping the course of the Reformation in Scotland. Henry VIII's initial response to the minority of Queen Mary was to propose a dynastic alliance. Negotiations concluded with the regency government at Greenwich in July 1543 were to lead to his son and heir, Edward, not yet six, marrying the infant queen of Scots. James Hamilton, 2nd Earl of Arran, leader of the English party in Scotland, duly encouraged parliament to take a favourable stance towards Protestantism by authorising the circulation of the Bible in English or in Scots that was to be read and heard, but not disputed or discussed. Concerned that this dynastic alliance could lead to political incorporation, the French party were convinced that Scotland's future as an independent kingdom required the continuation of the 'auld alliance', a sentiment readily endorsed by David Beaton, made a cardinal in France before his return to Scotland as archbishop of St Andrews in 1539.

Cardinal Beaton was personally responsible for burning 14 out of the 21 Scottish martyrs between 1528 and 1558.[3] However, he was murdered in May 1546 by Protestant lairds from Fife, seven weeks after he had George Wishart, an inspirational preacher, put to the stake at St Andrews. For Beaton, Wishart was not only a heretic, but an English spy, having come to Scotland in the wake of Henry VIII's resort to arms to harry Scotland into accepting the terms offered at Greenwich. For two years, Lothians and the Borders as well as parts of Fife suffered from 'Rough Wooing' in which considerable destruction was inflicted upon abbacies and other religious houses. After the cardinal was murdered, his assassins occupied St Andrews Castle where they attracted Protestant dissidents and enjoyed English protection well into 1547. In the interim, Donald Dubh had escaped from imprisonment in 1543 to lay claim to the Lordship of the Isles. With support from pro-English forces in Dublin, he planned a seaborne invasion to harry the west of Scotland in a manner similar to the 'Rough Wooing' in the east. But he died of a fever at Drogheda in 1545.

After Henry VIII's death in 1547, the regency government for his son Edward VI was headed by Edward Seymour, Duke of Somerset. Having led the initial 'Rough Wooing', he stepped up the military assault on Scotland. His forces routed and slaughtered almost 10,000 Scots, poorly led by Arran, at Pinkie near Musselburgh on 8 September. Somerset pursued a war of attrition on the eastern seaboard. However, Henry II of France despatched sufficient forces to remove English garrisons by 1549. The French king had already pressed for a dynastic union that was agreed at Haddington in July 1548. Mary, Queen of Scots was to marry Francis, his son and heir. After the accession of Mary Tudor in 1553, her marriage to Philip II of Spain posed a major threat to France in completing its encirclement by the Habsburg dynasty and its allies. As Mary, Queen of Scots, had a legitimate claim to the English throne through the marriage of her grandparents, Margaret Tudor and James IV, Henry II wanted to make both England and Scotland dependent kingdoms.

Installed as regent, the queen mother, Mary of Guise, preferred to consolidate French control over Scotland rather than antagonise Protestants who were gaining more influence among the merchants and craftsmen in the towns as among the lairds and some nobles in the shires. To avoid charges of heresy for flaunting their faith, Protestants tended to convene in 'privy Kirks' where sermons were preached and the sacrament of communion administered behind closed doors. The majority of such worshipers practised occasional conformity, expediently attending mass to maintain a public posture as Catholics. This practice was censured by John Knox, an ordained priest from Haddington, who had been inspired by Wishart to turn Protestant. Knox had joined the dissident group that occupied St Andrews castle after the murder of Cardinal Beaton. Once the castle was retaken in May 1547, he endured two years penal servitude in French galleys. From 1549 to 1553, he was a Protestant preacher in various charges in the north of England before going into exile in Geneva, where he came under the guiding influence of John Calvin, who taught that salvation was not a matter of free will but of predestination. Only God elected the faithful for salvation. Like Luther, Calvin stressed the primacy of scriptures over all other ecclesiastical authority. But he put greater stress on preaching the word than administering the sacraments. Particular emphasis was placed on ecclesiastical discipline to promote godly communities like Scottish 'privy Kirks'.

John Hamilton, archbishop of St Andrews, summoned a series of provincial councils from 1549 to 1559, to promote reform from within the Scottish Church through improved preaching, better education and restored discipline in religious houses. He was even prepared to move in a Lutheran direction with regards to justification by faith and a catechism in Scots. But doubts remained, especially at Rome, that the Church in Scotland was capable of meaningful reform. Hamilton made no attempt to harmonise internal reforms with the Council of Trent, which met fitfully in Northern Italy from 1547 to 1563, to establish clerical, doctrinal and liturgical standards for the Counter-Reformation under papal direction. Antipathy towards Mary of Guise intensified in 1556, when the parliament rejected her proposal to finance what was becoming a French army of occupation. A huge influx of lairds, deliberately misinterpreting the act of James I calling shire commissioners to parliament in 1428, ensured this rejection. Widespread antipathy to French influence had not yet translated into nationwide commitment to Protestantism, as was evident from the distinctly lukewarm support for the First Band or Covenant, issued in the name of the Lords of the Congregation in December 1557 that drew on traditional Scottish bands of association.

The prospects for a Protestant Reformation changed critically during 1558. Both before and after their marriage on 24 April, Mary and Francis had promised jointly to maintain the laws, liberties and privileges of the Scottish kingdom. However, Mary had been persuaded three weeks earlier to sign over both her kingdom and her claim on the English throne to the French monarchy if she died childless. The accession of Elizabeth Tudor in November moved England decisively away from Catholicism to Protestantism. Faced with hostility from Spain and France, Elizabeth was soon convinced that enabling Protestantism to flourish north of the Border would close the backdoor threat to England. On 1 January 1559, the Protestant Reformers posted the Beggars' Summons on the doors of friaries whose incumbents were threatened with violent dispossession. It also warned that reformation could become deformation with the destructions of religious house, paintings and ornaments. Deformation was instigated when Knox arrived from England in May to preach an inflammatory sermon in St John's Collegiate Kirk in Perth. Both the Lords of the Congregation and the regency government mobilised. After a truce was agreed at Perth, the Second Band or Covenant was issued. Though moving to equate patriotism with Protestantism, restricted subscriptions showed pragmatism still triumphing over principle. Nevertheless, the recruitment of Lord James Stewart, illegitimate son of James, boosted support for the Congregation.

The death of Henry II in July 1559 made Mary queen of France as well as of Scots. Support for the Congregation was building momentum. Protestant kin networks were certainly more active in promoting than Catholic kin networks were in resisting Reformation. Growing antipathy to the French occupation of key garrisons and to French dominance at the royal court sufficiently emboldened leading Protestants to represent the Congregation as the community of the realm. Although they were soon driven from Edinburgh, the dominance of French forces was terminated by naval and military assistance from England. The Lords of the Congregation negotiated a pact at Berwick in February 1560 whereby Elizabeth sent an army to besiege the French headquarters at Leith in April. The siege continued until the death of Mary of Guise in June. The Lords of the Congregation issued a Third Band or Covenant. This band, which played up Scottish antipathy to the French presence and clearly identified Protestantism with patriotism, won backing from around 50 leading nobles who included prominent Catholics, like George Gordon, 4th Earl of Huntly.

By July, commissioners from France and England arrived in Edinburgh to conclude a formal treaty for the withdrawal of all foreign forces from Scotland. The Lords of Congregation called a parliament to determine religious affairs, a flagrant act of defiance compounded by the wholesale intrusion of lairds who, as in 1556, claimed an extended but erroneous right to attend as shire commissioners. This parliament in August duly marked the Reformation as a distinctive break from Rome by abolition of the mass, rejection of papal authority and acceptance of a distinctively Protestant confession of faith that leaned more towards Calvinism than Lutheranism.

The blueprint for a Protestant Reformation, known as the *First Book of Discipline*, was submitted by John Knox and other leading reformers to the parliament in August 1560. The blueprint envisaged a godly commonwealth stimulated by active Christian congregations. This was to be achieved by university-educated ministers serving in every parish and working through a Kirk session with elders drawn from the local elite to promote discipline, schooling and social welfare. Bishops who did not conform to Protestantism were to be replaced by superintendents. Ministers were to be elected by their congregations to preach the word and administer the sacraments. Schooling was to be based on two enduring principles, universal education and equality of opportunity, to progress from parish and burgh schools on to university. Social welfare in town and country was to relieve poverty and distress, but only for the deserving poor. Discipline was designed to reinforce family values by punishing extramarital sex, working or playing sports on Sundays and non-attendance at church. Deemed anathema to such values, geared more to nucleated families of parents and children than extended families of clans and other kindreds, were witches and the Romany.

Reputed pacts of witches with the devil ran counter to the divine inspiration for Scots covenanting to bring about Reformation. Practising witchcraft and consulting with witches were made capital offences by parliament in 1563. Those prosecuted, tortured and executed as witches were overwhelmingly women, especially the old, the single and those with intellectual disabilities drawn overwhelmingly from the lower social orders. From 1571, the Romany who had first made their way into Scotland in the late fifteenth century, were branded as gypsies and treated as vagabonds. From 1574, they were subject to penal laws that threatened hanging, drowning or deportation. Such victimisation had no bearing on the blueprint for Reformation not being ratified in parliament. The Protestant Kirk's claim to the rents, teinds and other property of the Catholic Church in Scotland was rejected by nobles, lairds and burgesses with vested interests in these resources, whether as lay commendators or patrons of country parishes or as town councillors running schools and hospitals.

ENFORCING PROTESTANTISM

Mary, Queen of Scots, returned from France in August 1561, nine months after the death of Francis II. For four years she was prepared to be guided by her half-brother, the staunchly Protestant Lord James Stewart. Confirmed as Earl of Moray, he counselled patience when the queen pushed her claims to the English throne. As evident from the crushing of the Catholic Gordons at Corrichie in Aberdeenshire in October 1562, Mary sought to rule equitably and without favour. That February she had allowed the Protestant Kirk to claim a third of the revenues from rents and teinds still retained by Catholic clergy. Although she was not prepared to give up Catholicism, she built up her support among Protestants by not promoting Counter-Reformation.

Mary's fall from power in 1567 can be attributed to her remarrying on the first occasion disastrously on the second injudiciously. Mary sought to expedite her succession to the English throne by contracting a marriage, according to Catholic rites, with Henry Stewart, Lord Darnley, an Anglo-Scot from Yorkshire and also a grandchild of Margaret Tudor. Darnley proved an immature and unstable consort. When Mary denied his claim to be co-ruler, he took revenge on her Italian secretary, David Riccio, who was murdered in March 1566. George Douglas, 4th Earl of Morton mobilised his kinsmen and their associates, the Lindsays and the Ruthvens to do the actual deed. The birth of an heir, three months later, brought a brief reconciliation marked by a lavish public display at Stirling Castle in December, when the future James VI was baptised according to Catholic rites. However, Mary, who had restored a Renaissance court along French lines, was becoming increasingly reliant on James Hepburn, 4th Earl of Bothwell, a firm Protestant.

In March 1567, the lodgings of the queen's estranged husband in Kirk o'Fields in Edinburgh were blown up. Darnley was found dead in the garden. Strangulation marks around his neck were the only damages to his body. The Douglases, Lindsays and Ruthvens had taken revenge on their former ally. Mary was compromised by her frequently stated wish to be free of her husband and by the perceived complicity of Bothwell in arson and murder. After Protestantism was confirmed as the established faith of Scotland by a parliament again buttressed by the lairds, Mary and the recently divorced Bothwell were married according to Reformed rites in April. The nobility were conspicuous by their absence. Moray reasserted himself by mobilising sufficient Protestant confederates to defeat the queen's forces in June, at Carberry in Midlothian. Imprisoned in Lochleven Castle in Kinross, Mary suffered a miscarriage of twins. Bothwell fled to Scandinavia. The captive queen, having confirmed Moray as regent, was forced to abdicate by the confederate lords on 25 July. Four days later, her 13-month-old son was crowned as James VI.

Mary's relationship with Bothwell had scandalised Protestant reformers and left her open to criticism that still endures. Such criticism relies heavily on double standards. In taking a lover and being implicated in murder, she was not acting out of character for a Renaissance monarch. There was one essential difference from a king, however. A queen could not disguise or deny a pregnancy contracted through an affair. Mary, the least acquisitive Stewart monarch, escaped from Lochleven in May 1568. Forces that rallied to her in the west could not prevent her defeat by Regent Moray at Langside near Glasgow. After appealing unsuccessfully to Elizabeth to arbitrate between her and the confederate lords at the outset of 1569, Mary became a captive exile in England for the next 18 years, until she was executed for her alleged plotting against the last Tudor monarch.

After Mary's abdication, Scotland became embroiled in a civil war that lasted six years. Despite the claims of the king's men that they were defending Protestantism, which would be imperilled if Mary was released from captivity, their dispute with the queen's men did not have a distinct confessional bias. Protestants and Catholics fought on both sides. There was a high turnover of regents from the assassination of Moray at Linlithgow by the Hamiltons in January 1570 until Morton succeeded in November 1572 with strong backing from the English court. Morton consolidated the Reformation in 1573 by a parliamentary enactment that deprived Catholic clergy who had retained their livings but not accepted Protestantism. He enforced a settlement between both factions in the civil war at Perth in February 1573 that confirmed the change in the monarchy.

Morton's eight-year regency was notably disturbed by the rise of Presbyterianism in the Kirk after the return from Geneva of Andrew Melville, a meddlesome academic from Montrose, who became principal first of Glasgow University in 1574 then of St Andrews University from 1580. Melville revitalised the college structure at both universities. He introduced professors for specialist subjects rather than rely on regents to take students through all courses. In moving the Protestant Kirk firmly in a Calvinist direction, Melville was intent on making no concessions to the Crown in exercising spiritual jurisdiction over the Church. Melville laid out his revised blueprint for the Kirk in the *Second Book of Discipline* of 1578. The Kirk and the State were to be distinctive but complementary agencies working to sustain a godly commonwealth in Scotland. All clerical appointments were to be vested in the Kirk not the Crown or lay patrons. The Kirk was to retain responsibility for running education and social welfare, while the State authorised national taxes and local stents to provide bursaries for scholars, assist with poor relief and maintain the fabric of schools, universities and hospitals. Bishops and superintendents were to wield no more authority than ministers. Ecclesiastical authority was to be exercised through a series of courts, commencing with weekly Kirk sessions for every parish, then regular presbyteries for every district, occasional synods for every region and annual general assemblies for the whole kingdom.

In seeking elders to serve with ministers on all courts from Kirk sessions to general assemblies, Melville appealed to the lesser magistrates, the lairds in the countryside and the merchants and leaders of craft guilds in the towns. Any prospect of attracting widespread support from the nobility was forfeited when he, like Knox before him, laid claim to all the revenues and property of the Catholic Church as the true patrimony of the Kirk. The geographic appeal of Presbyterianism was limited. A scheme for presbyteries proposed in April 1581 actually cut back the provision of ministers. Only 600 of the parish churches were to be supplied; this left well over a third vacant or obliged to amalgamate. In a pilot project, 13 presbyteries were established in the Lowlands and the eastern Borders. No effort was made to plant them elsewhere.

Morton faced another serious challenge from 1578 with the arrival from France of Esmé Stuart, Lord d'Aubigny, who made a considerable impression on the youthful king. Although the Presbyterians considered him an agent for Counter-Reformation, he primarily worked to check English influence on Scotland. James VI created d'Aubigny earl of Lennox in 1580, when his kinsman, Captain James Stewart, accused Morton of complicity in Darnley's murder. Elizabeth Tudor demanded a fair trial for Morton and warned of Catholic conspiracies involving Lennox. James VI, Lennox and Captain Stewart responded in March 1581 by drawing up for public subscription the King's Confession, also known as the Negative Confession, which affirmed Protestantism and denied all contrary faiths and doctrine, especially Catholicism. Three months later, Morton was executed, Lennox was elevated to duke and Captain Stewart became earl of Arran.

The Protestant position in Scotland was furthered strengthened in April 1582 when Edinburgh, on the initiative of the town council, was established as the fourth Scottish university, but the first without a papal warrant. Lennox's influence over the king continued to give offence to Presbyterians, most notably William, Lord Ruthven, who led a raid in August that captured the king and compelled Lennox to depart for France. The general assembly in October fully approved the king's seizure and imprisonment in Ruthven Castle, Perthshire. James VI escaped from captivity in June 1583. Arran took over the regency. Lord Ruthven, made Earl of Gowrie by the captive king, was executed. Arran took revenge by having parliament assert the authority of the State over the Kirk in May 1584. When James VI achieved his majority in 1587, he embarked on his personal rule determined to curtail Presbyterianism, to control unruly nobles and, above all, to secure clear recognition from Elizabeth that that he was to succeed her on the English throne.

UNION OF THE CROWNS

James VI was an active polemicist, writing for a European not just a British audience. From 1597 to 1599, he made particularly important contributions on witchcraft and on the exercise of royal authority as a direct rebuttal to his learned tutor, George Buchanan, who had become one of the leading political theorists of the Renaissance. Buchanan, who had presided over the general assembly in 1567, had justified the rights of resistance exercised to depose

Mary, Queen of Scots and further advocated an elective monarchy subject to the community of the realm. Where Buchanan promoted limited or contractual monarchy, James advocated a more organic approach in which the monarchy was head of the body politic and answerable primarily to God rather than to parliaments or general assemblies. But his policies were not inflexibly tied to his writings, being tempered both by sceptical and pragmatic considerations, as was soon evident in relation to witchcraft.

Witches were deemed to have blown the naval invasion of England by the Spanish Armada off course around the British Isles in 1588. In the following year, the ship carrying James VI and his new queen, Anna of Denmark, to Scotland was forced to take refuge in Norway because of storms allegedly raised through the malign intervention of witches. Prosecutions and burnings followed in both Denmark and Scotland, with James VI concentrating his ire in 1590 against an extensive coven of witches in North Berwick. Hunts for witches resumed in 1597 when Presbyterians were in the ascendancy in the Kirk. However, James VI was becoming increasingly sceptical about the effectiveness of witch-hunts, their use of torture and their impact on his international standing.

James accorded a higher priority to reasserting his royal authority centrally and locally. His revocation in 1587 corrected losses suffered by the Crown during his protracted minority of 21 years. Of greater importance was the accompanying act of annexation which claimed for the Crown all ecclesiastical lands and revenues, with two important exceptions. Teinds continued to be viewed as revenue for spiritual not temporal purposes. But the Kirk continued to enjoy only partial use of the teinds to further its religious mission, education and social welfare. Lay commendators who held lands and revenues of abbacies, priories and friaries not only retained these resources but had them erected into temporal lordships bolstered by baronies, regalities and other heritable jurisdictions. Although James wrote against heritable jurisdictions, his pragmatic creation of temporal lordships recognised the importance of decentralised government, consolidated the hold of kindreds over kirklands and gave them a vested interest in not supporting Presbyterian claims to ecclesiastical lands and revenues. Although Presbyterianism became the established faith of Scotland in 1592, the autonomy of the Kirk from the State was not conceded. The king retained the right to choose the time and place of general assemblies, which James used to good effect to bring back bishops by 1597, albeit in a limited capacity to represent the Kirk in parliament.

As well as his creation of temporal lordships, James VI brought the lairds permanently into parliament as shire commissioners from 1594. Seven years earlier, he had imposed a general band applicable to all named heads of Border families and Highland clans making them accountable not only for the tenants on their estates, but for all their followers even if they lived on the estates of other landlords. By recognising the personal authority of chiefs and heads of families, James VI made them 'de facto' agents of local government, who were encouraged to resolve disputes through bonds of friendship and amity. Adding a further element of discipline for the Highlands was the obligation placed upon chiefs in 1597 to produce charters for their estates. In part, this was James VI reviving the policy of his predecessors in exacting compositions from chiefs with incomplete or questionable titles. But it was also an attempt to come to grips with the wider problem that few chiefs held charters to all the territories on which their clansmen were settled. This mismatch was the primary cause of feuds and illicit removals of livestock. There was a further difficulty on the western seaboard from the retention of fighting forces for mercenary service in Ireland. Although James was particularly exasperated by this problem, it did have its positive side in demonstrating to Elizabeth Tudor that Scottish support was necessary to allow her to extend her authority over Ireland. In turn, the English navy went a considerable way to making the *buannachan (mercenaries)* redundant in July 1595, when a large Highland mercenary fleet was sunk off the isle of Copeland in County Down.

In reminding Elizabeth Tudor of the paramount need for British solutions to disorders in Ireland, James VI was focused on his own succession to the English throne. His espousal of divine right monarchy enabled him to press his case to succeed Elizabeth, but also justified him – and, indeed, his successors – in suspending or dispensing with laws. Penal laws against Roman Catholics, imposed accumulatively from 1573, were usually dispensed with for persons of influence though never suspended for all members of that faith which survived in pockets from the north-east to the south-west. George Gordon, 6th Earl of Huntly, the leading Catholic noble, murdered James Stewart, 2nd Earl of Moray, in February 1592 and defeated royal forces sent against him at Glenlivet in October 1594. Rather than have his estates forfeited or his family forced to undergo a Protestant education, he was banished briefly then restored to favour and made a marquess in 1599. The king's lenient treatment of Huntly and other Catholics nobles again led to his abduction in Perthshire. The Gowrie Conspiracy of August 1600 was a rerun of the Ruthven Raid of 1582. John Ruthven, 3rd Earl of Gowrie, like his father before him, was implicated, albeit the prime mover against the king was his brother, Alexander, Master of Ruthven. On this occasion, James VI was promptly rescued and his abductors summarily executed. Although Melville and the Presbyterians were as supportive of the Gowrie Conspiracy as of the Ruthven Raid, they were politically isolated.

Having survived the Gowrie Conspiracy, James attracted support from leading counsellors of Elizabeth Tudor. He had extensive experience of royal government. His court had revitalised the Renaissance in Scotland through mathematics, gardening and mapping. His marriage to Anna of Denmark had provided a royal family. James VI of Scotland duly became James I of England in March 1603. This reversed the accustomed pattern of the previous eight centuries of English monarchs claiming overlordship of Scotland. James saw himself as the first Stuart monarch of Great Britain and Ireland. His plans to unite England and Scotland were denied parliamentary backing in both countries and had to be shelved by 1607. Nevertheless, he promoted a British agenda, initially through religious uniformity, then through foreign, colonial and frontier policies.

Manipulating the time and place of general assemblies to undermine Presbyterian opposition, James VI & I restored bishops in full to their temporal estates and spiritual office by 1610. He viewed bishops as essential to his exercise of imperial power in Scotland as in England and Ireland. His Stuart dominions were subordinate to no spiritual or temporal power by land or sea. The restoration of the bishops was complemented by the expulsion of Melville and other leading Presbyterians. The consecration of three Scottish bishops at Westminster in October 1610 did not subordinate the Kirk to the Anglican Church. No consecrated bishops in Scotland were still alive. Yet the essentially Anglican character of religious uniformity was underscored in 1611 on the publication of the King James Version of the Bible. Intended for use in all Stuart dominions, this Bible promoted Standard English, a confirmation that Scots, like Gaelic, was not an authorised language for salvation.

The restoration of the bishops also led to a return to the situation pre-Reformation when leading clerics became career civil servants. The most notable of these was John Spottiswood, archbishop of Glasgow (later translated to St Andrews), who contrived unity among Protestants by enforcing the penal laws against Roman Catholics. His principal target was a Jesuit priest working clandestinely first in his native north-east then in and around Edinburgh and Glasgow. John Ogilvie was captured, tortured, tried and executed in the course of 1615 for upholding the spiritual supremacy of the papacy over James VI & I.[4] Although no more Catholics were martyred in Scotland, the death of Ogilvie spurred on the missionary endeavours for Counter-Reformation that were sponsored from 1623 by the College of Propaganda at Rome. In the interim, contrived unity among

Scottish Protestants had sundered. James drove through liturgical innovations that became known as the Five Articles of Perth, where they were promulgated at a general assembly in 1618. By far the most controversial of these innovations was the requirement that all partakers of communion kneel before the bishop or minister when receiving the sacrament, a provocative return to the pre-Reformation role of priests as intermediaries between God and man.

The subsequent enforcement of the Five Articles by the bishops led to the re-emergence of privy kirks or conventicles for committed Presbyterians. Women of all ranks played a leading role in creating preaching circuits to sustain conventicles. James VI & I secured parliamentary ratification for the Five Articles in 1621, by judicious management of the proceedings and the votes. Control over the agenda was secured through a committee of articles in which the bishops, as royal appointees, were key to the selection of placemen from the nobles, shire and burgh commissioners. Legislation was packaged to ensure the passage of all Five Articles. Nevertheless, a substantial dissenting minority obliged James to drop plans for teind redistribution to raise ministers' stipends and for a draft liturgy to facilitate convergence between the Scottish and the Anglican churches. Albeit other British policies were marked by dissent, James faced no serious challenge as an absentee monarchy,

James VI & I rationalised Scottish and English diplomatic efforts, with the Scots leading in Northern Europe and the English elsewhere on the continent. James sought an even-handed approach to Habsburg interest in Spain, the Netherlands, Italy and the Holy Roman Empire (effectively Germany and central Europe) on the one hand, and to their opponents in France, the Dutch Republic, Denmark, Sweden and the German principalities on the other. This polarisation was largely confessional, with the Habsburgs prominent supporters of Counter-Reformation and their opponents usually Protestants of either the Reformed or Lutheran traditions. Catholic France lined up with the Protestant powers on the European spread of the Thirty Years War instigated in 1618. The French monarchy not only feared Habsburg encirclement but was fundamentally opposed to Habsburg notions of universal monarchy in Europe and the New World. James had sought to broker peace by marrying his daughter Elizabeth in 1613 to the leading Habsburg opponent within the Holy Roman Emperor, Frederick the Elector Palatine and sometime King of Bohemia. After the death of his elder son and heir Henry in 1612, James struggled to secure a Spanish match for his younger son Charles. When this project failed, in 1624, the future Charles I was married off to the French princess, Henrietta Maria. James now found himself being dragged into the Thirty Years War.

Scots engaged in the competitive drive for colonies in North America and the Caribbean by French, Dutch and Swedish as well as British adventurers. Although there had been attempted English settlements in America before 1603, it was James VI & I who launched successful British colonies from 1609, first in Virginia, then New England, Newfoundland and Bermuda. In 1621, James authorised Sir William Alexander of Menstrie (later Earl of Stirling) to launch the colony of Nova Scotia as a British complement to the neighbouring colony of New England to the south. Settlement under Scots law did not commence until 1628 and lasted for no more than six years.

The Union of the Crowns in 1603 facilitated common policing of both the Scottish and the English Borders. A riding troop commanded by Sir William Cranston meted out summary justice to reiving families. Members of notorious reiving families were expelled, mainly to Ulster after James VI & I followed up private Scottish plantations in Down and Antrim from 1606 with a general British plantation of the rest of the province from 1609. Plantation in Ulster, made possible by the successful conclusion to the Tudor conquest of Ireland in 1601, was conducted along similar lines to the English plantation of Munster in the 1580s: through the enforcement of English law and the large-scale displacement of native Irish. Although the Scottish plantations were predominantly settled by Lowland Protestants, Ulster also provided a refuge for prominent Lowland Catholics, such as the temporal lord, James Hamilton, Earl of Abercorn, who became a significant undertaker around Strabane in County Tyrone. Plantation, which also attracted Gaels from Easter Ross to Kintyre, expedited the breach of the Irish branch of the Clan Donald South from their Scottish kindred. Randal MacDonnell of Antrim, subsequently ennobled in 1618 as Viscount Dunluce (later as Earl of Antrim), became a prominent Ulster planter while remaining Catholic.

The Scottish branch of the Clan South was one of four clans expropriated by James VI & I. The MacGregors, notorious predators on the Lowland peripheries, were the first to be outlawed and dispersed. Their lands in the southern Highlands were lost to the Campbells of Argyll and of Glenorchy. Like the MacDonalds of Kintyre, Islay and Jura, the MacIains of Ardnamurchan and the MacLeods of Lewis were wracked by internal divisions. Although James could call on the services of the English navy as well as military assistance from Scottish burghs and from shires adjacent to the Highlands, expeditionary forces were expensive. Expropriation became a matter of private enterprise. The Campbells of Argyll acquired Kintyre and Ardnamurchan, the Campbells of Cawdor Islay and Jura. The MacKenzies moved across from Wester Ross into Lewis.

James and his councillors laid greater store on a legislative offensive to expedite the assimilation of the clan elite on the western seaboard into the Scottish landed classes, a process well underway without official prompting elsewhere in the Highlands. This offensive was marked by the Statutes of Iona that were generally enforced from 1609, with specific re-enactments following on from the failed rebellion of the Clan Donald South in 1615. The desire to spread Protestantism made the enactment to replace Gaelic with English as the language of education a non-starter; the Church not the State ran education. Enactments to curtail drinking and the purchase of guns, which would have saved the chiefs money, had an unacceptable social cost: they would have lessened patriarchal obligations for hospitality and protection. However, the legislative offensive did make meaningful changes to estate management. With the *buannachan* *(mercenaries)* now redundant, some were deployed to make lands more productive by shifting from small enclosed plots to large open fields. Others took to piracy or became racketeers as members of cateran (raider) bands. The majority seem to have migrated as soldiers and adventurers exploiting the opportunities for gainful employment opened up by the Thirty Years War. The legislative offensive required chiefs to report annually to central government for the conduct of their kinsmen and followers. On coming to Edinburgh, they usually incurred lavish expenditure on dress, entertainment and gaming. This led to debts accumulating on their estates faster than rents could be raised to pay off their creditors. Most chiefs had to mortgage or sell off lands to finance lifestyles that were now criticised by vernacular Gaelic poets.

Changes in landownership also featured in the annexation of Orkney and Shetland to the Scottish Crown by 1612. In the later sixteenth century, the Northern Isles had been run ruthlessly by the Stewart Earls of Orkney who had taken over from the less intrusive medieval bishops of Orkney. In 1609, Earl Patrick Stewart, as powerful as any leading Border reiver or Highland chief, was imprisoned in Edinburgh Castle for his oppressive exploitation of native udal laws of Norse origin. The abolition of udal law in 1611, as a prelude to annexation the next year, provoked an unsuccessful revolt which ended in the execution of Earl Patrick in 1615. The annexation of the Northern Isles, and their running according to Scots law, was a necessary first step to challenging the towns in Northern Germany and the Dutch Republic who controlled the trade in herring and white fish from Orkney and Shetland. Competition with the Dutch was replicated in Lewis. The development of Stornoway as a fishing plantation in the 1620s by Colin MacKenzie, 1st Earl of Seaforth, with the assistance of Dutch adventurers, was firmly resisted by the Scottish burghs. They regarded the seas around the Western Isles as their traditional fishing grounds.

RESPONDING TO INFLATION

Notwithstanding these disputes, the Dutch Republic had emerged as Scotland's most important trading partner after its Protestant provinces broke away from the Spanish Netherlands in 1579. In their pursuit of economic as well as political war against Spain, the Dutch Republic became the most formidable commercial power in Europe with a global outreach to the West and East Indies and on to Japan. Paradoxically, the Republic's rise to commercial pre-eminence was facilitated by the huge influx of gold and silver from Spanish colonies in Peru and Mexico. A sustained period of price instability and inflation ensued as not just Spain, but all of Europe, attempted to absorb the vastly enhanced supplies of gold and silver for conversion into coin. Economic power shifted substantially away from the Mediterranean towards the Atlantic.

The Scottish staple at Campvere in Zeeland was well placed to capital-ise on this shift. Zeeland was second only to its neighbouring province of Holland in driving Dutch overseas trade. Scots could now exchange their staple goods for sophisticated and exotic global products drawn not just from the Mediterranean but from America, Africa and Asia. The Scots made fur-ther gains for the country's carrying trade from the Baltic to the Caribbean which was modelled on Dutch best practice. Scottish ships provided flags of convenience for Dutch adventurers who came to dominate the trade in solar-evaporated salt from the Iberian peninsula. Scottish towns around the Firth of Forth became major suppliers of coal and salt to the Dutch Republic. Coal fuelled the pans in which seawater was evaporated for a lower grade salt, which had widespread domestic uses. Under the stimulus of Dutch demand, coal and salt became the major currency earners among Scotland's exports. Scottish coal was marketable not so much for its quality as for its ready avail-ability and its relatively cheap costs of production; likewise Scottish salt.

In Western Europe, particularly in the Dutch Republic and England, inflation stimulated economic diversity with the growth of manufactures particularly in towns which attracted and redeployed labour from agriculture. In Eastern Europe, landowners tightened their grip over agricultural production, imposed serfdom on their farmers and labourers, and left trade to Jews and enterpris-ing immigrants. Scots grasped this trading opportunity in large numbers, especially in the Commonwealth of Poland-Lithuania. Restrictions on the mobility of labour were also imposed within Scotland, however. Landowners around the Firth of Forth secured parliamentary backing to impose serfdom on colliers and salt-workers from 1606. Scotland remained a predominantly rural country. Two-thirds of a population of around 1 million at the outset of the seventeenth century engaged in agriculture or related services. The growing influence of urban crafts in manufacturing led to tensions over governance in towns. Accommodations were reached in Edinburgh, Perth, Glasgow, Dundee and Aberdeen, which allowed deacons of crafts to participate in the self-perpetuating oligarchies that ran the royal burghs. Scotland could not maintain stability without the export of at least 10% of the population as soldiers, traders and planters.

Emigration was as much about prosperity as poverty. Plantations in Ulster required capital as well as labour; the same applied to internal plantations. The creation of temporal lordships from 1587 stimulated an entrepreneurial response to inflation. George Keith, 5th Earl Marischal, who controlled much of the former estates of Monymusk Priory in Aberdeenshire, established Scotland's second civic university (after Edinburgh) and the second in Aberdeen in 1593. Simultaneously, he planted Peterhead as a fishing village which became a model for plans by the Crown to erect towns as oases of civility in Kintyre, Lochaber and Lewis from 1597. Over the next decade, the latter was attempted but aborted by adventurers from Fife with temporal lords to the fore. Owners of kirklands had more success in developing harbours in the west and south-west, such as that of Portpatrick in Wigtownshire in 1620, which secured Scottish dominance of the Ulster carrying trade.

Architecture remained a key indicator of enhanced lifestyles as dearth and famine were becoming less frequent. Edward Bruce, Lord Kinloss, developed undersea coal mining at Culross where he built his Abbey House from former monastic properties in 1608. It was Scotland's first country house. Elaborate, multi-storey, town houses were erected for the nobility in close proximity to the royal castles in Stirling and Edinburgh. Rising prosperity in the leading towns should not be overstated, however. Other than Edinburgh and Stirling, only the university towns of Aberdeen, Glasgow and St Andrews had substantial stone buildings for non-religious purposes. Even in Edinburgh, multiple-storey housing was still a rarity until the early seventeenth century, when Charles I tested the economic, political, social and religious resilience of Scotland to the limit.

Notes

1. From the perspective of a supporter of teams wearing green and white, the act abolishing football in 1424 laid the foundation for the eventual formation of Glasgow Rangers and Heart of Midlothian.
2. *A Source Book of Scottish History*, ii, pp. 98–9.
3. This Scottish total pales in comparison to around 350 English Protestants burned at the stake by Mary Tudor in England between 1553 and 1558, a number infinitely smaller than the 30,000 Protestants executed in the Netherlands during the 1530s and 1540s.
4. Beatified in 1929, John Ogilvie became the first post-Reformation Scottish saint in 1976.

4 Covenanters and Jacobites, 1625–1753

Charles I's British agenda, especially his pursuit of economic and religious uniformity, provoked revolution in Scotland by 1638. Scottish endeavours to impose contractual limitations on monarchy led to the wars for the three kingdoms in the 1640s. Scottish setting of the British political agenda was abruptly terminated by English republicans, led by Oliver Cromwell, who followed up their trial and execution of Charles I at the outset of 1649 with the occupation of Scotland during the 1650s. The Restoration of Charles II in 1660, which not only brought back the monarchy but also aristocratic power and Episcopalianism, was vigorously resisted in Scotland. Covenanting was recast as a subversive cause that activated both women and men to exercise their rights of resistance. Yet the removal of the Catholic James VII & II at the Revolution of 1688–91 and his replacement by his staunchly Protestant daughter, Mary, and her Dutch husband, William of Orange, was not readily accepted in Scotland. To curtail widespread opposition to his disaster-prone reign, William promoted political incorporation, a policy continued by his sister-in-law and successor, Anne, under whom the Treaty of Union was duly engineered in 1706–7. The Hanoverian Succession of 1714 confirmed the continental exile of the Stuarts whose cause met with little success in a series of risings and plots up to 1753. In the interim, Scots grasped opportunities in Empire that spread in the wake of Union.

TOWARDS A COVENANTING MOVEMENT

Charles I believed profoundly in his own sense of right and righteousness. He had no practical knowledge of Scotland, which he had left as an infant. In 1625 and 1630, he countenanced conventions of estates – parliaments with reduced numbers – to secure taxation. But he only held one full parliament during his 13-year personal rule, to mark his belated Scottish coronation in 1633, and never called a general assembly. He initiated his own downfall with his authoritarian Revocation Scheme, promoted and implemented on the most dubious of grounds. Charles had no formal minority or regency government. Yet by royal prerogative, that is, on his sole authority, he promoted a general revocation that threatened the validity of all titles to land.

Even after he scaled down his Scheme, he ineptly targeted the temporal lordships created by James VI & I that had become a principal means of rewarding royal counsellors. The nobility were further undermined when Charles sought to curtail heritable jurisdictions. Charles was also intent on a highly complex redistribution of teinds, allegedly to free the lairds from their dependence on the nobles. The lairds, now designated as gentry, were allowed to purchase their own teinds. This was not a full right of purchase, however, as teinds were to be redistributed to augment ministers' stipends, promote schooling, sustain social welfare and, above all, secure an annuity for the Crown. The valuation of teinds in every parish was labour-intensive, technically demanding and hugely undermined by active collusion between nobles, lairds, ministers and burgesses. Compensation for temporal lordships, heritable jurisdictions and teind redistribution could not be met from Crown finances or even annual taxes on land and money lent at interest. The bishops, who became increasingly identified with the Revocation Scheme, attempted to deflect attention by enforcing penal laws against Catholics coupled to renewed witch-hunts from 1627 to 1631.

The immediate impact of the Scheme was to render Scotland less governable. Dissent came to a head in the coronation parliament of 1633, when taxation was increased from a four- to a six-year subsidy and the tax on money lent at interest was raised from 5% to 6.25%. To promote a compliant parliament in Edinburgh, Charles had managed the elections of commissioners from shires and royal burghs. Proxies for absentee nobles were assigned to courtiers. He rigorously controlled parliamentary proceedings through the committee of the articles for which the bishops were again key to the election of members for the other three estates. Whereas James VI & I had only packaged the Five Articles in the parliament of 1621, the legislation in the coronation parliament stood or fell as a whole. Charles attended the vote in person and noted the names of all those who dissented. After a supplication in the name of the disaffected was leaked to the Court in 1634, John Elphinstone, Lord Balmerino, was put on trial under pressure from the bishops after John Spottiswoode, Archbishop of St Andrews, became chancellor, the first cleric to hold the principal royal office in Scotland since the Reformation. Balmerino's trial occasioned significant lobbying in Edinburgh by the disaffected in both December, when he was first indicted, and three months later when he was judged guilty for stirring up enmity between the king and his subjects for annotating the supplication. Convicted of treason and condemned to death,

Balmerino was later pardoned. His prosecution affirmed there was no conscientious right to dissent under Charles I.

By the trial of Balmerino, Charles I's pursuit of economic uniformity was producing a recession that led to renewed emigration to Ulster and an influx of Scots to the coal mines on Tyneside. Charles had launched a common fishery in 1630 to challenge Dutch dominance in the North Sea and exploit deep-sea as well as inshore waters around the British Isles for herring and white fish. Promoted as a British project despite objections from his council in Edinburgh, the common fishery was run by courtiers and London financiers. Royal burghs and coastal landlords, especially clan chiefs who unleashed their clansmen to exact landing fees, were continuously hostile. The fishery was also attacked by the Dutch fleet and by pirates based in Dunkirk.

The king's endeavours to equalise tariffs with England undermined the cost advantage of textiles, hides and skins enjoyed in continental markets. Raised customs on coal and salt from 1634 halved the cost advantage of these Scottish commodities over the English. This eroded differential, coupled to the greater risk of attack by Dunkirk pirates on the longer sea voyage from the Forth, led the Dutch to switch back their carrying trade to English outlets. Equalising tariffs on salt between Scotland and England restricted the volume of Scottish exports and doubled the costs for salt imported from Iberia that was deemed indispensable for curing fish, pork and beef for export.

Economic recession was compounded by ongoing price instability as German princes, to meet the rising costs of the Thirty Years War, clipped and debased silver coin. Problems of inflation were now magnified. Scotland, unlike England, had large amounts of foreign coin of indeterminate value circulating in the country. On the Union of the Crowns, James VI & I had fixed the exchange rates at £12 Scots to £1 sterling, and introduced a common coinage to facilitate trade within the British Isles and promote international confidence in Scottish currency. But James had allowed exchange controls at Scottish ports to lapse. Charles I made no effort to restore them. The common coinage was circulating not at rates of 12:1 but at 16:1 as dictated by London markets. Attendance at the royal court became even less attractive for Scottish politicians after a staggered devaluation of Scottish coin was aggravated by a debased new issue of silver coin in 1636.

Direct political action followed on from the king's simultaneous drive for religious uniformity aided and abetted by William Laud, Archbishop of Canterbury. In May 1635, Charles had authorised the publication of a Scottish version of the prayer book along with a complementary book of canons to regulate ecclesiastical behaviour. These tasks were entrusted to Laud's acolytes among the Scottish bishops. Published in Aberdeen at the outset of 1636, the

Book of Canons appeared first. It made no compromise with Presbyterianism, upholding the royal supremacy in ecclesiastical affairs and making bishops no longer accountable to general assemblies. It served notice of radical liturgical innovations in a *Service Book* that was published in Edinburgh in spring 1637. This was perceived as intentionally moving the Kirk beyond Anglicanism to threaten the very reception of Protestantism at the Reformation. When the king's council in Scotland authorised the first use of the *Service Book* in Edinburgh on Sunday 23 July, clerical and lay opponents of uniformity were ready to strike.

The introduction of the *Service Book* in St Giles Cathedral led to major rioting that spread to other churches in the city during morning and afternoon services. Although use of the *Service Book* was suspended on 29 July, the insistence of bishops that two copies be purchased for each parish led to further rioting in Glasgow on 10 August. By September, leading ministers, with Alexander Henderson to the fore in Fife, had co-ordinated local petitioning that dovetailed into a National Petition. The *Service Book* was condemned for lack of authorisation by a constitutional assembly, for undermining religious standards practised since the Reformation and for contents that were closer to popery than the Reformed tradition of the Kirk. The failure of Charles and Laud to make meaningful concessions again provoked extensive rioting in Edinburgh on 18 October. Two days later the National Supplication was issued by the disaffected leadership, which had secured the polemical assistance of Sir Archibald Johnston of Wariston, a devout lawyer, zealously committed to the triumph of Presbyterianism, and an insomniac of prodigious energy. The National Supplication first raised grievances against the bishops and associated the disaffected cause with covenanting.

This crisis by monthly instalments developed an organisational basis in November, when the nobles, gentry, ministers and burgesses respectively formed themselves into four Tables. In response, Charles I removed his council from Edinburgh. The Tables became a provisional government. A fifth executive Table was created from that of the nobility and a few representatives from the other estates in December. Membership remained fluid to allow activists in Edinburgh to report back to their localities and to prevent Charles targeting ringleaders for punishment. The Tables published the National Covenant, drawn up by Henderson and Wariston, on 28 February 1638. Ostensibly a conservative document, it made no outright attacks on the bishops or the recent liturgical innovations. Nor did it advocate Presbyterianism. But it was a manifesto for revolution.

Its first component rehearsed the Negative Confession (see page 77) of 1581 in association with a detailed, if selective, series of parliamentary enactments to maintain the true religion that culminated in the codification and collation of the penal laws against Roman Catholics in 1609. Scotland was thus part of a wider Protestant crusade against Counter-Reformation. Its second component stressed the religious and constitutional imperatives of covenanting between God, king and people. The religious covenant committed Scotland to a godly commonwealth preferably but not necessarily with royal support. The constitutional covenant imposed limitations on monarchy through parliaments and general assemblies. The most radical element was its third component, the oath of allegiance and mutual association. The oath required subscribers to give a binding commitment that they would:

> to the uttermost of our power, with our meanes and lives, stand to the defence of our dread Soveraigne, the Kings Majesty, his Person and Authority, in the defence and preservation of the foresaid true Religion, Liberties and Lawes of the Kingdome.[1]

In effect the king's person and royal authority were to be defended in so far as he accepted the religious and constitutional imperatives of the National Covenant. This conditional loyalty updated the same message from the Declaration of Arbroath that the king could be changed but the office of monarchy retained to serve the best interests of a now godly commonwealth.

WARS FOR THREE KINGDOMS

Copies of the National Covenant were sent round the country for subscription, backed up by persuasion from the pulpit and coercion in the streets during 1638. Charles I despatched James Hamilton, 3rd Marquess (later 1st Duke) of Hamilton to negotiate with the Tables. While Hamilton was able to stall on the calling of a parliament, he did concede that a general assembly should be held in Glasgow in late November. The Tables managed its composition by having not only ministers but sympathetic nobles, lairds and burgesses elected as ruling elders from the presbyteries and burghs. With Alexander Henderson as moderator over proceedings and Johnstone of Wariston as clerk in control of past records, the assembly moved against the diplomatically absent bishops as well as liturgical innovations since the Five Articles of Perth. When Hamilton, as king's commissioner, attempted to prorogue the assembly, he was openly defied by the vast majority of those attending, who in the course of four weeks established a Second Reformation that entrenched Presbyterianism, abolished episcopacy and banned the clergy from involvement in civil governance. They also won over Archibald Campbell, 8th Earl (later Marquess) of Argyll. War became inevitable.

The Tables had a blueprint for a national army that drew upon the professional engagement of Scots in the Thirty Years War. The Swedes, the Dutch and the French released Scottish troops to fight for the Covenanters – most notably, Alexander Leslie, a Field-Marshal in Swedish service who became the supreme General of the Covenanting forces. The Bishops' Wars lasted two years. George Gordon, 2nd Marquess of Huntly mobilised his kinsmen and associates in the north-east for the Royalist cause from the spring of 1639. Naval troops sent from London to assist him never got beyond the Firth of Forth. In June, Charles I marched to the Borders with sufficient English troops to parley a truce at Berwick, which allowed for a parliament and general assembly in Edinburgh. The parliament in August was short, inconclusive and rancorous with a significant presence of Royalists. They were absent from the general assembly in September that reaffirmed Presbyterianism.

A second phase of war commenced after Charles I raised troops and money in England. By June 1640, a Scottish Parliament, unsanctioned by the king, ratified the transition of the Tables into the Committee of the Estates, one part of which was to remain in Edinburgh, the other to attend the Covenanting army. Parliament abolished the clerical estate and increased the voting presence of gentry to two commissioners for all but the smallest shires. Subscription to the Covenant became compulsory for all holding public office in Kirk and State. The Covenanters moved into the north of England in August, roundly defeated the Royalist forces at Newburn in Northumberland, cut off the coal supplies from Newcastle to London and forced Charles I to call a parliament to remedy English grievances about authoritarian kingship. This parliament met the costs of Covenanting intervention. In the interim, uprisings in favour of the king in the north-east had been crushed.

Charles came to Edinburgh in person in August 1641. Over the next two months, he ceded control over the appointment of counsellors and judges. Real executive and judicial power was devolved to a series of committees dominated by Argyll and the radical mainstream. Charles gained no advantage from elevating Argyll from earl to marquess or creating General Leslie as Earl of Leven. A markedly negative aspect of the Covenanting Revolution was the authorised abolition of monuments deemed idolatrous that unleashed renewed deformation from the north-east to Galloway. No less destructive were the atrocities perpetrated on British settlers in Ulster following the revolt of Irish Catholics against Charles I. Catholic planters, such as Randal MacDonnell, 1st Earl of Antrim, sided with the king. However, the Irish Catholics were joined by some of Antrim's kinsmen, most notably Alasdair

MacColla, evicted from Colonsay by Argyll after the outbreak of the Bishops' Wars. Argyll became a prominent backer of sustained Covenanting intervention in Ulster as civil war broke out between Royalists and Parliamentarians in England. Argyll and the radicals exported revolution to secure the religious and constitutional attainments of the Covenanting Movement.

The threat that Charles I, who initially enjoyed the upper hand in the English civil war, would make common cause with the Irish Catholics spurred an alliance between Covenanters and Parliamentarians. The Solemn League and Covenant, negotiated at Edinburgh in August 1643, was a concerted endeavour 'to bring the Churches of God in the three Kingdoms to the nearest conjunction and uniformity in religion'. The revolutionary oath from the National Covenant was incorporated in the Solemn League making loyalty to the monarchy conditional on 'the preservation and defence of the true Religion, and Liberties of the Kingdoms'.[2] On the Scottish side there was the expectation that the true religion was Presbyterianism, but the Covenanters were content to participate in and duly accept the standards for faith, worship and governance determined by a predominantly English Assembly of Divines meeting at Westminster.

The Scottish Parliament reconstituted the Committee of Estates, again split between Edinburgh and the Army in England. The Covenanters under the Earl of Leven were decisive participants at Marston Moor in Yorkshire in July. The war now turned against the Royalists. The Scots, for the first time since Robert the Bruce in the aftermath of Bannockburn in 1314, were setting the British political agenda. Subscription to the Solemn League as to the National Covenant became mandatory for all holding public office in Scotland, but not in England where the Parliamentary forces were dividing between Presbyterians and Independents. The latter, like the Covenanters, wanted to win the war against Charles I. Rather than replace Anglicanism by Presbyterianism they preferred a loose gathering of Puritan sects that ranged from Baptists to Quakers. Unlike the religious autonomy attained by their Scottish brethren, the Presbyterians favoured a church subordinated to state control. They were more intent on pressing for peace than vanquishing Charles I. When the Parliamentary forces were reformed along professional lines, the Covenanters were marginalised. With Oliver Cromwell as sole commander, the New Model Army defeated the Royalist forces at Naseby in Northamptonshire in June 1645.

However, the biggest military blow to the Covenanters was the outbreak of civil war at home. Scottish Royalists, primarily clansmen and kindreds from the north-east who had accepted Protestantism under Episcopal direction, bolstered by support from the pockets of Roman Catholicism, were mobilised under James Graham, 1st Marquess of Montrose. He joined up with the forces under Alasdair MacColla sent over by the Irish Catholics. For 12 months the Royalists swept all before them through a brilliant guerrilla campaign. Although Argyll rallied the standing forces in Scotland, the Covenanters were defeated emphatically at Kilsyth in central Scotland on 15 August. Montrose gained no sustained support from Huntly and the Gordons in the north-east. He lost the services of MacColla and the Irish forces in the aftermath of Kilsyth as they attempted to wrest Kintyre, Islay and Jura from the Campbells. The Committee of Estates in Edinburgh duly recalled substantive forces from England under David Leslie, another veteran of the Thirty Years War. He caught Montrose off guard at Philiphaugh, near Selkirk, on 13 September. Montrose was forced into continental exile by the spring of 1646. MacColla retreated to Ireland that autumn. Both escaped the retribution meted out to their followers. In June, contingents of Campbells massacred the Lamonts after they surrendered their castles in Cowal. A year later, Leslie's forces slaughtered the MacDougalls once the siege of Dunaverty Castle in Kintyre was lifted.

The recalled Covenanting forces from England brought plague in their wake which ravaged the civilian population. Argyll also led a purge of civil and military offices of those who had collaborated with or were deemed sympathetic to Montrose and MacColla. Exhausted by warfare, Scotland faced renewed financial demands: a tax on consumable commodities, the excise, introduced in January 1644; and a monthly maintenance based on rental values, the cess, in March 1645. After Charles I surrendered to the Covenanting forces in the English Midlands in May 1646, he was transferred eventually to the Parliamentarians for £400,000 sterling (£4 million Scots), a fee agreed but never fully honoured as the Covenanters withdrew to Scotland in January 1647.

Once Charles was seized by the New Model Army five months later, conservatives rallied around Hamilton; his brother William, Earl of Lanark; and John Maitland, 2nd Earl (later 1st Duke) of Lauderdale. Argyll's kinsman, John Campbell, 1st Earl of Loudoun, went over to the conservatives. Once Charles I was imprisoned at Carisbrooke Castle on the Isle of Wight, Lanark, Lauderdale and Loudoun negotiated for his release in return for his conditional support for imposing Presbyterianism on England for a trial period of three years. They also proposed to move from confederation to full incorporation with England. This British Engagement proved immensely controversial. By drawing on aristocratic desires to wrest power from the radicals, Hamilton and his associates were able to carry the Scottish Parliament. Argyll rallied the general assembly to condemn the Engagement as a betrayal of the

Covenants. He won over Loudoun and some of the army's high-command. Grass-roots resistance to mobilisation at Mauchline Moor in Ayrshire was suppressed in June 1648. Hamilton failed to co-ordinate his planned invasion with Presbyterians and local groups resistant to the growing dominance of the New Model Army in England. Hamilton's military incompetence culminated in his resounding defeat at Preston in Lancashire by Cromwell in August. News of this defeat inspired Argyll and the radicals in the west to mount the Whiggamore Raid on Edinburgh at the outset of September. They regained control of the Committee of Estates and the Parliament after Cromwell's advance into Scotland led the Engagers, now under Lanark, to disband.

When Cromwell retired from Scotland, Argyll and the radicals began a new round of purging at the outset of 1649. The Act of Classes removed not only former Royalists but all Engagers from public office. To counter the aristocratic thrust of the Engagement, the radicals embarked on a vigorous reforming programme to phase out heritable jurisdictions, redistribute teinds and redress complaints about military quartering and tax collection. Cromwell and his fellow regicides executed Charles I in London on 30 January. Outraged by this unilateral act, the Covenanters retaliated by recognising the dead king's elder son as Charles II of Great Britain and Ireland.

Despite his reluctance to sign the National Covenant and the Solemn League, Charles II eventually arrived in Scotland in the summer of 1650. He was given a strict political re-education by Covenanting ideologues in preparation for his coronation at Scone on 1 January 1651. By this juncture, the Movement was deeply divided. A western grouping, which had come to prominence through Mauchline Moor and the Whiggamore Raid, protested against taking Charles II on trust. They were not prepared to relax the Act of Classes in the interests of national unity when Cromwell and the New Model Army returned to Scotland. Disputes over purging ungodly elements weakened the Covenanters at Dunbar on 2 September 1650. Forces commanded by David Leslie gave up their position of strength and succumbed to Cromwell in a defeat no less shattering to Scottish morale as that at Flodden in 1513. The purging Protestors, in the guise of the Western Association, pursued a separate campaign against Cromwell, which came to grief at Hamilton on 1 December. The pragmatic Resolutioners, who brought former Royalists as well as Engagers into a patriotic accommodation for Charles II, pushed into England but came to grief at Worcester on 2 September 1651. All of Scotland, except Argyllshire, was occupied over the next 12 months, an accomplishment beyond Edward I or Edward III during the Wars of Independence.

Scotland was incorporated as a junior partner in the Commonwealth following protracted meetings between English commissioners and representatives from the shires and burghs between January 1652 and April 1653. The union itself did not come into effect until May 1654, when the Commonwealth had given way to the Protectorate of Cromwell and his generals. Scotland, which was accorded no more than 30 Members of Parliament, was essentially ruled by the military and subdued through regional garrisons charged with tax collecting. Military expenditure mushroomed. The occupation was only seriously challenged between August 1653 and September 1654, however. The Royalist-inclined William Cunningham, 8th Earl of Glencairn, had considerable success when pursuing guerrilla warfare in the Highlands. But after Charles II sent John Middleton, the former Engager, to take over command, the Glencairn Rising became embroiled in quarrels.

Scotland under Cromwellian occupation was not governed radically; nor was justice dispensed equitably and the country was damaged materially. With the notable exception of Johnston of Wariston, there was little collaboration with the radicals of 1649. A witch-hunt instigated in 1649 had passed its peak by 1651, when it was wound down. Prisoners who survived forced marches after the battles of Dunbar and Worcester were shipped out to become servants indentured for seven years in Barbados and New England. Instead of curbing thefts of livestock on Lowland frontiers, racketeering MacGregors were awarded the exclusive right to levy blackmail. With toleration for all but Catholics and Episcopalians, Puritans migrated from England, particularly to garrison towns. But only Quakers stayed on, mainly in Aberdeen. Scotland was included within the Navigation Act of October 1651 directed against the Dutch. However, the first Anglo-Dutch War of 1652–4 severed trade with Scotland's leading overseas markets. Trade to the Baltic was at a standstill by 1653. Scotland had become a peripheral province in Northern Europe by the death of Cromwell in September 1658. The failure of the generals in the New Model Army to reach an accord with his son, Richard, paved the way for the Restoration of Charles II in 1660.

The Restoration, which was launched from Scotland, had an immediate impact on Scottish journalism. The civil wars of the 1640s had led to an explosion of polemical tracts, broadsheets and newsletters. The latter were confined to England, but Scottish polemicists were influential in launching *The Scottish Dove*, which remained sympathetic to the Covenanting Movement during its periodic circulation from October 1643 to November 1646. When the New Model Army occupied Scotland, occasional newsletters were published, notably the *Mercurius Scoticus* from Leith in 1652. However, the first newspaper published by Scots in Scotland was the *Mercurius Caledonius*, a short-lived commentary on current affairs from Edinburgh that celebrated the Restoration. Despite issuing only 12 editions between December 1660 and

January 1661, this Royalist newsletter paved the way for advertising in broadsheets and pamphlets which opened up the land-market, attracted support for colonial ventures and created consumer demand for goods and services in the Restoration era.

RESTORATION AND REBELLION

Following the Restoration, the Scottish Parliament awarded Charles a substantive annuity for life, which negated its need to meet frequently. The trial, conviction and public beheading of Argyll in Edinburgh, in May 1661, for his association with Cromwell, was later followed by that of Johnston of Wariston in July 1663. The Restoration in Scotland was driven on by former Engagers such as John Middleton (ennobled as the Earl of Middleton) and Lauderdale as well as by Royalists like Glencairn. They had backed away from the witch-hunt of 1661–2 after the licensed witch-finders were exposed for their judicial shortcomings. Glencairn and Middleton had already determined that there was greater mileage in prosecuting Highland clans for stealing livestock. Only a few clans in and around Lochaber and Rannoch Moor were so engaged, mainly on the Lowland peripheries. The vast majority of chiefs and leading gentry maintained good standing with central government by giving an annual account of their conduct in Edinburgh from 1661. Attention switched to religious dissent.

The change to Episcopalianism from Presbyterianism was facilitated by the refusal of the Protestors to countenance any disavowal of the Covenants and by the naivety of the Resolutioners in trusting negotiations to their duplicitous colleague James Sharp, who secured for himself the archbishopric of St Andrews. Bishops were restored to their temporal as well as their spiritual estates. However, no effort was made to reimpose liturgical innovations. North of the Tay, Episcopalianism was generally accepted. But the subordination of the Kirk to the State provoked significant dissent south of the Tay. All ministers were to be confirmed by a bishop. Those who refused to do so between October 1662 and February 1663 were outed from their parishes. Less than a third of ministers were forcibly separated from their former congregations from whom they were required to live at least 20 miles distant. Some chose exile in the Dutch Republic. Members of congregations who absented themselves from services held by their replacements faced punitive fines. Despite being subject to military reprisals, illicit conventicles in houses and in fields flourished. The increasing frequency of military activity in Lowland districts triggered the Pentland Rising, when conventiclers from the south and west marched on Edinburgh in 1666. This was no rerun of the Whiggamore Raid. The militant conventiclers were crushed at Rullion Green on 28 November. But the repressive behaviour of Glencairn and Middleton was discredited.

Lauderdale was now in the ascendant. He focused initially on implementing summary justice in the Highlands. In August 1667, John Murray, 2nd Earl (later 1st Marquess) of Atholl was commissioned to raise the first of the Independent Companies to keep a watch over passes into the Lowlands and to establish garrisons on the Highland borders. The excuse of curbing predatory raiding, usually carried out by renegade clansmen, led to the introduction of commissions of justiciary from March 1668 to expedite trials of all persons formerly brought before sheriff courts. This association of the military with judicial commissions, to police and prosecute disorders, not only became commonplace in the Highlands, but became widespread in the Lowlands. Over the next decade, Lauderdale duly exaggerated social disorder in the Highlands and religious dissent in the Lowlands to build up standing forces and shire militias able to operate anywhere in Scotland.

In order to include Protestors as well as Resolutioners within the Episcopalian establishment, Lauderdale offered conditional toleration by way of indulgences. Outed ministers were allowed to return and receive full stipends if they accepted episcopal confirmation and attended presbyteries and synods. While just under half of the outed ministers accepted indulgence, toleration was an ineffective check on conventicling which continued to thrive as a means of protesting now against the indulged as well as the Episcopal establishment. Lauderdale's last gesture towards conciliation was a proclamation offering indemnity in March 1674 to all non-conformists apart from those involved in the Pentland Rising. He reverted to repression within three months.

Notwithstanding regular deployment of standing forces and shire militias sustained by a monthly cess, conventicling had become entrenched among the laity in the Lowlands. Lauderdale's determination in 1678 to quarter a Highland Host, raised north of the Tay, on the west and south-west provoked a militant reaction. In May 1679, Archbishop Sharp was murdered in Fife. At the outset of June, government forces commanded by James Graham of Claverhouse (later Viscount Dundee) were defeated at Drumclog in Ayrshire. A substantive body of rebels was routed at Bothwell Brig in Lanarkshire later that month after the despatch of forces from England commanded by the king's illegitimate son, James, Duke of Monmouth. Bothwell Brig discredited Lauderdale, whose repressive policy towards the clans was also unravelling. Archibald Campbell, 9th Earl of Argyll, and his kinsman, John Campbell of

Glenorchy (later 1st Earl of Breadalbane) were supported by shire militias and Independent Companies in pressing territorial claims, the former against the Macleans in Morvern, Mull and Tiree and the latter against the Sinclairs in Caithness.

Lauderdale was eased out of power in favour of James, Duke of York, the brother of the king, whose conversion to Roman Catholicism had provoked efforts to exclude him from the throne in England. Prior to the duke's arrival in autumn 1679, a third Indulgence had been offered on the one hand and £1.8 million Scots were committed as cess to be levied over five years to suppress conventicling on the other. The reduced core of radical dissenters was led initially by Richard Cameron until he was killed in a skirmish at Airds Moss in Ayrshire in April 1680 and thereafter by Donald Cargill until his capture at Covington in Lanarkshire in July 1681. The Cameronians issued manifestos that reasserted their commitment to the Covenants, but not to an ungodly, tyrannical monarchy or an Erastian Kirk. The torturing of dissidents to secure confessions for conventicling was now commonplace as was summary justice against the Cameronians for their permanent guerrilla activity. James VII had little difficulty in persuading the parliament of 1685 to impose the death penalty on field conventiclers and charge anyone upholding the Covenants with treason.

The later Covenanting Movement could mobilise up to 14,000 men at Bothwell Brig and hold field conventicles at which an attendance of 2,000 was not uncommon. Their subversive political impact, no less than their unbending religious commitment, requires scrutiny, particularly as their activities extended from Scotland to Ulster, the English Borders, the Netherlands and even to Barbados. Subversion was justified ideologically to uphold popular sovereignty by Sir James Stewart, who invested rights of resistance in an active commonwealth not just the political nation (of nobles, gentry, burgesses and clergy). Lists of prisoners banished to America reveal marked changes in social composition as Covenanting shifted from a movement of power to that of protest in the later seventeenth century. Nobles were conspicuous by their absence. Lairds and merchants continued to feature; but a new prominence was assumed by substantial tenant farmers who were joined by artisans, craftsmen and labourers and given a militant backbone by discharged soldiers. Women, who were coming to prominence as tenant farmers and as skilled workers in textiles, printing and shop-keeping, played enhanced roles as couriers, agitators and clandestine organisers. Ministers were celebrated as itinerant preachers, but there was also a strong element of anti-clericalism provoked by the Indulgences. The driving force for the Cameronians was the militant laity.

Covenanting engagement reflected and drew strength from increased commercial activity. The periodic reallocation of open fields into strips of run-rig was giving way to fixed family holdings which prioritised marketing over consumption of grain and livestock, a shift marked by the mushrooming of fairs and villages. Competitive bidding for tenancies occasioned a growth in single-tenant farms. The accompanying surge in seasonal and casual labour for wages undercut paternalism in Highlands and Lowlands. Diversification from agriculture ranged from textile manufacturing, paper making and metallurgy on through extractive industries to fishing and whaling in the North Atlantic. Nevertheless, as evident from continuing migration overseas, more labour was coming on to the market than could be absorbed in Scotland. Wages were relatively static. Mercantilism, economic nationalism that favoured protected markets, was resurgent in Europe.

Navigation Acts imposed by the English Parliament between 1660 and 1671 impacted adversely upon Scotland, especially during the Second (1666–7) and Third (1672–4) Anglo-Dutch Wars. The Duke of York, who was instrumental in granting Scottish merchants dispensations from the Navigation Acts, also moderated mercantilist attempts to monopolise the fishing resources around the British Isles for English benefit from 1661. Separate fishing companies enjoying royal patronage operated respectively for Scotland from 1670 and for England from 1677. Scots actually gained from the English prohibition on importing Irish cattle in 1667, which gave their cattle droves a clear run in English markets. Initially Galloway dominated the droving trade but hardier beasts that travelled on the hoof from the Highlands and Islands came to the fore by the 1680s.

A committee of inquiry into trade instigated by York in 1681 identified the Dutch, the French and then the English as Scotland's most important trading partners. The Scottish Council was sceptical about calls to protect trade. Scotland lacked the political muscle to impose mercantilist measures. As an alternative to incorporating union with England, the duke promoted colonies in America. Two colonies were established. The first, at Stuart's Town on the Ashley River in South Carolina in 1682, was an undertaking of experienced transatlantic traders from Glasgow and entrepreneurial landowners, mainly from west and central Scotland, that was razed by Spanish forces in 1686. The colony established in East New Jersey in 1685 was a more durable venture around the town of Perth Amboy that attracted support from the Highlands, the north-east and the Borders.

The Duke of York won widespread acclaim for establishing his court at Holyrood in Edinburgh, notwithstanding the presence of Jesuits, the vanguard of the Counter-Reformation. He restored royal patronage for the arts and sciences at a time when Scottish excellence in law, botany, mapping, astronomy and medicine was gaining recognition in Republic of Letters, which had superseded the Renaissance by spreading learning through vernacular languages rather than Latin. York's cordial relations were strained by the Test Act in 1681. All in public office were required to uphold the royal supremacy in Kirk and State while accepting that the future king, as a practising Catholic, would be supreme governor of the established Episcopalian Church. When Argyll challenged this, he was charged with treason and forfeited, albeit he escaped from prison into exile.

Argyll's forfeiture allowed the Duke of York to inaugurate a brief, but unique, period of conciliation with the clans marked by a Commission for Securing the Peace of the Highlands, drawn from the clan elite as well as nobles and gentry from the Lowland peripheries. Between August 1682 and September 1684, the Commission exacted bands of surety, parish by parish, from every landowner in the Highlands. Their willingness to accept responsibility for the conduct of their tenants and dependants in order to suppress thefts of livestock contrasted sharply with the reception accorded to bands imposed on Lowland landlords to restrain their tenants and dependents from conventicling. The Commission tapped into the significant expansion of landowning occasioned by indebted chiefs and clan gentry preferring to mortgage and sell lands to more frugal kinsmen who had profited from the expansion of the droving trade.

The accession of James VII & II in February 1685 triggered an abortive rebellion by the Duke of Monmouth in England in association with Argyll in Scotland. Around 4,000 men, drawn primarily from clans in Lochaber were mobilised under John, Marquess of Atholl, to supress Argyll's rebellion. The overenthusiastic participation of these former Royalist clans undid the good work of the Commission for Securing the Peace. Central government resorted to repression. When the Mackintoshes of Clan Chattan, backed up by government troops, sought to resolve their long-standing feud over lands in the Braes of Lochaber occupied by the MacDonalds of Keppoch, the last clan battle was fought at Mulroy on 4 August 1688. The MacDonalds and their allies overcame the superior forces of the Clan Chattan. Punitive reprisals against them by the military were only halted by the outbreak of the Revolution against James VII & II.

Sectarian rioting on Christmas Day 1680 against York's professed Catholicism was resumed in Edinburgh in January 1686, following the conversion to Catholicism of two royal councillors, James Drummond, 4th Earl of Perth, and his brother, William, 1st Earl Melfort. The king was unable to secure toleration for his co-religionist in parliament. Having decided that his

Scottish Council was more pliable, he declared an Indulgence in September which offered discrete toleration to Catholics, Quakers and house conventicles. Rising public concerns were not quelled by the king's use of his prerogative powers to suspend the penal laws against Roman Catholics. A second Indulgence in February 1687 licensed meeting houses for Presbyterians. While the Cameronians remained committed to guerrilla resistance, expanded toleration allowed Presbyterians, with help from exiles returned from the Dutch Republic, to reconstitute an embryonic national church.

A more critical incursion from the Dutch Republic was the arrival of William of Orange in England at the invitation of leading Whigs and Tories in November 1688. William was married to Mary, the elder daughter of James VII & II. Both William and Mary were staunch Protestants. The birth in September of the king's son, Prince James, had signified Catholic continuity in the Stuart dynasty. Both Whigs and Tories opposed toleration for Catholics, especially as James VII & II was closely allied to Louis XIV, an exponent of absolute monarchy who had expelled French Protestants, the Huguenots, in 1685. William came to England to mobilise British support against Louis expanding the territorial bounds of France at Dutch expense. From the outset of the Nine Years War, William was consistently backed by the papacy who were opposed to the French king's promotion of Gallicanism, that is, autonomy for the Catholic Church in France from Rome. As James VII & II also favoured Gallicanism, the papacy backed the Revolution against him.

REVOLUTION TO UNION

In contrast to their action against Charles I 50 years earlier, the Scots were bystanders in a Revolution made in England. William's emphatic military presence forced James into exile in France. The English parliament offered the throne to William and Mary in March 1689. Whig sympathisers in the southwest of Scotland hounded out Episcopalian ministers from their parishes. In Edinburgh, another sectarian mob sacked the Chapel Royal at Holyrood and expelled the Jesuits. After Scots peers and gentry flocked to London to meet with William and Mary, their willingness to jointly accept the Scottish Crown led to a convention of estates being summoned for March. When the king's supporters, the Jacobites, led by James Graham, Viscount Dundee, left Edinburgh to carry their campaign to the country, there was no restraining influence on the Whigs. Whereas James II was deemed to have abdicated in England, James VII was actually deposed in Scotland. This was rationalised on 11 April 1689 through the Claim of Right, when the political nation, as in

1638 and 1643, asserted their collective right of resistance. James had fundamentally altered the constitution:

> to the subversion of the Protestant religion, and the violation of the laws and liberties of the Kingdom, inverting all the ends of Government, whereby he hath forefaulted the right of the Crown, and the Throne is become vacant.[3]

In order to expedite British mobilisation against Louis XIV, William had encouraged the Convention to consider an incorporating union with England. This issue allowed the Convention in July to turn itself into a parliament, which had exclusive power to commission bilateral negotiations. However, the prior offer of the throne to William and Mary left the Scots with little bargaining power when the English Parliament deemed that union was not a strategic concern. The Scottish Parliament was more concerned to unshackle itself from royal control. Giving teeth to this task was a group known as 'the Club', drawn mainly from the gentry and burgesses who looked back to the radical politics of 1640–1. The Club was prepared to delay a final constitutional settlement to ensure purposeful consultation between the royal court and the Scottish Parliament. The abolition of episcopacy led, as in 1640, to the enhancement of the estate of the gentry. But rather than just two, three or four, additional commissioners were authorised to be returned from the larger shires to parliament from 1693. The Club was unable to replicate the main constitutional gain of 1641 – parliamentary control over appointments to the executive and judiciary.

William agreed to replace Episcopalianism with Presbyterianism in June 1690 after the bishops reaffirmed their commitment to Jacobitism. Although the religious establishment was replaced in Scotland but reaffirmed in England, the Presbyterian Kirk like the Anglican Church remained subject to state control. This lack of Covenanting autonomy led to the Cameronians remaining outside the Kirk. General assemblies attended by ministers and elders were restored. William remained opposed to the persecution of Episcopalians; less than a fifth of their ministers were deprived. Following Indulgences for those prepared to swear allegiance to the new monarchy in 1693 and 1695, around 100 Episcopalian ministers took the oath as jurors. The majority of Episcopalians remained Jacobite, as supporters of the exiled house of Stuart. As late as 1707, at least 165 ministers who had not sworn the oath of allegiance held out as non-jurors in rural and urban parishes.

While the Revolution had been accepted with a relative lack of bloodshed in England, the main theatre of civil war was in Ireland which was hotly contested until victory went to William of Orange at Aughrim in County Galway on 12 July 1691. The Revolution was vigorously challenged in Scotland with the clans to the fore as supporters of James. Led by Viscount Dundee, the Jacobites defeated forces drawn mainly from Scots in Dutch service at Killiecrankie in Perthshire on 27 July. Dundee was killed towards the close of battle. The Jacobites failed to break out of the Highlands, being held at Dunkeld in Perthshire on 21 August and turned back at Cromdale in Aberdeenshire on 30 April 1690. However, the Jacobites in Scotland, unlike those in Ireland, were contained rather than defeated. They remained in arms in throughout 1691; but they were vulnerable to reprisals.

The Massacre of Glencoe on 13 February 1692 was engineered by Sir James Dalrymple (later 1st Earl of Stair). A committed unionist and joint-secretary of state, he endeavoured to keep Scotland as quiet as possible in order not to distract William from the Nine Years War. The massacre of a small Highland clan, the MacDonalds of Glencoe, was intended to demonstrate Stair's fitness to be the sole secretary for Scotland. He manipulated the ambition and avarice of the military high command. Archibald Campbell, 10th Earl (later 1st Duke) of Argyll, readily agreed to deploy troops from the Argyll Regiment into Glencoe at the outset of February. William of Orange conditionally authorised the massacre if the MacDonalds of Glencoe could be detached from neighbouring Jacobite clans. When news of the massacre leaked out, Stair was obliged to demit office, but he, the military high command and King William were never held to account or to make reparations.

To take the heat from the massacre of Glencoe, William licensed two significant enterprises in 1695 – the Bank of Scotland and the Company of Scotland trading to Africa and the Indies. Both were financed through public subscriptions. The Bank's remit was to stimulate manufacturing and commerce. In this it largely succeeded. The Company of Scotland, however, shifted its focus from trading to planting at Darien on the Panama Isthmus, a settlement that could potentially dominate trade to the West and the East Indies and control the overland route for Spanish gold and silver from Peru to the Gulf of Mexico. This shift was largely attributable to a London-based Scot, William Paterson, a founder of the Bank of England in 1694. A settlement at Darien was anathema to the Spanish Crown whose support for William was vital to his ambitions to contain Louis XIV.

The East India Company was no less concerned to preserve its monopoly trade to India and could count on support from Whigs and Tories in the English parliament. William duly reneged on his commitment to the Company of Scotland, which was not allowed to raise finances or acquire shipping in London, Amsterdam, Rotterdam and Hamburg. Darien became a solely Scottish venture, albeit shares worth £400,000 sterling (£4.8 million Scots) were promptly subscribed in Edinburgh and Glasgow. Funding was not matched by adequate planning. Two expeditions to Darien foundered. The majority of the colonists succumbed to disease. However, the Scots had arrived prepared to enter a confederal association with the native peoples who combined with the surviving settlers to defeat Spanish forces at Tubuganti in August 1700, prior to the colony being abandoned.

The Darien fiasco coincided with a demographic crisis in Scotland through prolonged famine that lasted from 1695 until around 1700 and even longer in some localities. The famine was felt acutely as dearth was no longer a regular occurrence. Even in peak years, the famine was never endemic. Towns, with greater purchasing power, fared better than rural areas dominated by arable farming. Districts where pastoral farming predominated were less affected. Prices for grain as for livestock had stabilised by the accession of Queen Anne in 1702. In the peak years of famine, the Scottish Parliament had prioritised long-term recovery through education over short-term relief.

Darien was of far greater political significance. The Court Party controlled by the political careerist James Douglas, 2nd Duke of Queensberry, was now confronted in the Scottish Parliament by the Country Party, intent on reparations from London. Under the leadership of the maverick James Douglas-Hamilton, 4th Duke of Hamilton, who supported the Revolution but flirted with Jacobitism, the Country Party mobilised public support through petitions from parishes and burghs that recalled the local supplications in 1637 that heralded the emergence of the Covenanting Movement. The Country Party attracted support from constitutional and social reformers as from former Club members. William's attempts to reassert royal control by pushing for political incorporation found few takers even within the Court Party and were rebuffed by the English Parliament that reaffirmed the Navigation Acts and appended an Alien Act for the removal of all Scots from civil and public office in the American colonies from 1696. William of Orange was to be succeeded by Anne, his sister-in-law and daughter of James VII & II. But Anne had no living children. Accordingly, the English Parliament determined unilaterally in 1701 that the succession was to pass to the nearest Protestant member of the house of Stuart, Sophia, Electress of Hanover, a granddaughter of James VI & I.

Prior to his death in March 1702, William was preparing to oppose France in the War of the Spanish Succession. A grandson of Louis XIV was contesting the vacant throne with the Austrian Habsburgs whom William supported. Anne and her English ministry were determined to commit Scotland to the war which was accomplished through the Scottish Council after the parliament to recognise the new queen was delayed for three months. As Louis had recognised Prince James Stuart as James VIII & III on the death of his exiled father in 1701, there was a real prospect that the War of the Spanish Succession could become the War of the British Succession, particularly after fresh negotiations for union, instigated by the Court Party in 1702–3, proved fruitless.

Overseas trade was increasingly viewed as the most important means of financing war. Fiscal burdens fell mainly on the customs and excise exacted on trade and consumption respectively rather on the land tax. The largest component of customs was levied on the colonial trade with the Americas. But this trade faced significant disruption from Scottish commercial networks that circumvented the Navigation Acts by tramp-trading, a practice the Scots had exported from the Baltic to the Caribbean, by counterfeiting of shipping documentation and by the judicial packing of colonial courts. The highly efficient carrying trade of these networks was becoming dominant in Irish markets and was even shipping out wool from England to rival continental manufacturers.

English desires to restrain Scots politically as well as commercially became more acute when the Scottish Parliament in 1703–4 refused to accede to the Hanoverian Succession. The Country Party, which had come into power after the general election of 1703, was inspired by the radical rhetoric of Andrew Fletcher of Saltoun to enact extensive limitations on the prerogative powers of Queen Anne's eventual successor. An outraged Anne encouraged her English ministers to terminate the Scottish Parliament. Members of the Court Party were opposed to limitations and intent on securing the Presbyterian Kirk while attaining greater career opportunities promoted Union. In this they were joined by a New Party (the Squadrone), a small but influential group of pro-Hanoverian Presbyterians who defected from the Country Party.

Their leader, John Hay, 2nd Marquess of Tweeddale, was unable to deliver the Hanoverian Succession. John Campbell, 2nd Duke of Argyll, was brought back from Flanders in 1705 to reinvigorate the Court Party and prepare the ground for an incorporating union. The English Parliament had fired the decisive legislative shot through an Alien Act which now applied in a domestic rather than imperial context. The Scots were invited to treat for union or face an embargo on importing livestock, coal and textiles to England. Compromised by Jacobite plotting, Hamilton proposed that the queen select the Scottish as well as the English commissioners. This played into the hands of the English ministry concerned about England's demographic deficit. England had insufficient manpower to fight war in Europe and America, to sustain domestic manufacturing and to expand Empire. Scotland was a ready reservoir. Garrisons at Carlisle, Berwick, Newcastle and Hull were stepped up to facilitate an invasion of Scotland by land and sea if necessary.

With the exception of George Lockhart of Carnwath from the Jacobites, the Scottish commissioners were appointed exclusively from the Court and the Squadrone. Primarily they were placemen who were not necessarily corrupt, but they were certainly inept as English negotiators admitted after Union was accomplished. The £20,000 sterling sent on by the English ministry to selectively pay arrears of salary and pensions for parliamentarians holding public office and the specific promise of £233,884 as reparations for Darien certainly facilitated the passage of Union. But in practice, these monies were used to shore up the vote for the alliance of the Court Party with the Squadrone, not to bribe members of the Country Party into voting for Union. Despite rioting in the streets of Edinburgh, Glasgow, Hamilton, Dumfries and Stirling, addresses from the shires and burghs – which surpassed the petitioning against Darien – and protests from the parliamentary floor, the political management of James Ogilvie, 1st Earl of Seafield, and John Erskine, 6th Earl of Mar, carried the day. They controlled proceedings and the order of voting. With opportunities for dissent minimised, the 25 Articles of Union passed through the Scottish Parliament in less than four months from October 1706 to January 1707. The Kirk was won over by inserting an act guaranteeing the Presbyterian establishment into the Treaty. Public antipathy to political incorporation remained, notwithstanding the despatch of spin-doctors, spies and *agents provocateurs* from London.

The Treaty of Union was not a magnanimous act of altruism in which England rescued an impoverished Scotland. Darien had not financially crippled Scotland. No more than £153,000 sterling in venture capital was lost on the Panama Isthmus as just over 38% of the shares were actually subscribed. The losses from Darien were more than compensated by returns from the carrying trade as from inward and outward investment through commercial networks operating in the Dutch Republic, Sweden and northern Germany. The Scottish balance of trade appeared far from healthy, with imports hugely exceeding exports. But the adverse balance was calculated on trade taxed not on trade conducted. The balance took no account of imported goods reexported or processed by manufactures or of the invisible earnings from the thriving Scottish carrying trade. The financial acumen of Scottish commercial networks was powerfully demonstrated as the Treaty passed through the Scottish and English Parliaments in 1707. Scottish networks exploited fiscal loopholes by investing £300,000 sterling in brandies, wines, salt and whalebones (for manufacturing into bodices and stays) which they exported to England tax-free after the Union became operative on 1 May.

Constitutionally the United Kingdom was created with a common monarchy, a specified Hanoverian Succession and a common parliament. The main issues determined by the Treaty of Union concerned political economy. A common market was created throughout the United Kingdom. In this market, Scotland was comparatively under-resourced and undercapitalised and lacked a competitive edge in manufacturing. Nevertheless, by allowing for the free flow of capital, English investors could no longer be prevented from investing in Scottish ventures. The Scots were now guaranteed access to the American colonies of the Crown. All parts of the United Kingdom came under the same trading regulations and were liable to the same duties. In effect, the Scots had to adjust to English commercial regulation and meet higher rates for customs and excise. The Scottish carrying trade was specifically targeted on exports of wool from England, a practice that was now proscribed throughout the United Kingdom. The immediate beneficiaries were English not Scottish manufacturers.

Because Scotland had been guaranteed access to English and domestic colonial trade, it was not unreasonable to expect that Scotland should pay a share of the English National Debt which had financed the wars against France since 1694. However, this debt was around £20 million when the Union was negotiated. Scotland was indemnified with a capital Equivalent of £398,085 sterling that was to be paid over seven years as recompense for higher public burdens, for standardising the coinage and as reparations for Darien. A rising Equivalent of £2,000 annually for seven years was also to be paid to promote the manufacture of coarse woollens and then fishing and linen. As the Equivalents were to be raised by higher levels of customs and excise, the Scots were effectively paying for their own compensation, reparations and development funding.

Scottish concerns were further aggravated when the initial British Parliament of 1708 passed measures for improving Union. The establishment of a Court of Revenues for Customs and Excise extended English fiscal regulation to Scotland and gave an edge to smuggling as an expression of political protest. The imposition of the English Treason Law on Scotland facilitated easier conviction of Jacobites and made forfeiture lasting through the tainting of the blood, a concept alien to Scots Law. The abolition of the Scottish Council deprived the country of its executive and its central intelligence agency. Gun-running and credit transfers by Jacobites became more difficult to monitor.

Scottish representation in the new British Parliament was restricted to 16 elected peers in the House of Lords and 45 MPs in the House of Commons. In 1709, Queensberry, who had been rewarded with a British peerage as

Duke of Dover, was denied the right to vote for the elected peers. Two years later, his rival Hamilton was created Duke of Brandon. Hamilton was not only denied the right to vote for peers, but he was also barred from taking his seat in the Lords to deter other Scots from seeking British peerages. Scots were outraged when the Tory ministry, in direct contravention of the Union, introduced an augmented malt tax before the formal conclusion of the War of the Spanish Succession by Treaty of Utrecht in 1713. Seafield (now Earl of Findlater) and other Scottish politicians who had actively supported the Union now began to work closely with those politicians who had opposed it. The motion debated in the Lords was not to dissolve the Union but to instigate a formal debate towards the same end. The Union was only saved by four proxy votes.

COMPETING PATRIOTISMS

The immediate beneficiary of the ongoing unpopularity of Union was Jacobitism. As well as major risings in 1715–16 (the Fifteen) and 1745–6 (the Forty-Five), and two minor risings in 1708 and 1719, there were sporadic plots either to assassinate leading ministers or to overthrow the British government. As a sideshow in European diplomacy, the Jacobites received inconsistent support from France, Spain, the papacy, Sweden and Russia. Nevertheless, Jacobitism was a major theme in Scottish politics and a constant irritant to successive British governments for over six decades.

The dynastic appeal of Jacobitism was grounded in the hereditary principle of kingship. The royal house of Stuart was the rightful trustee of Scotland in the same way that Highland chiefs and Lowland heads of families were the customary protectors of their kindreds. Dynastic legitimacy was considered the source of justice, the basis of government that was imperilled by the sundering of genealogical continuity, first by William of Orange in 1689 and then by the Hanoverian Succession of George I in 1714. In Scotland, adherence to Roman Catholicism was a minority pursuit (less than 5% of the population). The confessional allegiance of Scottish Jacobites, especially in their heartlands of the Highlands and the north-east, was overwhelmingly Protestant, but Episcopalian. The refusal of the vast majority of Episcopalians to abjure the exiled Stuart had led them to reject toleration from the British government in 1712. Non-jurors, like Roman Catholics, were subject to penal laws.

Popular antipathy to the Union saw in Jacobitism an appropriate vehicle to reassert Scottish patriotism. The identity of the Scottish people was expressed through the momentous attainments of scholars, soldiers and adventurers no less than monarchs, an identity that also drew on epic heroism as of William Wallace, the leader of the Scottish community of the realm during the Wars of Independence in the late thirteenth century. Appeals to patriotism became part of a continuous process of redefining Jacobitism that was not always to the taste of the exiled house of Stuart. This led to strategic tensions that were particularly evident in the Fifteen and again in the Forty-Five.

John, Earl of Mar, who had steered the Union through the Scottish Parliament, was removed from office as Secretary of State for Scotland at the Hanoverian Succession. He was able to play on the Scottish Jacobites' need for a prominent leader at the Fifteen. He failed to channel widespread discontent with the Union into a successful patriotic rising. Jacobites had taken control of the towns of Perth, Dundee, Montrose, Aberdeen and Inverness and their respective rural hinterlands from the outset of the rising. Rather than consolidate in the central Lowlands by moving from Perth on Edinburgh, Mar sent a detachment across the Firth of Forth to liaise with Scottish and English Borderers who, at the insistence of Northumberland gentry, marched into England, a course which ended in emphatic defeat at Preston on 13 November 1715, the same day as Mar suffered a decisive reversal at Sheriffmuir near Dunblane. Although the Jacobites did have a military commander with a dash of brilliance in the Forty-Five, Lord George Murray was constantly undermined by a fatal personality clash with the charismatic, but strategically inept, Charles Edward Stuart, the elder son of the exiled 'James VIII & III'. The Jacobites again secured Aberdeen and even established a provisional Scottish government in Edinburgh, covered with benign neutrality by the thrice-weekly *Caledonian Mercury*. Since its founding in 1720, it was more patriotically inclined and more critical of the Whig establishment than the rival *Edinburgh Courant*, established two years earlier.

The initial success of Prince Charles in winning the battle of Prestonpans in East Lothian on 21 September 1745, then marching his troops from Edinburgh as far south as Derby, had flattered to deceive. Prince Charles had failed to consolidate in Scotland before invading England. The lack of foreign support undermined the confidence of English Jacobites, while the wholesale adoption of Highland garb led to their complete failure to identify with the prince's Scottish army. By the time of retreat at the outset of December, Jacobite lines of communication had been overextended and provisioning was extremely difficult. Despite their victory at Falkirk on 17 January 1746 there were no secure bridgeheads for assistance from France or Sweden. The Highland army's incursion into the English Midlands had persuaded the commanders of the superior British forces by land and sea that Jacobitism should be annihilated. After an emphatically brutal defeat at Culloden near

Inverness on 16 April 1746, the Jacobite leadership lost the political will to sustain patriotic campaigning.

With no sustained organisation to co-ordinate Jacobite activity in Scotland between the Fifteen and the Forty-Five, religious dissent and smuggling, which led to occasional rioting rather than rebellion, offered alternative means to express opposition to Union. The passage of the Toleration and the Patronage Acts in 1712 remained a source of tension and division for Presbyterians. These acts followed on from a judicial appeal by an Episcopalian clergyman, James Greenshields. His preaching and use of an Anglican liturgy in Edinburgh in defiance of the local presbytery led to his imprisonment by the town council, a decision upheld in the Court of Session but lost on appeal to the House of Lords in 1711. This legislation on ecclesiastical matters was the first substantive breach in the Presbyterian establishment as embodied within the Treaty of Union. Presbyterians were further outraged at being required to swear an Anglican oath of loyalty for public office. Taking communion according to Anglican rites became a sacramental test that barred conscientious Presbyterians from civil and military offices in England and the Empire.

Endeavours of patrons, drawn overwhelmingly from the landed interest, to impose ministers on vacant parishes against the wishes of the congregations led to sporadic and localised protests. General assemblies controlled by legalists and placemen were prepared to uphold the rights of patrons and ride roughshod over congregations. Presbyterian dissent found a denominational outlet when Ebenezer Erskine, minister of Stirling, and a few associates seceded to establish the Original Schism of 1733. The more accommodating Relief Church followed after Thomas Gillespie was deprived of his charge at Carnock in Fife by the general assembly of 1752 for not deferring to patrons. As these Seceders accepted the Hanoverian Succession they were exempt from penal laws, as were the Cameronian who remained prominent anti-Unionist as well as anti-Jacobites. Their continuing militancy was noticeably evident in Galloway where wholesale enclosures to increase landlords' profits from the droving trade were resisted vigorously in 1724 by a group known as the Levellers for their destruction of dykes and their social subversion.

The threat of rioting, which had led the British government to postpone the augmented malt tax in 1713, duly became a reality when a revised tax was implemented in 1725. While brewers provoked disturbances in west and central Scotland, the most notorious protest was the Shawfield Riot in Glasgow when the mansion of the local MP, Duncan Campbell, was razed because he had not vociferously opposed the malt tax. The military's inept handling of the mob magnified disorder. The magistrates and the town council were blamed by the British government and, after a brief period of incarceration in Edinburgh, punitively fined by the Scottish judiciary. General George Wade, despatched from England to restore order, went on to enforce a military occupation of the Highlands to contain Jacobitism, which had not featured as an incendiary factor.

Smuggling, which was a perennial source of disturbances in ports with customs houses, such as Leith, Montrose, Aberdeen and Glasgow, was intimately bound up with the Porteous Riot in Edinburgh. The city guard opened fire on a mob attempting to free a convicted smuggler in 1736. The mob regrouped, then seized and lynched John Porteous, as captain of the city guard. Although the mob had included contingents from Fife and other contraband districts, the political fallout was less pronounced than after the Shawfield Riot. Order was restored without punitive action being taken against the magistrates or town council. The riot was largely attributable to the lack of co-ordination between the military and the Scottish judiciary. Again no Jacobitism was detected.

Smuggling, which lessened the tax that accrued as customs and excise, compounded the 20-year delay by the British government in fully redeeming the Equivalents. Ongoing fear of Scottish Jacobitism contributed to the eventual provision of development funding that was channelled from 1727 through the Board of Trustees for Fisheries and Manufactures in tandem with the Royal Bank of Scotland. The Bank of Scotland was not trusted as the conduit for these funds because of its reputed past association with Jacobitism. The Board's venture capital to promote fishing and textiles was limited. Initially set at £6,000, it was mainly applied to the raising of manufacturing standards for linen and then wool. Sheep farming districts in the Jacobite heartlands of the Highlands and the north-east were excluded from access to woollen bounties.

Patriotism was undergoing a British rebranding. Loyalty to the territorial nation became a more pressing concern than allegiance to the exiled house of Stuart or the incumbent house of Hanover. British patriotism profited from the recovery of Scotland from recession as imperial opportunities expanded exponentially in the Americas and reached new horizons in Africa and Asia.

Droving of black cattle in the aftermath of Union took off with unrestricted access to expanding markets stimulated by the growth of London into the imperial metropolis as well as Europe's largest city, by naval demand for salt beef and by the growth of manufacturing towns in England. Although the Jacobite heartlands in the Highlands dominated this trade, droving had a negative impact in financing the absenteeism of chiefs and clan gentry, their accumulation of debts from increased consumer spending and their raising of rents. However, droving was a positive stimulus to banking. Sustained inflows of cash were invested in local fishing and textile initiatives. The painful experience of the Darien Scheme notwithstanding, Scotland, like the rest of the United Kingdom, was caught up in the mania for speculative ventures in stocks and shares that fed the South Sea Bubble. Having temporarily pushed up the prices of landed estates, its bursting in 1720 caused widespread bankruptcies. The Bank of Scotland was to the fore in promoting commercial stability through sound lending which continued under the dual banking system operative from 1727.

The Royal Bank had authorised capital in excess of £150,000 to the Bank of Scotland's £100,000. Scotland soon benefited from their rivalry. Pioneering note issues, overdrafts and deposit accounts during the 1730s facilitated commercial enterprise on the basis of credit rather than secure funds, a basis which attracted inward investment from England where banking practices remained conservative. As well as advancing credit for colonial traders in tobacco, sugar and rum, increased funding was now available for exports of linen and woollens directly to colonial markets through Glasgow and other Scottish ports rather than indirectly through London, Bristol and Liverpool. The principal colonial exports from Scotland – light woollens copied from the Mediterranean, linens priced for quantity not quality, salted and cured herrings – were geared primarily to clothe and feed the burgeoning slave plantations in the American South and the Caribbean.

Unrestricted access to the American colonies enabled Glasgow merchants to secure dominance in the tobacco trade by the 1740s, primarily by expanding the store system under which the merchant rather than the planter bore the risk of transatlantic shipping. Advances of credit on future tobacco sales in Europe were tied to the purchase of merchandise from the colonial store, a practice particularly suited to the expansion of small plantations along the Chesapeake and into the hinterlands of Maryland, Virginia and the Carolinas. Whitehaven was so eclipsed by Glasgow that the Cumbrian town actually petitioned for repeal of Union in 1710. Glasgow merchants took advantage of drawbacks on customs for re-export by shipping out huge quantities of tobacco to the Isle of Man and then bringing small amounts back illicitly to ports in the south-west of Scotland.

Scottish entrepreneurs extended the store system into the Caribbean to enhance profits from sugar and rum. The Treaty of Utrecht opened up imperial opportunities for Scottish entrepreneurs in the sugar trade from 1713. Scots as well as English planters benefited from the expulsion of the French from St Kitts and from the eradication of any Spanish threat to the more extensive working of sugar in Jamaica. Scots also gained a significant foothold in the African slave trade through the concession of the *asiento*, the monopoly to supply Spain, to the recently formed South Sea Company, which subsequently devolved the contract for carrying slaves to Campeche in the Gulf of Mexico to Scottish shippers. Sugar no less than tobacco became a major driver of urban and rural improvements in the early eighteenth century, especially after the resilience of the Scottish economy was tested by widespread famine in 1742–3. Central government now actively promoted drawbacks for linen exports – drawbacks which gave Scottish colonial entrepreneurs a vested interest in maintaining the Union and the Hanoverian Succession. The growing importance of Empire to Scottish prosperity was key to declining Jacobite commitment even among the clans, especially as imperial engagement had a profound impact on political management.

The limited offices and other places of profit in Scotland tended to be monopolised by Presbyterians and committed Whigs, especially after political management was devolved to Archibald Campbell, Earl of Islay (later 3rd Duke of Argyll) in 1725. Placement in Empire was different on account of the pervasive contacts of John Drummond of Quarrel. Having begun his career as an Edinburgh merchant, he moved to Amsterdam where he established himself as the leading continental financier for the British forces during the War of the Spanish Succession. Thereafter, Drummond shuttled between Amsterdam, Edinburgh, Paris and London. He helped shape the direction of the East India Company after he settled in London from 1724. Though he favoured Union, his strong Episcopal and Jacobite connections made him the ideal imperial complement to Islay's domestic political management. Drummond, who served as MP for the Perth burghs from 1727, enjoyed the backing of Prime Minister Robert Walpole who had factored in Jacobites as expendable manpower to maintain the British presence in the Caribbean and secure the frontiers of American colonies such as Georgia and North Carolina. Until his death in 1740, Drummond was the chief mover in placing Scots regardless of their political or religious affiliations in both the military and the mercantile branches of the East India Company. The Governor of Madras, James MacRae, from an impoverished family in Ayr, became the first Scottish nabob in the 1720s. Drummond also aided Scottish adventurers in Madras and Bengal from where they tramp-traded through the Indian Ocean to the South China Seas. Gaining placement in India was no guarantee of prosperity, however. The chances of any adventurer returning with a fortune were about 1 in 500.

Nevertheless Scottish networks tainted with Jacobitism did prosper from Empire. Indeed, the Duffs from the north-east, based in the shires of Aberdeen and Banff with further mercantile interests in the towns of Elgin and Inverness, repatriated funds through London from three Empires – the

Spanish and the Swedish as well as the British. With fortunes founded on private banking, landed enterprise and overseas trade, the network's leading laird, William Duff of Dipple, was ennobled in 1734 as Lord Braco (later as 1st Earl of Fife) in recognition of his British rather than his Scottish patriotism. The Stirlings of Keir, landowners near Glasgow and in the shires of Stirling and Perth, focused their endeavours on the West and East Indies. Sums repatriated from tramp-trading in India to Britain by 1748 were used, in part, to improve and expand the family holdings in central Scotland, but primarily to acquire further plantations in Jamaica. By 1753, the family were quit of Jacobitism.

BRITISH COMMITMENT

After the Fifteen, prominent Jacobites were forfeited by legal attainder rather than by the due process of law. However, the Scottish Jacobite elite remained well connected to their Whig counterparts. There was a nationwide determination that landed families and their commercial associates should not be utterly ruined. In the Lowlands, forfeiture was partially obstructed by the Scottish courts allowing the process of sequestration, based on bad debts, to take precedence. Estates sequestered were usually put under the charge of a kinsman of the person forfeited. But forfeiture had also enabled speculative interests, notably the York Buildings Company of London, to purchase Jacobite estates with a view to asset-stripping timber and mineral rights. Among clans where chiefs and leading gentry had been forfeited, rents continued to be paid to them in exile. Attempts of government troops to lift rents in Wester Ross in October 1721 were violently resisted.

In the wake of the Forty-Five, the British government pursued a final solution to the Jacobite problem, particularly in the Highlands, by active terrorism directed against the clans by land and sea. Indiscriminate punitive action, initiated by the Hanoverian victor at Culloden, William Augustus, Duke of Cumberland, verged on genocide. This was condoned not only by chiefs of Whig clans but by chiefs whose clansmen had defied them to fight for Jacobitism. Livestock was driven off and fishing boats holed to induce starvation. Apart from occasional retaliatory assassinations in Lochaber, banditry became a form of social protest for renegade clansmen who lifted livestock from Lowland peripheries. A more widespread practice of civil disobedience was the payment of rents from forfeited estates to chiefs and clan gentry exiled on the continent. This practice led to the show trial of James Stewart, a veteran of the Forty-Five, who was sending rents to France and legally resisting the eviction of his clansmen by the government factor in Appin. Within six months of the murder of Colin Campbell of Glenure in May 1752, Stewart was wrongly accused, tried and executed as an accessory. The last Jacobite executed in Britain was Dr Archibald Cameron, an aide and companion to Prince Charles after his flight from Scotland in September 1746. Apprehended in his native Lochaber while preparing the ground for what proved the last Jacobite plot in Scotland, he was incarcerated in the Tower of London prior to his execution in June 1753.

Following adverse press publicity for the atrocities in the months after Culloden, the British government moved away from extirpating to civilising the clans. The legislative programme promoted from 1747 was marked by acts disarming the clans and proscribing the wearing of tartan. These acts applied to all Highlanders, not just Jacobites. In the mistaken belief that the authority of chiefs was institutional rather than personal, the British government abolished heritable jurisdictions. The real intent of this enactment, however, was to reward chiefs and other landowners who had opposed Jacobitism. Archibald, 3rd Duke of Argyll was empowered to distribute around £493,000 (more than double the actual reparations for Darien) for jurisdictions that had largely become anachronistic. Argyll was also intent on demonstrating that British patriotism trumped Scottish rebellion. Two venture companies ensued – the British Linen Company, which promoted manufacturing primarily through banking services, and the British Fishery Company, the first in which the Scots had voluntarily participated in for over 120 years. Landed enterprise at home, no less than commercial engagement with Empire, now made improvers and adventurers British patriots regardless of any past family connection to Covenanters or Jacobites.

Notes

1.   *A Source Book of Scottish History*, iii, pp. 95–104.
2.   Ibid., pp. 122–25.
3.   Ibid., pp. 200–07.

5 Enlightenment and Enterprise, 1753–1884

Scotland emerged from the civil war between Jacobites and Whigs into an era of Enlightenment in the arts, law, medicine, science and technology. Scotland prospered within a United Kingdom, expanded to include Ireland in 1801, and as a key imperial partner in Asia, Africa and the Caribbean, notwithstanding the loss of the American colonies by 1783. The application of science and technology, the most enduring legacy of the Enlightenment, promoted enterprise which took Scotland through two stages of industrialisation, the first marked by textiles and chemicals from the 1770s and the second by coal, iron and steel, railways and shipbuilding from the 1820s. With agricultural improvements leading to removals and relocations, population drifted irrevocably away from the countryside to the towns. Despite extensive emigration overseas as well as to the rest of the United Kingdom, population levels continued to grow, with improved nutrition and large-scale immigration, particularly from Ireland. Urbanisation aggravated religious issues with the growth of dissent, non-churchgoing and sectarian discrimination and heightened political awareness through class divisions, electoral reforms and growing pressure for state intervention on social matters.

The Enlightenment rationalised the most fundamental shift in the social structure of Scotland away from hierarchical communities in favour of class interests. Chiefs and heads of families came to view themselves by education, marriage and imperial engagement as members of the Anglo-Scottish upper classes. Managers, financiers and professionals considered themselves as the middle classes discretely distanced by dwellings, schooling and transport from the workers. Manual work underwent a major change in labour rhythms from the seasonal requirements of agriculture to the daily shifts in factories, foundries, mines, railways or shipyards. Despite pollution, destitution, insanitary housing, drunkenness and epidemical diseases, the working classes by 1884 retained a community spirit based on solidarity in the face of exploitation.

CONSTITUTIONAL REFORM

The Enlightenment in Scotland is associated with common sense on the one hand and scepticism on the other; with a community focus for theoretical and applied learning; and with an experimental approach to problem solving across the whole range of human experience. Leading luminaries of Enlightenment, based predominantly but not exclusively in Edinburgh, have been identified as a progressive Whig influence. Intellectually, their contribution to learning was distinctive, but not detached from the European Republic of Letters which featured Jacobite no less than Whig intellectuals. Scholarly endeavours were supported and guided by printers, booksellers and patrons. Initially the latter were aristocrats and town councils, but latterly, as Scotland became locked into patronage networks in London and the rest of the United Kingdom, industrialists and imperial adventurers. Scottish intellectuals exchanged and refined ideas through learned societies and clubs. Their writings were circulated through public and private libraries in town and country to a receptive, literate population. By 1753, *The Scots Magazine* had a 14-year track record of debating advances in science as well as discoursing on history, philosophy and political economy.

The Moderates, who had come to prominence in the Kirk of Scotland by 1753, promoted themselves as an Enlightened influence. They maintained their dominance by management of church courts from presbyteries to the general assembly which debated annually issues of Scottish, British and imperial significance that led occasionally to progressive accomplishments. In 1778, the Court of Session ruled that slavery was not recognised by Scots Law. This landmark case was brought by Joseph Knight, a former slave baptised and legally married in Scotland, against his former master, John Wedderburn of Ballindean. The judges determined that dominion over a negro in Jamaica was unjust and could not be supported in Scotland. It was agreeable neither to humanity nor to Christianity.

William Robertson, a historian of note and Principal of Edinburgh University as well as a power-broker among the Moderates, was the most prominent spokesman for a polite Scotland liberated by the Union, an accomplishment which enabled the country to participate in the onward march of civilisation. He was not arguing that civilisation commenced in 1707, merely that the Union complemented the Revolution of 1689–91 that restored Scotland on the pathway to civility. Despite triumphalist Whig linking of Protestantism, property and progress with the Revolution, Adam Ferguson, the foremost Scottish thinker on the sociology of politics, remained sceptical about the perfectibility of the English constitution. Ferguson held back from equating change with progress and from accepting improvements as bringing material benefit to all. Ferguson and his fellow members of the Poker Club formed to agitate against Scottish exclusion from the Militia Act of 1757, and saw themselves as the moral guardians of the British constitution established at the Revolution and consolidated by the Union. Scots should be treated as equal and trusted partners though repeatedly denied a militia in 1760, 1762, 1776 and 1782. Nonetheless, British identity was promoted assiduously as a common commitment to liberty and Protestantism.

A more prescient critique of not just the British state but its claims to Empire had already emerged within Jacobite circles. Having participated in the failed risings of 1715 and 1719, Field Marshal James Keith had subsequently become a military commander in Spain, Russia and Prussia. Writing between 1748 and 1756 – mainly from Sans Souci in Potsdam where he was installed as a confidant of Frederick II of Prussia – Keith offered a Jacobite perspective on applied Enlightenment that was grounded in his military expertise in Eurasia. He promoted as both rational and liberal the destruction of the Turkish Empire in Europe as of the Spanish Empire in the Americas. This was not only advantageous to the leading European powers, but also carried the further prospect of moral reformation without which France, Britain and the Dutch Republic were bound to lose their own empires in the Americas. Keith was unconvinced that Britain, under the corrupt oligarchy that passed for parliamentary government, practised or encouraged virtuous patriotism.

A firm believer in probity in public life, James Stuart, 3rd Earl of Bute, the first Scot to become Prime Minister of Great Britain, briefly held office from May 1762 until April 1763. His support for George III's efforts to steer politics and patronage rekindled aversions to Scots last heard at the Forty-Five that were diverted by the controversy provoked by James 'Ossian' Macpherson's rich embellishment of Gaelic oral tradition relating to the classical heroes of Celtic mythology. Macpherson provided an exemplar for Romanticism whose fascination with the primitive and the irrational fundamentally questioned the Enlightenment's tempering of reason with emotion. This controversy was overtaken by issues of taxation and representation raised by the American Revolution, which stimulated moves for parliamentary and burgh reform.

The main electoral abuse in a parliamentary system based on property not people was the ability of nobles, as feudal landlords, to influence elections in the counties. In the burghs, the self-perpetuating oligarchies that ran town-councils marketed votes and plundered funds for the common good. A convention in Edinburgh to reform electoral abuses was attended by 23 out of the 33 Scottish shires in 1784. Burgh critics of the parliamentary franchise, for whom the *Caledonian Mercury* was a receptive platform, called another convention in Edinburgh, attended by 33 out of the 66 burghs. The focus of this burgh convention soon turned to internal reform. Neither convention espoused democracy. There were just 2,665 electors in the 45 Scottish Parliamentary constituencies in 1788. Elections tended to be managed rather than contested.

The loss of the American colonies led to the re-emergence of the Tories into British prominence. Their mainstay in Scotland was Henry Dundas (later Viscount Melville), an Edinburgh advocate. His promotion of legislation to oversee the workings of the East India Company from 1784 opened up imperial avenues of patronage to sustain the Tories in government and enhanced his own influence as the dominant political manager in Scotland. Following the Revolution of 1789 and then war with France from 1793, Dundas, first as Home Secretary then as Secretary for War, viewed Ireland as the back door to invasion as Scotland had been from the onset of the War of the Spanish Succession in 1702. Political incorporation was again seen as the solution but not for the United Irishmen, maligned as Jacobins for their support of the French Revolution. Their radical pursuit of Irish autonomy with assistance from France was crushed in 1798. The incorporation of Ireland into the United Kingdom by 1801 was not so much an Enlightened as a reactionary British endeavour.

The initial Scottish response to the French Revolution, while less nationalist, was arguably as radical as the Irish. The patriotic bridge between Jacobites and Jacobins was paved by the iconic poetry of Robert Burns. Like other initial sympathisers with the French Revolution, Burns contended that the Union of 1707 was accomplished primarily by the perfidy of a usurping monarchy and by the bribery of corrupt Scottish politicians greedy for English gold. Burns, like many in Scotland who welcomed the French Revolution, was a freemason committed to the pursuit of a just, perfect and regular society. Freemasonry, co-ordinated under the Grand Lodge of Scotland in 1736, remained distinctive and considerably more inclusive than its English equivalent. In his striving for international brotherhood, Burns was acutely conscious that the tree of liberty planted by the French Revolution was a cause further advanced in Scotland than from London to the Tweed:

Wi' plenty of sic trees, I trust/ The world would live in peace man/ The sword would help to make a plough/ The din of war wad cease man.[1]

The Scottish Friends of the People established in 1792 and their later offshoot the United Scotsmen maintained fraternal links with the United Irishmen, which exposed them to reprisals marked by show trials, selective executions and transportation to Australia. The most celebrated radical was Thomas Muir of Huntershill, an advocate who made his reputation defending the poor and the oppressed. His call for annual parliaments and a franchise geared to democracy rather than property alienated the majority of country and burgh reformers, even though the radicals had followed their lead in holding a series of constitutional conventions in Edinburgh to improve the Union and the accountability of parliament. The first two, in December 1792 and in May 1793, were Scottish concerns; a third was attended by members from the London Corresponding Society in November. Muir was charged with sedition for his purportedly treasonable association with the English radicals in London, the French Revolutionaries in Paris and the United Irishmen in Dublin. Rather than fight the flimsy case against him by forensic legal pleading at his trial in August 1793, Muir opted to make powerful political speeches to confirm his standing as a tribune of the people. His transportation for 14 years to Botany Bay became the benchmark for other radicals. The last radical transported was George Mealmaker, the leader of the United Scotsmen, in 1797. Radicalism fragmented and went underground. The United Scotsmen were defunct by 1802.

From the American to the French Revolution, newspapers in Scotland increased from 8 to 27. Press reports spread public aversion to the French reign of terror, in which the monarchy and much of the aristocracy were beheaded by guillotine. The *Aberdeen Journal* (established in 1747) provided weekly coverage of events from Paris. The subsequent outbreak of war in 1793 led the Tories to identify opposition to the French Republic and the rise to power of Napoleon Bonaparte with British patriotism. Anyone suspected of reforming sympathies was denied patronage if professional and credit if tradesman. Royal birthday celebrations in Scottish towns were associated with intoxicated rioting. Urban meal mobs were not uncommon in times of shortage. Such breaches of the peace in the 1790s were deemed as radical plotting, even though a major stimulus to rioting was the imposition of Corn Laws in 1790 to protect the rents of the landed interest. British reaction was further consolidated by the formation of the Goldsmith's Hall Association in Edinburgh (which provided the jury for Muir's trial) and the Constitutional Association in Glasgow. Encouragement was also given to the spread of the Orange Order, established to oppose the United Irishmen. By 1805, the *Glasgow Herald*, which was not unsympathetic to the independence of the American Colonies when originally issued in 1783, was firmly on the side of British reaction. Radicalism was further contained by the tax breaks for industrial distilling of grains for whisky and gin. The complementary lowering of duties on spirits and the proliferation of public houses for their consumption turned the distillation of the much higher quality malted barley into an illicit trade in the Highlands and the north-east. While Robert Burns extolled the alliance of whisky and freedom, endemic drunkenness diminished personal and political capacities to resist reactionary politics disguised as patriotism.

Patriotism was publicly encouraged through recruitment of volunteer companies to contain disorder at home and prepare against French invasion. Scottish Jacobins were rigorously excluded, but recruitment was radicalised after Scotland was eventually granted a militia in 1797. The landed and commercial elites could hire substitutes, but the general population faced conscription, a situation which led to rioting at Tranent in East Lothian and later at Bathgate in West Lothian. On both occasions colliers were to the fore, but their protests were rapaciously suppressed by the military as were combinations and strikes by workers struggling to maintain living standards.

The first urban strike of significance, that by Glasgow weavers in 1787 during the recession occasioned by the American Revolution, was ruthlessly terminated by the military. Strikes took on added significance after Napoleon's blockade of Britain tied economic to political warfare from 1796. Although the Court of Session required Glasgow magistrates to fix fair wages for striking weavers in 1812, the decision was disregarded by the employers with support from the British government. The strike leader, Alexander Richmond, rehabilitated himself with employers by turning informer against combinations of workers. In order to taint trade unions with seditious activities, Richmond became an *agent provocateur*. Bills calling for mobilisation in support of a provisional government were posted in Glasgow in April 1820. Weavers in the Calton district of Glasgow went on strike and workers from Strathaven in Lanarkshire marched to the Cathkin Braes on the outskirts of the city. A desultory band intent on besieging the Carron Iron Works was routed by cavalry at Bonnymuir. Three ringleaders from the 47 that were tried for treason were executed at Stirling Castle.

The cause of reform among the upper and middle classes revived as the Tory reaction rapidly ran out of credibility in continuing to use force to suppress radical activity throughout Britain after the conclusion of the Napoleonic Wars in 1815. Whig reformers had been heartened by the removal of Dundas for financial irregularities as First Lord of the Admiralty in 1806, by the abolition of slave trading in the British Empire in 1807 and by the founding of the Commercial Bank to free up Scottish sources of credit in 1810. The Whig belief in progress through Union was now tied to a British reform agenda for a more liberal constitution that was to be accomplished through parliamentary legislation, a view supported diligently by the *Edinburgh Review* from 1802 and by *The Scotsman* newspaper from 1817. Religious impediments to full citizenship were removed through the repeal of the Test and Corporation Acts (1828) and the passing of the Catholic Emancipation Act (1829). The franchise for parliament and municipal corporations was expanded to ensure wider accountability and representation for the propertied interests from commerce and industry as well as land by the First or Great Reform Act (1832) and the Burgh Reform Act (1833).

The franchise benefited the emerging middle class who occupied single-tenant farms in the counties and substantial households in the burghs. Political representation increased, but Scotland still had only 65,000 electors. The number of Scottish constituencies rose from 45 to 53 by increasing representation for the major burghs and creating constituencies for the manufacturing towns of Paisley, Greenock, Falkirk and Kilmarnock. Direct voting ended the managerial control of town councils in elections. Feudal landlords enhanced their influence on county elections by having their tenant farmers vote publicly, a practice only curtailed by the introduction of the Secret Ballot in 1872.

Religious and parliamentary reforms were not the only breaches in the British imperial establishment. Slavery was abolished throughout the British Empire in 1833. Of the £20 million compensation paid to plantation holders and their financers, about 16% of the capital repatriated to the United Kingdom came to Scotland. Of the 684 verified Scots from Caithness to Galloway who claimed compensation, over a fifth were women. This was not just a matter of inheriting estates or legacies as women made claims as executors, trustees and creditors.[2] Albeit women were less active than men, exploiting slavery in the West Indies was primarily an issue of class not gender. Imperial adventurers were still active in the opium trade from the East Indies to China. In marked contrast to elite women profiting from slavery and its abolition, working women in Scotland were struggling to throw over the shackles of serfdom. Women and girls worked in cramped and dark locations as carriers from the coal face to the pit head in the mines of central Scotland. Women in the north-east sold fish from heavy creels in rural hinterlands where they sought safety in numbers and carried knives to fend off unwanted sexual advances. Women hand-knitters in Shetland were obliged to sell their produce for goods from the stores of local merchants, a form of exploitation known as truck. This intertwining of gender and class struggles helped fuel the emergence of Chartism by 1838.

Chartism in Scotland, as in England and Ireland, was an attempt at working class solidarity to uphold collective bargaining on wages and conditions by trade unions. The Chartists adopted the Jacobin programme for annual parliaments and adult male suffrage and enhanced this with demands for a secret ballot, equal electoral districts, and removal of property qualifications for and the payment of MPs. They stressed the importance of education for an informed electorate. Branches continued to proliferate into the 1840s from the Northern Isles to the Borders. Despite Chartist engagement in strikes, class solidarity was not sustained even on a Scottish basis. Yet the Chartists set the agenda for democratic representation. The Second Reform Act in 1868 pushed up the electorate to around 230,000 by granting the vote to adult male householders in the towns where seven more parliamentary constituencies were created. This modest move towards democracy consolidated the alliance of landed Whigs and middle class reformers in the Liberal Party.

SOCIAL REFORM

Constitutional reform opened up the prospect of social reform through meaningful intervention by central government as an aspect of applied Enlightenment. This prospect was advocated by Sir John Sinclair of Ulbster, MP and a progressive landlord in Caithness, who edited the *Statistical Accounts*, which provide qualitative commentary as well as quantitative information of a broad range of human activity for every parish (936) and the five universities in Scotland. Compiled predominantly by the ministers of the established Kirk in the 1790s, this endeavour was repeated between 1834 and 1845 when the general assembly sponsored the *New Statistical Accounts*.

Until the mid-eighteenth century, public health was primarily a localised concern of town-councils in the burghs and of barony courts and other heritable jurisdictions in the countryside. Hospitals were institutions for containment rather than cure of disease, that also cared for the aged and infirm. Mental illness was neglected. The provision of poor relief and education, though governed by a statutory framework, was primarily the concern of the Kirk. In urban and rural parishes the supervision of communities by Kirk sessions was shared, respectively, with the town councils and landowners who had a legal duty to underwrite financial provisions for welfare and schooling. This basic provision was challenged by the growth of religious dissent and class consciousness. Despite hair splitting theological differences, the Original Seceders along with the Relief Church appealed especially to the middle classes. The upper classes were drawn to Episcopalianism after jurors and non-jurors reconciled their differences by 1804. Parish resources were hugely strained by population growth, removal and relocation.

The first Scottish census, carried out under the auspices of the Kirk's general assembly in 1755, estimated a total population of 1,265,380 with Perth, Aberdeen, Midlothian, Lanark and Fife the most populous counties. By the first official state census in 1801, the Scottish population had risen to 1,608,420, but the order of the most populous counties had changed to Lanark, Perth, Midlothian, Aberdeen and Angus. By the census of 1881, the population had grown further to 3,735,573 and the most populous counties were now Lanark, Midlothian, Aberdeen, Angus and Renfrew, confirming the urban dominance of Glasgow in the west of Scotland, and the cities of Edinburgh, Aberdeen and Dundee in the east. Predominantly rural counties had experienced more fluctuating patterns of growth particularly in Galloway and the Borders, the Northern Isles and the Highlands, with Argyll from 1841 and Inverness from 1851 haemorrhaging people.[3]

Enlightenment thinking on health, welfare and education applied mainly to institutional developments. The first Edinburgh Medical Society, which was founded in 1731, was remodelled in 1737 as the Society for Improving Arts and Sciences then revitalised in 1751 as the Edinburgh Philosophical Society. Its comprehensive interests in useful intellectual inquiry paved the way for the Royal Society of Edinburgh, founded in 1784. The development of the Edinburgh Medical School and its philosophical offshoots was driven by the patronage of aristocrats and civic authorities no less than by Enlightened luminaries. Alexander Monro senior, then Professor of Anatomy at Edinburgh University, worked purposefully with George Drummond, Lord Provost of Edinburgh, to establish the city's Royal Infirmary which attracted international renown for its vital contribution to clinical teaching and later for its development of psychiatry under Alexander Monro junior. The medical school also pioneered the study of tropical medicine in Scotland which was later taken up by Glasgow University and Marischal College in Aberdeen in order to equip graduates from Scottish medical schools to sustain British imperial expansion in the Americas, Africa and Asia.

Medical provision was not necessarily open to all citizens, however. Infirmaries, such as that of Greenock established in 1806, restricted access to subscribed investors and their associates. Access to other institutions also exhibited a class bias that was based on compulsion for the poor, as evident in Moorhead's Hospital, the workhouse operational in Dumfries by 1753 and in the lunatic asylum founded in Montrose in 1779. The town council of Aberdeen funded free medical care for over 100 inmates and outpatients in a workhouse and infirmary from 1741 that proved so attractive to beggars that strict policing and rigorous means testing were introduced after 1753. Foundling hospitals, such as that established in Glasgow in 1801, had a more subtle class bias. Accommodation for single mothers, drawn primarily from the ranks of household servants, was usually paid by the male employers with whom they had a sexual dalliance.

Poor relief struggled to adapt to mass unemployment, with 10,000 out of work in Paisley for more than a year and 1,200 regularly walking the streets of Edinburgh by 1843. Temporary relief in terms of food and materials was available for the unemployed in emergencies, particularly those providing a service to their community as shop-keepers, ferrymen and tradesmen. The able-bodied poor unwilling to work were denied relief other than by begging. Even where relief was granted, the poor were expected to rely on their personal endeavour and the kindness of friends and relatives, to fend off destitution. Funding through the Kirk was usually inadequate. This meant a recourse to assessment, as a compulsory levy for up to six months with the landowners paying half and their tenants the remainder. Voluntary contributions were also affected by non-churchgoing and by the sectarian response to the influx of Irish Catholics during the economic downturns after 1815. The Kirk also supported self-help through friendly societies and savings banks. Although Henry Duncan, minister of Ruthwell parish in Dumfriesshire, pioneered the latter in 1810, within nine years he became convinced that the communal and enduring assistance offered by friendly societies was more beneficial than the individual and exhaustible savings lodged in banks.

In Glasgow, where problems accompanying urbanisation were most acute, the town council established a common central fund for all city parishes in 1774. Claims for poor relief increasingly moved beyond the scope of resources available. Thomas Chalmers, a prominent Evangelical in the Kirk, began a social work experiment in the parish of St John in the east end of Glasgow in 1819. Opting out of the city common fund, he provided for the poor voluntarily through urban districts supervised by deacons. The money amassed from the excess of poor contributions was used to run parish schools which all social classes were encouraged to attend, as well as Sunday schools for children in employment. Although his experiment lasted only five years, Chalmers did foster a meaningful sense of community within his predominantly working class parish.

The ideal of at least one public school in every parish had been backed up by parliamentary legislation in the seventeenth century, which sought to balance the demand for teachers between richer and poorer parishes by laying down a fixed salary range that went from well over £5 to just over £11 sterling. However, no provision was made to increase salaries when costs of living rose. The supply of teachers was helped temporarily by an influx of persons training part-time for the ministry or by qualified ministers waiting for a parish. This led to a high turnover in staffing, a drop in teaching standards and irregular attendance by scholars. Fees were kept low for basic numeracy and literacy, as for Latin and grammar to allow the more able to progress from parish to burgh public schools or even directly to university. The Education Act of 1803 altered the fixed salary scale from under £17 to over £22. Where more than one school was required in a large rural parish, the salaries for both masters was just over £33, but only one benefited from the new compulsory provision of a house and garden. This encouraged landowners not to go beyond the minimum requirement and prolonged the need for charitable schools as provided by the Society for Propagating Christian Knowledge. Its mission since 1709 was to inculcate Presbyterianism, loyalty to the Hanoverian dynasty and basic literacy in English through ambulatory schools that travelled around extensive rural parishes. The Society began to use Gaelic as a medium of instruction from 1766 and published the first authentic Scottish Gaelic translation of the New Testament in the following year and then the whole Bible in 1801. Non-sectarian, ambulatory schooling was extended throughout the Highlands by the Gaelic Society Schools established through public subscription in Edinburgh (1811), Glasgow (1812) and Inverness (1818). Their promotion of basic literacy and bilingualism actually accelerated emigration by the time public funds were running short in the late 1820s.

Alternative schooling in the form of private tuition expanded, particularly where organised by Presbyterian dissenters. Catholic seminaries and Episcopalian academies for training priests and educating sons of the gentry were of necessity ambulatory. Town councils reshaped their educational facilities to offer new subjects, which earned teachers higher fees and were deemed more in keeping with the needs of a commercial society. Banff established three new schools besides the traditional public school for grammar and Latin by 1762. One school taught writing, book-keeping, mathematics and navigation; a second taught English language; and the third taught white and coloured seam and other vocational courses deemed suitable for girls normally excluded from parish and burgh schools. Class interests were carried further in Edinburgh where there was a range of finishing schools for the daughters of landed and commercial elites. Four English schools created in 1759 to supplement the High School were soon reserved for their sons.

This class and gender bias was also evident in higher education. The universities were heavily dependent on their close working relationships with the aristocracy, civic authorities and especially the political managers of Scotland. These ties of patronage to learning were notable in determining the excellence of scientific provision at the universities of Edinburgh and Glasgow as at Marischal and King's Colleges in Aberdeen. However, David Hume, the preeminent Scottish philosopher, was ruled out of professorships at Edinburgh in 1744 and at Glasgow in 1751 because of his scepticism about religion. James Hutton, who laid out the scientific principles for the study of geology from 1785, was never offered an academic post. The University of St Andrews was intellectually moribund. The college of St Leonards was allowed to fall into disuse by 1772. In order to sell medical degrees internationally, St Andrews had a chair of medicine but no medical school.

All five universities retained elementary classes for students who came directly from parish schools. Fees for the classics and philosophy were kept low and bursaries were available to sustain equality of opportunity, particularly for those progressing to professional degrees in divinity, law and medicine. Academies funded by public subscription acted as ginger group for universities who only abandoned lectures in Latin from the 1730s. They catered primarily for the middle classes and built upon a cultural ethos which favoured neither the exclusive oversight of schools by the established Kirk nor the financial control exercised by town councils. The first purpose-built academy was opened at Perth in 1761. By 1790, the new academy at Elgin was based on the building plan of that at Montrose and on the teaching curriculum of that at Inverness, which had been funded by capital repatriated from the West Indies. Whereas academies required their schoolmasters to teach several and diverse subjects, the universities now offered specialist professors in different subjects.

John Anderson, Professor of Natural Philosophy at Glasgow University, was determined that there were no grounds for complacency. His last will and testament of 1795 created a place of useful learning for the city that reached out from Scotland to France as well as England. Anderson envisaged an alternative university that inspired those willing to learn about scientific principles, regardless of class or gender. He favoured open rather than selective access and, for the first time in Scotland, encouraged women to engage with higher education. The Andersonian Institute's chief inspiration came from across the Atlantic, notably the Public College of Philadelphia (later the University of the State of Pennsylvania) promoted by Benjamin Franklin in 1749 as a more practical place of learning than existing American universities. Anderson promoted harmonious working relations with the entrepreneurs shaping the industrial future of Scotland. Chartered as the Royal College of Science and Technology, the Andersonian Institute was playing a formative role in equipping Scots for service in an expanding British Empire by the 1820s.

Yet this very role was questioned by the royal commission enquiring into the condition of the Scottish universities between 1826 and 1830 that eventually laid the basis for legislation which standardised governance, length of academic years and degree programmes in 1855. Done not so much to harmonise as compete with Oxford and Cambridge in England, restructuring led five years later to the unification of King's and Marischal Colleges into the University of Aberdeen. Vested academic interests, which had blocked past attempts at unification from the eighteenth century, were not entirely quashed. James Clerk Maxwell, who became the foremost Scottish scientist of the nineteenth century, was released from his post at Marischal College. His work as a mathematical physicist contributed to the development of cable telegraphy in the 1860s and subsequently created the theoretical foundations for the technological application of electric power, telephony and radio.

University reform in 1855, which ended the Presbyterian monopoly on academic posts, came in the midst of a legislative programme for social reform that was triggered by the Disruption of 1843. The Free Kirk walking out of the established Kirk realigned class and denominational influences. The Poor Law Amendment Act of 1845 institutionalised recourse to assessment and placed the overall supervision of poor relief on a Board of Supervision, with inspectors in every parish. Boards of landowners or town councillors, some ministers and elders and a few elected ratepayers, oversaw relief in every parish. The Board of Supervision supported the construction of urban poor houses that also served the rural hinterlands of small towns. The Act made it essential to provide proper medical care through qualified doctors for workhouse inmates. Medical provision was loaded in favour of the deserving poor and their dependants. Relief was still viewed as a charity rather than a right, but attitudes to poverty were changing in being identified with health and sanitation rather than sin. Poor and destitute confined to mental asylums continued to be stigmatised, however. In 1867, the Public Health Act for Scotland was grafted onto the Poor Law framework. Parochial boards did not readily adapt to becoming local sanitary authorities.

The Catholic Church had popularised temperance. A mass meeting on Glasgow Green in 1842 was invited to sign the pledge in favour of total abstinence from alcohol: 50,000 people, Catholics and Protestants, signed up. The Free Kirk pressed for the Licensing Act of 1853 that imposed Sunday closing on public houses and cut drinking times in the rest of the week from 18 to 14 hours daily. Duties on spirits were increased markedly. Licensed grocers were cut to the same hours. Children under 14 years were banned from purchasing drink in 1862.

State intervention was most emphatic in education. The stock of Scottish schooling had been augmented by the creation of parliamentary schools in 1838. The Disruption led to additional denominational schools and better teacher training. A parliamentary act of 1861 raised schoolmasters' salaries to between £35 and £80, with pensions equivalent to two-thirds of salary awarded for the first time. But inadequate fees, meagre facilities and concerns about literacy as the electorate expanded led to the Education Act of 1872. A Central School Board was charged to run Scottish education. In every parish, public schooling was entrusted to an elected board to which parliamentary schools were soon transferred. Private schools were acquired by purchase, but rarely those for the expanding middle classes. Denominational schools only came under the remit of school boards by agreement. Attendance at school became compulsory. The leaving age was set at 14 years for basic schooling. There was no uniformity in elections to the boards or assessed rates for education, poor relief and public health. The Act improved buildings, equipment and attendance as well as salaries, but school rates remained high if not excessive in rural areas where there was a lack of higher schooling. English became the sole medium of instruction. Overzealous teachers made overgenerous use of corporal punishment to deter pupils from using Scots or Gaelic.

RELIGIOUS OBSERVANCE

Prior to 1843, Moderates and Evangelicals in the Kirk had long-standing differences over the appointment of ministers by landlords as lay patrons, even if they were not actually Presbyterians – differences that were compounded by theological concerns about the dilution of orthodox Calvinism and the failure to promote adequate spiritual missions at home and abroad. The Evangelicals, who came to the fore in the general assembly of 1833, pushed through the Veto and Chapel Acts. The first allowed congregations to challenge the choice of ministers by patrons, the second let ministers serving in mainly urban chapels of ease or extension churches participate in church courts. After ten years of conflict, in which the State upheld rights of patronage and denied chapel ministers representation in church courts, a substantive minority – a third of the ministers and around two-fifths of the membership – led by Thomas Chalmers left the Kirk at the Disruption. The new Free Kirk was not conceived as a voluntary institution but as a spiritually revitalised establishment in waiting. Its strength lay among the urban middle classes and in the Highlands. Whereas the urban middle classes had the means and resources to commence an ambitious programme of church building, Highlanders became embroiled in controversy with landlords refusing to grant sites for churches.

The moral compass of the Free Kirk was evident in such ethical issues as the repeal of the Corn Laws in 1845, but less so in extending the abolition of slavery from the British Empire in 1833 to the United States. Anti-slavery attracted American speakers of renown – such as the former slave Frederick Douglass – who put the Free Kirk on the defensive in 1845–6 for accepting money from slave states. The Free Kirk also faced further challenge from the middle classes who backed the voluntary organisation of health, welfare and education once the Seceding and Relief Churches merged in 1847 as the United Presbyterian Church of Scotland. The Free Kirk responded by developing initiatives financed by public subscriptions and supplemented by philanthropy in Aberdeen, Edinburgh and Glasgow, notably ragged trouser or industrial schools to feed as well as educate destitute children, residential reformatories to enable delinquent children to become responsible citizens and urban parishes in which communities determined priorities for welfare and schooling.

Community welfare and schooling remained particular concerns for the established Kirk whose membership among the working classes was on the rise before patronage was abolished in 1874. Church discipline was more relaxed as poor relief, public health and education became matters of secular governance. No longer compulsory, Sabbath observance remained customary. Non-churchgoing was a growing feature in Scottish life as were civil and irregular marriages not solemnised by any religious denomination. Calvinism in Scotland was on the defensive. Biblical criticism, particularly from Germany, stressed the fallible and contradictory nature of human documentation. Evolution theory as well as geological studies questioned the validity of biblical teaching on the earth's creation. Historical materialism, as espoused by Karl Marx and other German thinkers, laid the secular basis for scientific socialism. All Presbyterian churches were affected by musical and liturgical controversies as practices of worship were stimulated by American evangelists, most notably Ira Sankey and Dwight Moody from Chicago when touring Scotland in 1874.

The religious denominations most responsive to liturgical change were the Episcopalians and the less well-resourced Roman Catholics who sustained welfare and schooling within their own communities. Episcopalians, who drew on non-juring tradition north of the Tay that strove to return to the piety and purity of the early Church, spoke out against sectarian discrimination in industrial towns by 1830. Their numbers revived through their integration into the global Anglican community from 1867 and, more significantly, through migrations from England and Ulster into the universities, public administration, financial services, factory management and skilled trades. Catholics endured rampant sectarianism as Irish migration swelled into west and central Scotland following widespread famine across the North Channel in the 1840s. The Catholic community also suffered from internal divisions, which were particularly explosive in Glasgow by the 1860s, as efforts of immigrant priests to impose an Irish identity were resisted by Scots from the traditional heartlands of the faith in the Highlands and the north-east. Episcopalians, who viewed themselves as the true heirs to the medieval Church, were not supportive of the restoration of Scottish diocesan titles for the Roman Catholic hierarchy in 1878. The restoration refocused differences between Irish and Highland factions, but also promoted expansive liturgical worship. The Catholic presence in Scotland was subsequently given a stronger continental flavour by the growing presence of Polish and Lithuanian miners and, above all, by a large influx of Italians, mainly as caterers, who transformed the dietary and socialising habits of Scots with ice cream parlours, fish and chip shops, and cafés.

RURAL AND URBAN PLANNING

Social legislation in the nineteenth century applied urban remedies to rural locations. The Enlightenment, however, had favoured harmonious and constructive planning in town and country. The first significant test of this approach came when 13 forfeited Jacobite estates were annexed to the Crown, a measure accomplished in 1752 but not implemented until 1760. Intended as models for exemplary practice, the Annexed Estates were overseen by commissioners charged to propagate loyalty to the Hanoverian dynasty, diversify the Highland economy and promote Presbyterianism. The commissioners included in their ranks civic leaders and noted improvers who sponsored authoritative reports on fisheries, manufactures and mineral resources. However, financing was dependent on the cash surplus from the capital raised from the sale of forfeited Jacobite estates in the Lowlands, not on an annual grant from central government. Rents on the Annexed Estates, after initial survey and valuation, were frozen by the commissioners. The resultant erosion of capital impeded long-term projects. Inherited debts were continued, not cleared. Bureaucracy flourished through lack of accountability and energetic management. No commissioner would appear to have personally visited any Annexed Estate. Following the end of the Seven Years War in 1763, the Estates primarily became an agency to relocate demobilised soldiers and sailors. Fourteen years of planning effectively ended in 1774. Offers of long leases giving greater security of tenure for improving farmers were curtailed to facilitate the movement of labour into industry and to conserve landed interests in anticipation of the full-scale restoration of the Jacobite disinherited. By disannexation in 1784, there was a general recognition that the estates were only distinguished for their comparatively bad condition. Although the commissioners did not transform the Highlands, they did accelerate the break-up of traditional, communal townships through the creation of single-tenant farms, planned villages and crofting communities. The consequent removal and relocation of people served as a template for clearance for restored Jacobite as well as loyalist Whig landlords.

Rationalised by the political economy emanating from the Enlightenment, the clearance of people was propagated as integrating the Highlands into the British Empire. Commercial farming of first cattle then sheep by single rather than multiple tenants removed surplus farmers and labourers from the land or relocated them into crofting communities that too often became rural ghettos for quarrying, burning seaweed to produce kelp and fishing. The civil engineer Thomas Telford was employed to direct central government's programme of road, bridge and canal construction to stem what had become a tidal flow of emigration from the Highlands. Telford warned in 1802:

> it is a great Hardship, if not a great Injustice, that the Inhabitants of an extensive District should all at once be driven from their native Country, to make way for sheep Farming, which is likely to be carried to an imprudent Extent.[4]

It was the duty of government to consider the Highlands as an extraordinary case by curtailing the excesses of profiteering landlords. This prognosis fell on deaf ears, as evident from the notoriously brutal clearances in Sutherland in the next two decade. Cattle farmers, their labourers and families were removed from interior glens and straths to make way for sheep walks. Some of the evicted were relocated into coastal crofting communities to pursue a livelihood from fishing, for which they were ill-equipped. In the interim, Telford's flagship project, the Caledonian Canal, expedited access for more highly capitalised and technologically advanced north-east fishing boats into west coast waters. The Crinan Canal opened up urban markets in the central Lowlands for Argyllshire slates and Islay distilleries, but did not halt migration to British cities or North America.

The first phase of Clearance, associated with the creation of crofting communities, gave way to a second phase from the 1820s marked by the removal of these communities for sheep walks and shooting estates. With the industrial production of inorganic salts and alkalis leading to a collapse in demand for organic kelp, with changing taxes legitimising the commercial distilling of malt whisky from 1823 and with diminishing calls on manpower for imperial service by land and sea, the state of crofting communities was increasingly parlous. The contrary nature of herring shoals affected the viability of communities engaged in fishing. The eradication of slavery in the British Empire in 1833 diminished the market for herrings in the West Indies. The only relatively buoyant aspect of crofting was in such extractive industries as slate, lime and timber. Crofting communities were over-reliant on potato cultivation and seasonal or episodical migration to the Lowlands to find employment in arable agriculture, heavy industries or construction work. But here again Highlanders faced stiff Irish competition as casual labourers. The critical condition of crofting was first exposed by the potato famine of 1836–7, which was relieved largely from Glasgow through funds raised in British cities.

Landlords were increasingly on the defensive after potato blight occasioned the Great Highland Famine of 1845–50. Journalists provided frontline accounts of destitution and limited resistance to evictions. The general, but by no means universal, reluctance of landlords to finance adequate work programmes was combined with their particular aversion to the Poor Law Amendment Act of 1845. In marked contrast to the contemporaneous Irish situation, the Great Famine did not become a demographic disaster in the Highlands. Again relief funds were mobilised through British cities and supplemented by contributions from North America. A Central Board of Management based in Glasgow and Edinburgh sponsored destitution roads and other infrastructural developments that enhanced the value of landed estates. Population continued to decline in the Highland counties. With prospects for crofting limited, the Board of Supervision came down firmly in favour of assisted emigration by 1851. Sheep farms as well as crofting communities were now losing out to deer forests for sporting purposes. Ironically, new avenues for migration to Australia and New Zealand led to Highlanders becoming engaged in very profitable sheep farming, which made the production of wool from the Antipodes highly competitive on the British market. Such competition hastened the conversion of sheep walks into sporting estates.

Recreational land use received a major boost when Queen Victoria and Prince Albert acquired Balmoral on Deeside during the 1850s. The purchase of large sporting estates by industrialists, such as Ardtornish on Morvern by Octavius Smith a London distiller in 1860, was secondary to acquisition of estates by Highlanders or entrepreneurs from a Highland background who had made their fortune in Empire, such as James Matheson who had acquired the island of Lewis by 1844 from the spoils of his belligerent opium trading into China. The first radical challenge to the propertied interest occurred on this estate in 1874. Crofters on the island of Bernera contested the authoritarian behaviour of the factor of Lewis in the fields, in the streets and in the courts. Their persistence, despite the threat of military reprisals, restored their common grazings in Lewis and blocked evictions. In the process, they created the template for successful crofting agitation that had spread to Skye by 1882, where evictions and the denial of access to common grazing were resisted first in the Braes on the Sound of Raasay and later in Glendale where local law officers were assisted by contingents of Glasgow police with military forces in reserve.

Landowners in Highlands and Lowlands were no longer building the classical mansions designed with elaborate magnificence, especially by Robert Adam in the latter eighteenth century. Instead, they favoured heavily decorated, domestic castles in the Scottish baronial style which represented a retreat behind battlements from past economic and social leadership in creating planned villages – perhaps as many as 250 – that came to be dispersed throughout Scotland in the eighteenth and early nineteenth centuries. Planned villages were characterised by their geometric layouts, wide streets and hygienic standards. Landowners advanced credit and advertised widely throughout the United Kingdom for settlers. The primary role of planned villages was entrepreneurial: to relocate and redeploy labour, not just for casual and seasonal work in agriculture but to diversify employment opportunities in textiles, fisheries, extractive industries, chemicals and distilling. Planned villages, which dispersed markets and stimulated consumerism, served as a vital bridge between agriculture and industry that offered a staged process rather than a sudden jump to urbanisation.

Around the Moray Firth and in the north-east, where planned villages proliferated from the 1720s, newly founded settlements near the coast switched from textile production to fishing, a task facilitated by parliamentary grants to encourage exports, to remove restrictions on salt for curing and, above all, to construct harbours using residual moneys from the Annexed Estates. In 1786, the mantle of exemplary Highland development was taken over by the British Society for Fisheries. Of their four planned villages, only Pultney in Caithness was still thriving by the 1820s, partly because of its proximity to the fishing expertise in Wick and partly because of its diversification into distilling. A ferocious and destructive storm in 1848 in the waters between Wick and Peterhead stimulated the building of harbours with adequate lighting that gave safe access at low tides and from where open boats built to a clinker design with two masts for sails – such as the Fifie, the Scafie and ultimately the Zulu – could engage in deep-sea fishing. Continuous investment was integral to sustainability. If deficient, planned villages could and did degenerate into housing for agricultural labour or into seatowns where serfdom had been occasionally imposed upon workers to maintain fishing.

The counterpoint to this regressive development was the depth and diversity planned villages gave to industrialisation, particularly when promoted by David Dale, the foremost textile entrepreneur in the later eighteenth century, who pioneered the switch in production from cottages for linen and wool to factories for cotton. In the west of Scotland, he founded New Lanark in partnership with Richard Arkwright, the English inventor of the water frame that had transformed productivity in cotton factories throughout Britain.

The most exemplary factory village in terms of living conditions for workers was at Catrine in Ayrshire, which Dale established with Claud Alexander
of Ballochmyle, who had made his fortune in India. The leading importer of
bird-nest yarn from India was James Menteith, with whom Dale founded
the village of Blantyre in Lanarkshire, whose workforce was largely made up
of Highlanders displaced by the Clearances. Dale's missionary zeal for industrialisation led to his promotion of villages in Newton Stewart in Galloway,
Oban in Argyllshire and Spinningdale in Sutherland. Planned villages were
integral to the production of linen almost quadrupling from 1730 to 1775.
Colonial markets were absorbing up to 40% of direct exports, about the same
to England and Ireland, with no more than 20% retained for domestic use.
The relocation of industry with the development of steam power and the
subsequent rise of the heavy industries – iron, coal and shipbuilding – and of
railway networks made the factory village either redundant or absorbed into
the urban conurbations which came to dominate central Scotland.

The conurbations and city sprawls of the mid-nineteenth century should
not detract from earlier endeavours at urban renewal in the three leading
Scottish cities. New towns in Edinburgh, Glasgow and Aberdeen were projected as Enlightened representations of the UK and of Scottish engagement
with Empire. In Edinburgh and Glasgow, renewal was accomplished by urban
expansion. In Aberdeen there was a more pronounced element of inner-city
redevelopment, which was also featured in towns such as Ayr and Perth.
Public architecture, especially the works of William Playfair in Edinburgh,
Alexander Thomson in Glasgow and Archibald Simpson in Aberdeen, which
varied in style from severe classical to flamboyant baronial, blended together
in comparative harmony as a counterpoint to nocturnal images of cities as
places of doom, destitution and despair.

First proposed in 1752, Edinburgh's new town did not get underway until
1767. Streets to the north of the old town were laid out according to a grid
pattern that was adjusted and continued well into the nineteenth century.
Extolling the Hanoverian dynasty in slate and stone proved a costly exercise
both financially and socially. Although the tenements of the old town also
featured in the new, the communal living of the former was effectively abandoned in favour of the aspiring middle classes. The lower orders were primarily present as servants and shopkeepers, not as residents. The lead in urban
planning was actually taken by Glasgow. The grid planning of the Merchant
City, initiated in the 1720s by tobacco lords and sugar barons to celebrate
their colonial enterprise, was a piecemeal undertaking that was not completed
until the 1790s. A more soundly capitalised expansion westwards in the first
three decades of the nineteenth century primarily celebrated the Hanoverian

dynasty rather than the transatlantic connection, which still underwrote the city's wealth. Expansive British patriotism of the drive west reduced the rateable value of the inner city and made the relocated middle classes less inclined to contribute to the relief of destitution.

In Aberdeen, the scale of operations was smaller but no less challenging. Streets were refashioned by compulsory purchase and demolition of existing properties and by the construction of a major viaduct that duly ran from west to east with arcaded shops and housing. The principal thoroughfare, Union Street, named to celebrate the political incorporation of Ireland with Britain in 1801, took 15 years to complete. The city faced bankruptcy and the town council parliamentary censure by 1817. Dundee was the only Scottish city not to be associated with new town development. However, civic improvements were made to the harbour and docks in the aftermath of the Napoleonic Wars. Dundee became the main Scottish centre for imports of Baltic and Russian flax and for exports of coarse linen to North America and the Caribbean for sacking and clothes for slaves. From 1850, the industrial expansion of jute was complemented by whaling, which provided the oil to soften fibres. Jute production, mainly through a female workforce, increased to meet demands for canvas, tents and tarpaulins from sailing ships and for wagon and gun covers, as for sandbags in the series of wars in Europe and America from the 1850s to the 1870s.

Dundee, along with Glasgow, Aberdeen, Edinburgh and Perth, had secured police acts in advance of the Burgh Reform Act of 1833 to facilitate not only urban security, but also wider and cleaner paved streets illuminated by gas lighting. Burgh Reform, in turn, encouraged the gradual acquisition of policing powers in lesser towns. By 1850, elected commissioners were taking over responsibility for public health and water supplies paid from the rates, the local tax exacted annually from valuations of commercial and domestic properties. The Commissioners of Police tended to work in harmony with town councils and encouraged philanthropic contributions from individuals and societies to improve civic life by drinking fountains, public parks and better housing.

Glasgow, the city with the greatest urban problems, was the most innovative in taking public initiatives. In the first half of the nineteenth century its population quadrupled and continued to increase exponentially in the second half. Reluctance of landowners to release land for speculative house building encouraged further construction of tenements. As the city pushed westwards, the council created Scotland's first purpose built, public park at Kelvingrove in 1852 for recreational relief from urban congestion for all classes. Urban reformers, concerned about the exploitation of the working classes by capitalist employers, produced social photographs that sketched the human misery to be found on a daily basis in the streets and lanes of the inner city. Damp and insanitary housing, inadequate lighting and impure air pushed the over-worked and underpaid towards artificial stimulants, not just cheap wines and spirits but narcotics such as opium. In response, the city implemented radical measures to reform sanitary conditions from 1859. The piping of pure water from Loch Katrine in the Trossachs, a considerable feat of gravitational engineering accomplished over four years, provided Glasgow with the best public supply in the United Kingdom. With the appointment of a medical officer of health in 1863 and with railway developments razing the worst of the slums, the City Improvement Scheme steadily raised standards for comfortable living from 1866. Glasgow had been ravaged by cholera in 1832 and again in 1847–8, but its return in 1865–6 was easily contained.

TRANSFORMING AGRICULTURE AND INDUSTRY

The landscape as well as the built environment was transformed from the later eighteenth century: afforestation, enclosures, parklands, dry stone dykes and single tenant farms with steadings, barns and bothies became commonplace. The botanical distinction between leguminous and non-leguminous crops, which provided the scientific basis for crop rotation, was readily transmitted by Scottish MPs impressed by the more advanced state of English agricultural practice. National societies, such as the Honourable Society of Improvers, which operated from 1723 to 1745, was succeed by the Edinburgh Society for Encouraging Arts, Sciences, Manufactures and Agriculture in 1755. To further encourage agricultural transformation as a fashionable pursuit, the Highland and Agricultural Society was established in 1784 to bring improvements in the Highlands up to the same level as the Lowlands. Pioneer improvers, usually with external sources of income as judges, army and naval officers or as imperial adventurers, drove on agricultural change as was the case with Sir Archibald Grant of Monymusk in Aberdeenshire from the 1730s to the 1750s. Having been obliged to resign as an MP on becoming bankrupt through his engagement with the York Buildings Company of asset strippers, Grant continued to engage in speculative ventures of doubtful provenance. He was heavily dependent on capital repatriated from his sugar plantations in Jamaica. Piecemeal surveying of his estate from 1719 indicates that his improvements were more haphazard than scientific.

Surveying, though used in the building of military roads in the Highlands from the 1720s, only attained commercial significance from the 1750s. Surveyors pointed out settlement potential, highlighting the neglect of cultivation, inadequate drainage, misuse of field divisions and the arbitrary location of day labourers' holdings. Estate improvement was often not the first priority in their remit. Aesthetics and landscaping prevailed if charged to find the best site for a family seat.

William Dick, a blacksmith, had trained in London as a veterinary surgeon in the 1790s before moving back to the Edinburgh. He established a veterinary college that maintained momentum for commercialised pastoral farming from 1823 by placing emphasis on breeding rather than just rearing livestock. Hitherto the only recognised Scottish breed was the Ayrshire dairy cattle. Beef cattle attracted premium prices after the Aberdeen-Angus was bred initially at Alford from the 1820s, going on to become a recognised world leader by the 1870s. Urban markets were then supplied by meat slaughtered close to farms in the north-east rather than driven on the hoof from the Highlands. Technological innovation was transformative. The light plough designed by James Small from Berwickshire was generally introduced from the 1760s. Andrew Meikle from East Lothian devised the threshing machine in 1786. These inventions both redeployed and increased the demand for labour as did the steam-powered reaper invented in 1827 by Patrick Bell from Angus. Mechanisation was limited by its expense, its weight and its lack of mobility. Horsemen, shepherds and dairy maids commanded the top rungs of the moderate wages and housing on offer.

The primary driver of rural transformation, the acceptance of new machinery and the relocation of labour came from the stimulus of the market, notably the movement of prices for grain and livestock onto higher plateaux. This was largely accomplished between the 1760s and the 1780s principally because the prior increase in agricultural productivity in England was less than population growth. Prior industrialisation in England also increased the ready market for Scottish grain and livestock. Upward price movement was the key to convincing tenant farmers to engage in agriculture not just as a scientific enterprise but as a capitalist pursuit. By the 1840s, East Lothian was viewed as being as productive as the leading English counties of Norfolk and Lincoln. However, agriculture faced international competition from the wheat-producing prairies of the Canada and the United States, which also began to ship refrigerated beef to Britain from 1874. Refrigerated beef and lamb from Argentina, together with refrigerated lamb and dairy produce from Australia and New Zealand, came regularly to Scotland thereafter. Imports had a marked effect on rents and tenancies, from arable farms in East Lothian to pastoral farms in Galloway. As prices for produce lowered, working class consumers benefited from the chain of retail groceries started in Glasgow in 1871 by Sir Thomas Lipton, whose parents had left Ulster during the great famine of the 1840s. Lipton directly imported butter, bacon and eggs from Ireland, refrigerated beef from the United States and tea from his plantations in Ceylon. Demographic

growth, primarily through foodstuffs of better quality rather than inocula-
tions against diseases such as smallpox, provided labour for industrialisation.

For industry, as for agriculture, the UK common market remained vital as
did technological innovation, venture capital, managerial expertise and skilled
labour from England. Industrialisation was based primarily on iron and textiles in England. Scotland had a more integrated development through chemicals and textiles, the former being vital to the bleaching, dyeing and printing of
the latter. Adam Smith's *An Inquiry into the Nature and Causes of the Wealth of
Nations* (1776) stressed the importance of labour to wealth creation. Improved
divisions of labour were the key to productivity that underpinned the factory system. Smith did not anticipate the transformative role of technology,
which was the achievement of the Jacobite intellectual Sir James Steuart of
Goodtrees. His *Inquiry into the Principles of Political Economy* (1767) relied on
his practical observations of manufacturing in continental Europe during
protracted exile from Scotland. Where Smith was an ethical apologist for free
trade, Steuart advocated the light touch of government on economic levers to
ensure industrial technology raised living standards as well as productivity.

While Smith was Professor of Moral Philosophy at Glasgow University,
James Watt served there as a technician. Watt's invention of the separate con-
denser for the steam engine allowed lateral power to be converted into rotary
motion. This was only adapted for industrial use in 1773 after he moved to
Sheffield in Yorkshire where he received backing from Dr John Roebuck, who
had already established the first chemical works in Scotland at Prestonpans
in East Lothian in 1749. Widespread use of Watt's engines was facilitated by
his later move to Birmingham in partnership with the manufacturer Matthew
Boulton. Steam power transformed the location of the textile industry in
Scotland away from rural sources of water power to urban centres. English
inventions that transformed spinning removed the bottleneck that had limited the expansion of linen, wool and, above all, cotton production. Cotton
imports, initially tied to sugar and rum by West Indian merchants, tripled
from 1770 to 1788. Factories became centres of cotton production, mainly
in the shires of Lanark and Renfrew. As mills converted from water to steam
power, large factories were constructed around Glasgow where the integration
of the West Indian sugar and cotton trade with textiles and chemicals consolidated the repatriation of colonial capital for industrial manufacturing.

Mechanised spinning increased the demand for hand-loom weavers from
1807 until 1815. As the flying shuttle mechanised the weaving process, the
construction of spinning mills and power looms fell away by 1825. Large firms
tended to be undercapitalised and highly vulnerable in a bank crisis, there
being at least nine of these between 1793 and 1826. Cotton firms began to

dispense with labour. A water-mill factory in the 1790s could employ around 1,000 workers. Factories with power looms rarely employed more than a 100 workers by 1830. Cotton remained an important specialised industry, particularly in Paisley. Regional specialisation in textiles was further enhanced by mechanisation. John Kay, the English inventor of web spinning, was prominent in installing steam engines for jute production in Dundee in the 1820s. John Maberley, a London speculator, pioneered the application of power looms to linen weaving in Aberdeen. Mechanisation in woollen sock production also ensured that Aberdeen retained dominance in the hosiery trade throughout Britain. Border woollens upsurged from the 1830s as mechanisation was applied to weaving as well as spinning. Textiles remained a major source of employment for women, as chemicals did for men.

Even before the application of steam power moved textiles towards urban centres, chemical works were already concentrating there through the enterprise of engineers such as George Mackintosh, who had migrated from the Highlands in 1777 and with his son Charles went on to produce colour fixatives and dyes in Glasgow and Paisley. Charles Mackintosh, the inventor of waterproofing, was also in partnership with Charles Tennant from the Borders to produce chlorine as a dry bleaching agent from 1799. Bleaching had hitherto required large fields to lay out cloth to be treated organically with kelp ash and sour milk. With industrially produced, inorganic compounds this process could now be completed within a factory in five hours rather than five days in a bleach field. Tennant's chemical works at St Rollox in Springburn was the largest in the world by the 1830s.

Chemical works, which produced coal gas for street lighting from 1781, were major polluters in the central Lowlands, as was the extensive working of iron and coal, the key commodities in the heavy industries that developed from the 1820s. In the eighteenth century, iron production was initially confined to the Highlands, where coal blast furnaces fuelled by charcoal were adjuncts of the timber deficient English industry. Such furnaces were relatively short lived, the exception being at Taynuilt on Loch Etive in Argyll which operated from 1753 to 1874. The Carron Company established near Falkirk with English capital and expertise in 1759 was a far more extensive operation with furnaces, forges, processing mills and a colliery. The first successful venture to exploit native iron ores, it was also technologically innovative in using coke for smelting. The Carron Company was successful when it confined production to domestic utensils and tools, less so in pursuit of ballistic contracts. Its signature carronade, which was used on land and sea during the Napoleonic Wars, originally had frequent technical mishaps due to imprecise calibration, making it more dangerous to operatives than to enemy targets. The American War of Independence first stimulated the growth of pig iron production especially in the west of

Scotland. Processors using forges tended to import bar iron from Russia and Sweden and send primary produce south. There were limited efforts at secondary processing to produce malleable iron for manufactured goods.

The phenomenal growth of iron as a heavy industry can be attributed to geological as well as technological factors. Vast deposits of black band ironstone discovered in Lanarkshire in 1801 were used to supply the hot blast furnace invented by James Neilson, manager of the Glasgow Gas Company in 1828. This invention allowed the massive reserves of iron to be smelted at least 55% more efficiently when furnaces were heated to 300 degrees Celsius. There was further exponential growth when coal replaced coke to give a blast temperature of 600 degrees. Low royalties to landowners and low wages to workers cut costs. Between 1830 and 1844, the number of hot-blast furnaces almost quadrupled and output of pig iron increased more than tenfold. Scottish pig iron was sold cheaper than English or Welsh until 1870, when the high levels of prosperity reached by the industry, with 160 furnaces capable of producing in excess of 1.2 million tons, were never to be surpassed. Output was geared less to domestic demand than to exports to England and Empire. Scottish pig iron was not sufficiently strong for casting in marine engineering or armaments. Scotland largely missed out on the overwhelming and ongoing demand for railway track.

Steel production suffered from the unwillingness of Scottish manufacturers to mix brands of pig iron as was done in Wales and the United States. Scottish pig iron had an insufficiently low phosphorous content for steel processing. The establishment of a Scottish Steel Company was the accomplishment of chemical and electrical engineers. Sir Charles Tennant of the St Rollox works combined with William Siemens, the German born inventor of the regenerative furnace, to produce steel at Cambuslang from 1873. Lack of integration between iron and steel works pushed up costs.

The take-off in the coal industry was inextricably linked to that for iron. Prior to the 1820s, the major demand for coal was for domestic consumption that rose with urbanisation. Demand was enhanced by industrial use in the ubiquitous steam engines in textile factories and chemical works. Despite the termination of serfdom for colliers in 1799, labour supply was not self-sustaining and working conditions remained appalling well after the parliamentary prescription on the employment of women and children under ten years of age in 1842. Miners tended to be housed in rural ghettos even less congenial than crofting communities. Sectarianism was rife after Irish Catholics were deployed as strike breakers. Although outlawed in 1831 and again in 1854, the elastic practice of truck, tying wages and advances in wages to purchases in company stores, remained prevalent in the coal mining and iron industries. The co-operative movement, begun in 1848 at Kilmarnock in Ayrshire, was an effective counter to truck, especially after the spread of its shops was consolidated by the founding of the Scottish Co-operative Wholesale Society in 1868. High prices in company stores remained both an irritant to industrial relations and an impediment to the recruitment of labour.

Internal transport was becoming less problematic. The building and upkeep of roads and bridges were no longer a matter of compulsory labour. The alternative of turnpike trusts with roads, bridges and labour financed through tolls, initiated in Midlothian in 1714, only gained gradual acceptance by the 1770s. The quality of the toll roads was certainly improved when John Macadam used tar, produced from the distillation of coal, to provide a top surface more conducive to mobility than compacted stones. With limited capital invested by trustees and limited revenues accruing from tolls, the creation of a road network was a slow process. Domestic coal supplies, building material for city expansion and passenger traffic between Edinburgh and Glasgow motivated the fitful construction of the Forth–Clyde Canal from Grangemouth to Bowling between 1768 and 1790. The Union Canal from Grangemouth to Edinburgh opened in 1822. The Monklands Canal, instigated in 1769 to expedite supplies of coal to Glasgow, was operational by the 1790s. Scottish waterways lacked capital, range and depth – the one exception being the creation of a ship canal between Dumbarton and Glasgow that was integral to industrial shipbuilding on the River Clyde by the 1820s.

The viability of the canals as industrial carriers did not last beyond the 1840s when they came under direct competition from the railways which spread throughout Scotland to a much greater extent, were more flexible in their construction and far faster in getting goods to markets. The railways actually originated in waggon ways powered by horses from mines to ports. The Monklands–Kirkintilloch Railway linked into the central Scotland canal network in 1826, operating as a branch line to extend and expedite coal extractions. The Glasgow–Garnkirk line, constructed between 1827 and 1834, broke the monopoly of the coal-masters in carrying coals to the city. It was the first to use steam locomotives and from its outset carried passengers. The railways reduced transport and marketing costs for the iron industry. Profits accruing from stocks and shares attracted further capital investment which made the railway industry self-sustaining.

Passenger traffic became especially significant. The first intercity connection between Glasgow and Edinburgh was made in 1842 with local and trunk lines connecting Dundee. Four years later, cross-Border travel was accomplished by the North-British Railway Company; a line from Edinburgh to Berwick in 1846 then linked through Newcastle to London. This east coast line was supported by a mid-Borders link through Annandale to the west of Scotland, the achievement of the Caledonian Railway Company which pushed railway connections through Perth and Forfar to Aberdeen by 1850. Inverness was reached from Perth in 1863 by a separate endeavour, the Highland Railway funded through its own Caledonian Bank. Scotland was now opened up to industrial challenges from the rest of Britain, which had certainly not been the case with the road and canal networks. The very survival of local markets, extractive industries and coastal ports was tied increasingly to the railways. Locomotive works commenced in combination with marine engineering on the River Clyde from 1843. Companies began building their own trains after the Glasgow and South Western Railway established their locomotive works at Kilmarnock in 1856.

Marine engineering was integral to Glasgow's dominance over Belfast, Newcastle and Liverpool in shipbuilding. Steam propulsion was first successfully trialled on the Clyde by Henry Bell's *Comet* in 1812. Within six years the North Channel was opened up to passenger traffic. Demand was localised until engine efficiency improved when screw propellers under ships replaced paddles on their sides. Leisure travel for the middle classes became a further stimulus to shipbuilding, especially as coastal waters were made safer for the tourist as for the trader by the series of lighthouses constructed, mainly by the Stephenson family, for the Northern Lighthouse Board. By the 1830s, coastal trading and passenger-carrying iron steamships were being built by the Napier family. David Napier was the first entrepreneur to combine engineering and shipbuilding. His cousin Robert developed a veritable academy for marine engineering and shipping from 1835 that devised compound engines to enable oceangoing voyages under steam by 1852. Wood and sail continued with particular sophistication in Aberdeen. However, the completion of the Suez Canal linking the Mediterranean to the Gulf of Arabia ceded advantage to the iron steamships as ocean carriers from 1869. Shipbuilders had become international shippers. Scottish ships were purpose-built for the migrant trade to the Antipodes, to run blockades by the Northern Union forces to stop supplies to the Southern Confederates during the American Civil War and to facilitate imperial trade.

Transforming agriculture and industry led to greater sophistication in financial services. Commencing in Aberdeen in 1749 and followed up in Glasgow, Perth and Dundee, 28 provincial banks were founded by 1772, which compensated for the lack of branch banking by the three national banks. Nevertheless, by 1771, the Bank of Scotland, the Royal Bank of Scotland and the British Linen Company operated a clearing house which recognised their own notes and those of other reputable provincial banks through twice-weekly exchanges. Accordingly, the collapse of the Ayr Land Bank in 1772 did not trigger a national bank crisis. This was a provincial bank founded in 1769 because the lending policies of the three national banks were insufficiently generous. Competing without the protection of limited liability, the

Bank engaged in rabid speculation on the London stock exchange. There was no further loss of provincial banks. Joint-stock banking was pioneered from 1816. The Clydesdale Bank, established in Glasgow in 1838, was the most significant of the 20 foundations that came into existence by 1845, when no new Scottish banks were allowed to issue their own notes. Despite a financial crisis in 1847 and again in 1857, the Clydesdale continued to expand by promoting branch banking and acquiring less successful joint-stock banks.

Asset management became a noted feature of life assurance companies established mainly in Edinburgh – Scottish Widows (1815), Standard Life (1825) and Scottish Equitable (1831). Increased global trading led to the emergence of specialised dealers for stocks and shares. Three separate stock exchanges for Aberdeen, Edinburgh and Glasgow came into operation in 1844–5; Dundee followed in 1879. Windfall funding from the abolition of slavery in 1833, attracted primarily to the Glasgow exchange, was heavily invested in railways. Commercial ventures overseas continued to carry higher risks, particularly in Africa where, for over four decades prior to his death in 1873, the celebrated missionary Dr David Livingstone from Blantyre repeatedly called for Christianity, Commerce and Civilisation to facilitate imperial expansion.[5]

The Scottish American Investment Company, initiated by financiers from Edinburgh and Dundee, stepped up overseas investment in North America from 1873. Investments in railroads broadened into an industrial and commercial portfolio that included cattle ranches and fruit farms. In 1876, Alexander Graham Bell, from Edinburgh, patented and tested the telephone in the United States. Developments in telecommunications, like other innovations in engineering, were primarily the achievement of American and continental rather than British manufacturers. British governments were content to regulate public utilities. The General Post Office, hitherto responsible for delivering letters and parcels, was given control over communications by telegraph in 1868 and by telephone in 1878. Inward investment, especially from the United States, was becoming attractive. The Singer Manufacturing Company, producing sewing machines since 1851, had opened an outlet in Glasgow by 1867. Such was the demand that Singer created a huge industrial complex at Kilbowie in Clydebank by 1884 that became the world's largest producer of sewing machines.

CIVIC PATRIOTISM

Class conflict and community disintegration were major concerns for Scotland's pre-eminent novelist Sir Walter Scott. A Presbyterian who converted to Episcopalianism and a sentimental Jacobite, Scott refashioned

Unionist perspectives for the population at large not just for his fellow Tories. Notwithstanding his stage management of the royal visit of George IV to Scotland in 1822 as a tartan extravaganza, Scott, as evident from his *Tales of a Grandfather* (1828), offered a version of Scottish history from the Wars of Independence to the last Jacobite rising that was based on informed scholarship. He was wary of the subordination of Scottish political, commercial and ecclesiastical interests to that of England. He successfully promoted the maintenance of separate Scottish banknotes in 1826. Scotland's distinctiveness within both the UK and the British Empire had hitherto found expression through national institutions, mainly in Edinburgh, for the visual arts, antiquities and curling. Scott's reworking of civic patriotism was inspirational for the short-lived National Association for the Vindication of Scottish Rights (NAVR), whose campaign for recognition of equal partnership in Union and Empire during the 1850s was endorsed by the *Glasgow Herald*. Despite the NAVR's lack of constitutional accomplishment, it aligned civic patriotism with home rule.

Civic patriotism was instrumental in building the Wallace Tower on the Abbey Craig overlooking Stirling between 1861 and 1869. Reputedly, Sir William Wallace's heroics in the Wars of Independence had enabled the Scots to enter the Union of 1707 as a free and independent nation! Scottish distinctiveness was further reasserted from 1873 through diverse national bodies that brought aristocratic patronage and middle class organisation to sports played mainly by the working classes. Civic patriotism was given a political edge by the decisive political shift in favour of democracy in 1884. The Third Reform Act extended the franchise to all adult males with their own settled addresses, who paid their rates and did not claim poor relief. The Scottish electorate increased to around 560,000 voters as did constituencies, rural as well as urban, from 60 to 72.

Notes

1. https://www.robertburns.org/encyclopedia/LibertyTreeof.523.shtml.
2. Legacies of British Slave-ownership database, The LBS Centre, UCL : https://www.ucl.ac.uk/lbs.
3. *Scottish Population Statistics*, James G. Kyd ed. (Edinburgh, 1952), pp. 82–89.
4. *A Source Book of Scottish Economic and Social History*, Roy H. Campbell & James B.A. Dow eds, (London, 1968), pp. 44–47.
5. Livingstone's missionary endeavours were eclipsed by Mary Slessor, an Aberdonian brought up in the slums of Dundee. Within a decade of arriving in West Africa in 1876, she was internationally acclaimed for protecting native children, promoting women's rights and providing vocational education.

6 Unionists, Civic Patriots and Nationalists, 1884–1999

Between 1884 and 1999 Scotland underwent relentless change. War, environmental degradation, depopulation and deindustrialisation were largely negative, while expanded leisure opportunities, urban renewal, air transport and information technology have tended to be positive. Unionism bolstered by British nationalism based variably on the monarchy, Protestantism, social privilege, class solidarity and the welfare state retains a powerful presence in Scotland. Scottish distinctiveness within the United Kingdom continues to find expression through law and education and more emotively through civic patriotism, broadcasting, organised sports and army regiments. In contrast to regressive variants based on race, religion or language, nationalism in Scotland is inclusive, peaceful and progressive. It welcomes migration from the former Empire as from the European Union (EU) which has offered a wider context for the free movement of people, goods and ideas than the United Kingdom. The rise of Scottish nationalism has coincided with decolonisation, the discovery of North Sea Oil and growing disillusionment with centralised decision making in London since 1945. The creation of a Scottish Parliament in 1999 adjusted rather than dismantled the United Kingdom as a unitary state: a limited measure of home rule does not equate to independence.

REALIGNMENT

The Third Reform Act perpetuated the Liberal dominance of parliamentary politics in Scotland, which endured from the First Reform Act in 1832 until World War I. Liberalism was grounded in free trade and on political, social and religious individualism, especially that espoused by the Free and the United Presbyterian Kirks. However, the Liberals were split by a major dispute over free trade and imperial preference – the latter involved tariff barriers against all imports other than from the British Empire. A group of Liberal Unionists broke away in 1886 to associate with the Tories, rebranded with mixed success as Conservatives since the 1830s. This split followed on from the defection of aristocratic Whigs opposed to land reform and home rule in Ireland. The perception that Ireland was more favoured instigated the founding of the Scottish Home Rule Association in 1886, a political expression of civic patriotism in which Liberals joined with organised labour.

Two prominent founders were Robert Cunninghame-Graham, writer, traveller and laird, with a hinterland that stretched from cattle ranching in Argentina to tireless campaigning for workers' rights at home and abroad, and the no less charismatic miner's leader Keir Hardie. They were instrumental in forming the Scottish Parliamentary Labour Party in 1888. Cunninghame-Graham, then MP for West Lanarkshire and the first socialist to sit in the British Parliament, was president; Hardie was secretary. The party offered a distinctively socialist programme of comprehensive public ownership to 'enable the workers to exercise their voting power to their own advantage'.[1] By 1893, the party merged with the Independent Labour Party (ILP) presided over by Hardie, who had moved to London to become a journalist and an MP. In 1901, Hardie set up the British Labour Representative Committee, which led the formation of a parliamentary Labour Party for the United Kingdom. The ILP, which continued to advocate home rule for Scotland, allied in 1900 to the Scottish Trade Union Congress (STUC) which, from its inception three years earlier, was entirely separate from the Trade Union Congress (TUC) for England and Wales that favoured militancy and centralisation. Socialist calls for class confrontation and nationalisation throughout the UK attracted a far lower response in Scotland, where no more than three Labour MPs were returned in general elections between 1906 and 1914.

The Liberals remained committed to Scottish home rule, which was raised formally but rejected in the British Parliament on more than a dozen occasions between 1886 and 1914. For the Liberals, like the Labour Movement, home rule was a ritual motion that tempered but did not alter their British and imperial concerns. More progress in administrative devolution was made under Conservative governments hostile to home rule. With the running of Scottish business by the Lord Advocate anachronistic in an age of state intervention, a separate Scottish Office was conceded in 1885. Elected county councils were introduced four years later.

Women were not granted the vote in 1884 even though their presence at all education levels from primary school to universities was increasing. Not allowed to graduate until 1889, women were steadily entering the medical and legal professions. They constituted the clear majority of school teachers by 1911, but their pay was half that of male colleagues. Lack of voting concessions, even to educated women, ushered in a more militant phase for the suffragettes, who moved from constitutional petitioning to direct action. Maureen Wallace Dunlop from Inverness was the first suffragette to go on hunger strike when incarcerated in Holloway Prison, London in 1909. Later that year, the prison governors in Perth and Barlinnie in Glasgow were prepared to force-feed suffragettes on hunger strike. The leading moderate in Scotland by 1906 was Dr Elsie Inglis, physician and surgeon in Edinburgh, who pioneered medical education for women and improved care for mothers and children in maternity hospitals. Scottish suffragettes were generally more conciliatory, more democratic and more welcoming of male support than their militant counterparts in England. Nevertheless, in 1913, the Royal Observatory in Edinburgh was bombed, grandstands at Ayr and Perth racecourses were burned down and the cottage in which the national bard Robert Burns was raised in Alloway narrowly escaped the same fate at the hands of suffragettes.

The political grouping initially advantaged by the Third Reform Act was the Highland Land League (HLL) formed in 1882, which was inspired by Irish militancy and attracted support from radicals operating mainly in Glasgow, Edinburgh and London. No longer averse to customary rights in India and Ireland, the Liberal government commissioned the former diplomat and Borders landowner Francis Napier, Lord Napier and Ettrick, to take testimony from crofting activists, Lowland sympathisers, estate factors and clergymen in 1883–4. The Napier Commission favoured the rehabilitation of communal townships to promote agricultural viability. This was not acceptable to crofting activists. Following further pressure from the HLL, supplemented by the return of a handful of crofting MPs in the general election of 1885, the Crofters' Holdings Act was duly passed the next year. Crofters were granted security of tenure but not of income, a situation not changed by further crofting communities created in response to land raids from Lewis to Lochaber. People continued to haemorrhage from the Highlands. The Liberal government had baulked at the compulsory relocation of land from deer forests in 1895. Two years later, the Conservative government created the Highland Congested Districts Board, but failed to provide adequate finance to buy out landlords.

By this juncture, the Liberals could no longer rely on unstinting support from the Free and United Presbyterian Kirks. Staunch adherence to orthodox Calvinism was becoming the preserve of a Highland rump, split between the Free Presbyterians who left the Free Kirk in 1893 and the minority not prepared to accept the union of the Free and the United Presbyterian Kirks in 1900. The Conservatives, long protective of the established Kirk, reaped the electoral benefits. The Liberals were largely compensated by their acquisition of staunch support from Irish Catholic voters. Liberal handling of Irish issues was deemed more adept and less risky than channelling support towards the embryonic Labour Party to which Irish Catholics were generally but not uniformly averse.

The Boer War in South Africa between 1899 and 1902 enabled the Liberal Party under Sir Henry Campbell-Bannerman from Glasgow to reclaim the moral high ground. The British Army's recourse to concentration camps occasioned atrocities. Mainly women and children perished through malnutrition and insanitary conditions. The Liberals achieved an emphatic victory at the general election of 1906 on a platform of social reform. Campbell-Bannerman died in 1908, the year old-age pensions were introduced. Health insurance and unemployment benefits followed in 1911 when a Small Landholders Act extended the provision for crofters in 1886 to the whole of Scotland. Vesting legislative supremacy in the House of Commons curtailed the House of Lords' capacity to block reform. Legislation for the collective good ensured that the vast majority of miners, textile workers and engineers continued to place their faith in social reform through the Liberal Party.

While the Liberals remained the dominant parliamentary party, this was not the case in local government. Benefiting from their merger of town councils and police burghs in 1892, the Conservatives became the leading presence in the Progressive Movement which transformed leading town and cities, especially Glasgow, through the public provision of parks, laundries and swimming baths. The creation of extensive, electrified tramways with cheap fares facilitated the mobility of labour between coalfields and shipyards and to suburban dwelling. Andrew Carnegie from Dunfermline, who made his fortune in railways and steel works in the United States, provided philanthropic support to build public libraries and assembly rooms throughout Scotland. The Progressive record on housing and health was less commendable. Redevelopment was still primarily the work of private enterprise. The vast majority of families in Glasgow and district continued to live in one or two rooms. Death rates for children remained high, as did lung diseases for people of all ages in congested districts. Poor housing, the relatively high cost of food and manifestly insecure employment led to the mass migration of highly skilled workers from the Lowlands.

Glasgow reaffirmed its standing as the second city of the Empire by a series of international exhibitions in 1888, 1901 and 1911 in Kelvingrove Park for trade, industry and the arts that were attended respectively by 5.7 million, 11.5 million and 9.4 million people. Flamboyant and exotic Unionist projections of Britain and Empire in 1888 were upstaged by the art work from the Scottish Impressionists, known as the Glasgow Boys (most notably, Sir John Lavery and George Henry). Art again transcended British Imperialism in 1901, but there was limited opportunity to project the Glasgow Style, a blend of art nouveau with the arts and crafts movement particularly associated with Charles Rennie Mackintosh and his wife Margaret MacDonald – a style ignored in 1911 when Scottish interests within a unified Britain were soberly presented. Edinburgh, which held restrained international exhibitions in 1886 and 1908, played a leading role in cultural realignment. Robert Louis Stevenson, from the celebrated family of lighthouse builders, produced writings of historical complexity, psychological ambivalence and transnational adventuring that were in stark contrast to the cultural introspection, parochialism and sentimentality of the 'kailyard school' in Scottish literature. Patrick Geddes, a city planner of international renown, promoted a decorative perspective which organically blended Scottish history with Celtic myth and legend to challenge the staid historical representations in city chambers, national and municipal galleries.

Over three-quarters of the Scottish population of almost 4.8 million in 1901 lived in towns of 2,000 or more people. Industry was the driving force for urban growth. Although the heyday of cotton had long past, linen and more especially woollen production was still significant in many towns throughout Scotland. Dundee and district remained the world's largest centre for jute and Coats of Paisley were the world's biggest thread makers. The distilling and blending of malt and grain into Scotch whisky attained new global markets through entrepreneurial drive and imaginative advertising. Brewers were no less adventurous. In locations where cholera and dysentery were rife, it was safer to drink bottled beers than take the local waters. Chemical works were more focused on supporting a steel industry increasingly dependent on imported raw materials than diversifying into pharmaceuticals, where German and American manufacturers were becoming dominant. In 1890, most of the Scottish industry underwent amalgamation into the United Alkali Company, based in the North of England. Light engineering had mixed fortunes. The first British cars were made at Dumfries in 1896 by the civil engineer Sir William Arrol, six years after he completed the iconic cantilever railway bridge across the Firth of Forth, and by the locomotive builder George Johnston. The first car plant in Britain was at Alexandria in Dunbartonshire, for the Argyle car in 1906. Although the Scottish car industry could not compete with mass production in the United States, Albion Motors in Glasgow switched to robust commercial vehicles in 1909 and later diversified into passenger buses.

The dominance of the west of Scotland in the heavy industries of coal, iron, steel and shipbuilding was becoming less secure. Supplies of black band ironstone in Lanarkshire were running out. Iron makers continued to concentrate on the basic production of pig iron with imported ores, which pushed up production costs. They preferred to diversify into the booming coal industry rather than push for integration with steel makers focused on the provision of plate for shipbuilding, for which there was high demand by 1899. The Steel Company of Scotland was overtaken by David Colville & Sons whose greater efficiency, quality control and profitability made it a major British manufacturer. Increased industrial demand for coal was supplemented by an expanding home market as wages for workers improved and the middle classes acquired larger houses and flats. Fuelling steam trains on the expanding railway network was the major driver of domestic demand. Exports led growth, particularly to continent outlets and in providing fuel for steamships with coal stored in bunkers along the main shipping routes to power the dominant British merchant fleet.

Growth in exports shifted productive employment in favour of the Fife, Clackmannan and Midlothian coalfields. The industry underwent major transformation as landed proprietors gave way first to iron-masters then to public companies of engineers, accountants and lawyers. Industrial relations remained difficult, but they did bring to the fore formidable trade union leaders such as Keir Hardie in Lanarkshire. The need for greater mechanisation, for pumping and winning coal and for improved systems of haulage and ventilation, were the main factors in declining productivity. As mines went deeper and underground galleries became longer, issues of safety became more critical. Investment in safe working did not match that in machinery. Naked lights rather than electricity were still used in pits. Limited rescue services for fire-fighting too often led to disasters. In August 1913, 26 men were trapped by smoke and fire in the Cadder mine, near Glasgow. The central rescue service for Scotland was located at Cowdenbeath in Fife, over four hours away. One miner survived.

The expansion of the rail network, particularly into the Highlands, provoked a vigorous debate on transport charges that favoured passengers over industrial goods. Railways and steamships opened up tourism and consumerism in the Highlands for the aspiring middle and the skilled working classes from the Lowlands. Leisure was further encouraged when the relatively new art form of photography was turned into pictorial postcards. As steam trawlers and drifters were securing world leadership for Britain in the fishing industry, the extension of the railway network to outlying ports consolidated packaging and marketing from Glasgow and Edinburgh. Aberdeen controlled over half the Scottish trade, as the foremost seaport from where fish were taken by rail for sale in London and other English cities. Significantly expanded rail use between 1885 and 1912 spread locomotive production from Glasgow to Inverurie in Aberdeenshire. In shipbuilding, the Clyde retained its edge in construction and design, despite marine engineering coming under serious challenge by 1897 from the invention of the diesel engine that was designed in France and tested in Germany. There was a growing need to import steel plate to keep down costs. International competition increasingly meant shipbuilders were reliant on sales in British and imperial markets, often to their own shipping companies. Prior to 1914, the Clyde was becoming reliant on naval orders, as imperial rivalries, particularly with Germany, instigated an arms race.

WAR AND ORDER

World War I from August 1914 until November 1918 was the product of imperial rivalries between Britain, France and Russia on the one hand and Austria-Hungary, Germany and the Ottoman Turks on the other. It was a global engagement more in terms of people mobilised than of actual military theatres. Britain looked to its Empire for auxiliary manpower, with India making as noted a contribution as Australia and Canada. Scots soldiers served mainly in continental Europe on the Western Front against the Germans, in the Alps against the Austrians and Hungarians, at Gallipoli and in the Middle East against the Turks. The main naval theatre was the North Sea avenues into the North Atlantic where Scots served in the merchant marine as well as the Royal Navy. Around 690,000 Scots either volunteered or were conscripted (from May 1916) for active service. Casualty figures, difficult to determine accurately, remain contentious. The Scottish population in 1911 was just under 4.8 million – less than 10% of the UK. Scottish casualties were not necessarily in proportion though, not as high as one-sixth of the British total. War memorials in cities, towns and villages commemorate the enormous scale of casualties suffered by all classes and communities.

The British commander on the Western Front, Field-Marshal Douglas Haig, was a Scot who adhered rigidly to trench warfare as the key to victory, despite horrific casualties. As ships were less identifiably Scottish than regiments, losses at sea were more difficult to quantify. Nonetheless, Fraserburgh in Aberdeenshire can claim the highest proportion of naval casualties in Britain. The yacht *Iolaire*, bringing sailors back to Lewis for New Year in 1919, was wrecked on rocks at the approach to Stornoway. Only 75 sailors survived out of an official passenger list of 280. Women were also among the casualties of war, not just those serving in uniform as auxiliaries in the army, navy and air force, but also as nurses, especially those engaged through the Scottish Woman's Hospital Committee instituted by Dr Elsie Inglis in 1914, who went on to serve with her from France to the Balkans and on to Russia. Civilian casualties were considerably less in the United Kingdom than overseas. The only danger in Scotland, apart from transport accidents and explosions in munition factories, was from the air. But rare attacks by zeppelins, large cylindrical airships, in 1916 were largely unsuccessful.

There was considerable repatriation of physical and mental casualties, those traumatised, shell-shocked and gassed, as well as those crippled and maimed. Mental casualties were treated in asylums separate from civilians. The British government did not wish to have soldiers, sailors and airmen tainted with lunacy. Limited official tolerance was accorded to conscientious objectors. Average life expectancy for civilians actually increased through improved diet from controls on food production and better organised health care. All were caught out by the influenza pandemic in 1917–19 that wiped out 27 million people worldwide. The equivalent killed in World War I was 18 million.

The British government, initially the Liberals then in coalition with the Conservatives from 1916, were unstinting in commandeering material and human resources to secure victory. Paddle steamers were pressed into service as minesweepers and troop carriers. Fishing boats dealt with mines and their nets were used to protect harbours from submarines. Constructing additional tracks and crossings where required; the railway companies prioritised the movement of troops, livestock, munitions, and coal over other goods and passenger services from Scapa Flow in the north to Gretna in the south, from the largest naval base to the largest munitions factory in Britain. Munitions along with the building and servicing of warships and merchant vessels became the major growth points in the Scottish economy as supplies of iron, steel and coal came under government direction. Farmers were also guaranteed minimum prices for wheat, oats and potatoes.

A key element in the war effort was the use of women to replace men who volunteered or were conscripted as soldiers and sailors. Such replacement in agriculture expanded the involvement of women as farmers and labourers. In industry, it led to radical new employment patterns. Women were employed in engineering works, in shipyards and as bank tellers and tram drivers. They also served as caterers in transit camps and supply bases for the army and navy throughout Scotland. Concerns for morality and welfare of young women led to mature ladies forming Women's Patrols. Middle class women formed Girls Clubs to harness the energies of young girls between the ages of 13 and 16. The clear models were the Boys Brigade, established under the auspice of the Free Church in 1883, and the non-denominational Boy Scout movement founded in the wake of the Boer War.

The Scottish Women's Rural Institute was established in 1917. Its active endeavours to revitalise rural communities and engage women in food production attracted government sponsorship. Women's Guilds, which had been established as a Church of Scotland initiative in 1887, continued to spread throughout Scotland in wartime, encouraging city stores to sell local produce and offering shelter for orphans. A working class variant was the Scottish Co-operative Women's Guild, formed as an adjunct of the Labour Movement at Glasgow in 1890, which came to enjoy mass urban membership by offering educational opportunities, nutritional advice and collective action that ranged from medical provision for children to better conditions for women workers.

Women were to the fore in the radical agitation on Clydeside, mainly in and around Glasgow, from 1915 until 1919. Rent strikes in November 1915 were led by housewives and munition workers, organised in local committees, who were joined by shipyard workers and engineers. Mass rallies, initiated by committed activists such as Mary Barbour, opposed rent increases by landlords faced with higher interest charges on mortgages. These same landlords had a poor record in repairing and maintaining their properties. The British government responded in December by hastening the passage of legislation which reduced rents to pre-war levels and lowered interest rates on mortgages. The rent strikes were the most successful aspect of 'Red Clydeside'.

Agitation had actually commenced among engineers seeking a modest pay rise in February 1915, when shop stewards including Willie Gallacher from Albion Motors came together to organise a month of overtime bans. Their unofficial action laid the basis for the Clyde Workers' Committee (CWC) which came to prominence in opposing the Munitions Act in May. In determining that munitions production must be stepped up and direction passed from the military to businessmen, the British government curtailed the right of workers to shift jobs. Unskilled men and women were recruited to boost production – recruitment viewed as the dilution of skilled labour. William Weir, notoriously hostile to trade unions at his engineering works in Cathcart, became director of munitions in Scotland. He expected workers to welcome compulsory direction and dilution of labour as patriotic citizens. Newspapers sympathetic to the CWC, such as *Forward*, were suppressed. Gallacher and other leaders were temporarily incarcerated. The CWC was revitalised by the introduction of military conscription in January 1916, which they regarded as further diluting skilled labour.

However, the CWC was not opposed to the war, unlike Mary Barbour, who founded the Women's Peace Campaign, and John Maclean, the school teacher from Mull who broke with the CWC on this issue. Maclean, an outstanding orator who faced charges of sedition in 1916 and 1918 and endured short periods of imprisonment, was the most visionary radical to emerge from 'Red Clydeside'. Unlike Gallacher, who adhered to the central dictates of the Communist Party for the direction of British labour, Maclean viewed communism as a means to create a separate Scottish Socialist Republic. In the wake of the Russian Revolution in 1917, Maclean became the Soviet consul for Scotland. However, the Russian Revolution, like the French Revolution in 1789, provoked reactionary British patriotism. The CWC never called a strike over conscription.

In the aftermath of the war, the 40 Hours Strike led to mass agitation and the raising of the red flag in George Square on 31 January 1919, with tanks and troops at the ready to suppress any hint of a violent uprising in Glasgow. The strike was called over the amount of working hours, that were to be reduced on the return of demobilised soldiers and sailors to the labour force. Whereas government and employers were prepared to countenance a 48-hour working week, trade unions and the STUC were arguing for 40 hours and the CWC made a pitch for 30 hours. Reputedly 70,000 participated in an unofficial strike. Conservative forces drawn mainly from the middle class mobilised as strike breakers. Employers established civic guards to combat industrial pickets. Rioting in the city centre was primarily due to the over-reaction of the Glasgow police. Soldiers held in reserve preferred to fraternise than to intimidate. Although proposals for a 40-hour week were rejected, the government passed a housing act later in 1919 that improved living conditions.

This measure was part of a legislative package to compensate the ultimate sacrifice made at home and abroad during the war. Clear responsibility was assigned to local government in Scotland, aided by subsidies from central government in London, to provide the decent housing for the working classes that the private sector had signally failed to deliver. The Land Settlement Act of 1919 gave the Scottish Office the means to create crofts and revitalise crofting communities. Compulsory powers to counter obstructive landlords were never deployed systematically, but sufficient investment was made to dampen down land raids by ex-servicemen. The British government was considerably more generous in funding the Forestry Commission, set up in 1919. Timber had been seriously depleted by the demands for props in the trenches.

Large amounts of former agricultural land were acquired for forestry, primarily in Scotland. Small landholdings or crofts were provided for foresters as a check to migration. Deer forests were left largely unscathed.

Restoring pre-war practices closed down employment opportunities for women; but the removal of sex disqualifications from 1919 eased the route of women into the professions and upheld their right to work after marriage. The Education Act of 1918 provided free secondary education for all, with a common curriculum for boys and girls other than in practical subjects. Faith schools for Episcopalians and Roman Catholics received state funding and came within the remit of Scottish Education, which generally introduced selective schooling that favoured academic courses over vocational training, albeit less than 5% of scholars went on to university. A Fourth Reform Act in 1918 conceded votes for males over 21 years of age and to most women over 30 who could demonstrate they were householders through marriage or in their own right or university graduates. Another ten years elapsed before universal suffrage was implemented for males and females over 21. Mary Barbour, who became a pioneer of family planning, was in the first cohort of women who became city councillors in Glasgow when returned for the Labour Party in 1920. Three years later, Katherine Stewart-Murray, Duchess of Atholl, was elected for the Scottish Unionists in Kinross and West Perthshire. The first woman MP in Scotland had actively opposed suffragettes.

REGIONAL DIRECTION

Extension of the franchise brought about a major shift in parliamentary politics. The wartime coalition decisively won the general election in 1918. In the following six elections prior to the outbreak of World War II in 1939, the Liberals were always behind the Labour Party, which came to the fore in Scotland by winning 29 seats in 1922. Its strong ILP contingent ensured Ramsay MacDonald, originally from Lossiemouth in Moray, became parliamentary leader. MacDonald, with backing from the Liberals, formed the first Labour government in 1923, the party having increased its Scottish presence to 34 seats. Its most significant achievement was the housing legislations steered through parliament by ILP stalwart John Wheatley, hugely influential in winning over his fellow Irish Catholics to the Labour cause. By guaranteeing both funding and rigorous building standards, Wheatley laid the groundwork for the massive expansion of affordable municipal housing over the next 14 years. Liberal backing sustained MacDonald's second minority government in 1929, when the Labour Party gained 36 seats in Scotland, its strongest interwar showing. With politics polarising along class lines, the Liberals were no longer viewed as the party of social reform.

The shift in working class allegiances was compounded by the Irish situation as the country was first plunged into civil war in 1919 then partitioned in 1921 when six counties in Ulster remained British. Ulster agitation against Irish home rule had led Conservatives and Liberal Unionists to merge as Scottish Unionists in 1912. With the formation of the Irish Free State, home rule no longer gave the Liberals traction with Catholic voters of Irish origins and allegiances. The Liberals' religious base in Scotland was further weakened by the amalgamation of the Church of Scotland and the United Free Kirk in 1929. The minority left to continue the United Free Kirk was not substantial. The dominance of Scottish Unionist sympathisers in the general assemblies of the Kirk before and after 1929 generated populist calls to curtail emigration of Irish Catholics and repatriate those engaged in criminal activity. The condemnation of Irish migration as a menace to Scottish nationality in the assembly of 1923 was motivated in part by state funding for Catholic schools after 1918, but primarily to extend restrictions on aliens, in play from 1905 against Jews and Italians, to the Irish. Scotland was in the grip of a post-war economic slump. Unemployment was rapidly growing and the country's population fell by 39,517 between 1921 and 1931, the first fall since official records began in 1801. It was due as much to renewed emigration, with around 400,000 Scots leaving, particularly skilled tradesmen and their families to the United States and Canada, as to losses in World War I and the subsequent influenza pandemic. The Scottish population had actually grown by 121,593 between 1911 and 1921, when the English replaced the Irish as the largest migrant group.[2]

Sectarian undercurrents in Scottish Unionist support were further evident in their long-standing association with the Orange Order that accrued votes, particularly in the west. The Unionists deployed the notorious Protestant gang the Billy Boys to steward electoral meetings in Bridgeton and neighbouring districts in the east end of Glasgow in 1931. The Scottish Unionists were not so much a sectarian as an imperial party disinclined to support home rule for Scotland. Their concession to administrative devolution was to have a Secretary of State in charge of the Scottish Office from 1926. In gaining 48 seats in 1931, their best post-war electoral performance, the Unionists tapped into middle class concerns about social order first raised by Red Clydeside and their aversion to socialism at home and abroad. Their most effective spoiling tactic was to support the Conservatives going into coalition with MacDonald, a move that split the Labour Party and secured Unionist dominance in Scotland during a decade of depressed trade worldwide.

In reacting to mass unemployment, economic depression and widespread emigration, successive British governments ruled out nationalisation of key industries. When railways were further merged in 1923, control over the four new conglomerates was vested in London without any appreciable improvement in wages, services and revenue streams. Mining was returned to private ownership in 1920. A bitter strike followed in 1921 when landowners and company managers cut wages and extended hours. Britain returning to the gold standard in 1925 pushed up exchange rates for sterling and lost foreign markets for coal. With output and prices falling as industrial relations deteriorated, the TUC called a General Strike in May 1926. Striking miners and railway workers took to sabotage, notably in Fife, Midlothian and Lanarkshire. The government appointed civil commissioners backed up by the police and Royal Navy to maintain supplies of food and fuel. They kept transport services running by recruiting middle class volunteers from managers and professionals to shopkeepers and university students. After nine days, the TUC called off the strike to reassert trade union control over workers. Unofficial strikes continued in the coalfields for six months.

Industrial relations in Scotland remained generally poor: the combined result of autocratic management and more assertive trade unionists, especially on Clydeside. Class solidarity was hampered by demarcation disputes between workers, particularly in shipbuilding and engineering. The short-term boom in shipbuilding to restore international trade was dissipated by 1921. Shipbuilders integrated their companies with steel works and shipping concerns. The company run by William Beardmore further diversified into aeroplanes, automobiles and tanks; but not from a position of financial strength or extensive research and development. Networking among owners and managers gave a distinctive Scottish dimension to the heavy industries, but reorganisation and rationalisation were becoming the order of the day. The shipping magnate Sir James Lithgow along with engineer William Weir, now Lord Weir of Cathcart, promoted Scottish industry in an imperial context. Lithgow became chair of the National Shipbuilders Security, a limited company established with government support in 1930 to remove British overcapacity. During the next eight years, shipyards in economic difficulties, including Beardmore's, were bought over and closed

Unfavourable currency exchange rates as well as subsidised shipping among British competitors led to a substantial fall in overseas orders that was regarded as catastrophic by 1930. Nevertheless, shipbuilding and shipping underwent a modest revival. Substantial subsidies from central government to sustain a British presence in the transatlantic passenger trade ensured that two majestic liners, the *Queen Mary* and the *Queen Elizabeth*, were completed on the Clyde in 1934 and 1938 respectively. Scottish shipbuilders and shippers benefited from a growth in both imports and exports to and from the Empire carried almost exclusively in British ships. The domestic significance of Empire was again celebrated at Glasgow in 1938. The Exhibition at Bellahouston Park, unlike its predecessors in Kelvingrove, made a loss though it attracted over 12 million visitors. However, the major stimulus to shipbuilding was naval rearmament.

Electric power generation and distribution, which had been run by private companies since 1901, came under public control in 1926. The new Central Generating Board instigated a national grid for Britain. A series of regional grids was in place by 1933, albeit they were not linked operationally until 1938. The General Post Office, which had control over radio waves from 1912, licensed wireless manufacturers to form the British Broadcasting Company (BBC) in 1922. Its first director was William Reith, a dour Scottish Presbyterian with an engineering background. Reith set the benchmarks for public broadcasting – to inform, to educate and to entertain. As evident when the BBC acted like a state broadcaster during the General Strike, Reith was a pillar of the British establishment. Nevertheless, the BBC – a Corporation rather than a Company from 1932 – was daily received as a British institution for the public good. Television was broadcast continuously from 1937, but not according to the system invented 11 years earlier by John Logie Baird from Helensburgh in Dunbartonshire. During his 15-year tenure, first as general manager then as director-general, Reith fostered Scottish distinctiveness under a regional controller. Broadcasting centres at Glasgow and Aberdeen in 1923 were soon followed at Edinburgh and Dundee.

Public broadcasting of British values was challenged both internationally and domestically. The international challenge was led by the United States, especially in relation to music and film. Jazz, big bands and swing were the dominant sounds in the ubiquitous Scottish dance halls. Moving pictures, especially after talk was added in 1929, led to the mushrooming of cinemas in urban Scotland. More cinemas were constructed in Glasgow than any other city in Europe. Films showcased glamour in clothing and hairstyles for both sexes and cosmetics for women which boosted trade in departmental stores, sewing machines, hairdressers and beauty parlours. The domestic reaction against British and American cultural influences was led by the Scottish Literary Renaissance that flourished from the mid-1920s through the 1930s. Its output ranged from mythical historical novels to film documentary as a mechanism for social reform. Its vituperative leader and poetic genius was Hugh MacDiarmid, a man of political extremes from Langholm in Dumfriesshire, who sought to blend spoken Scottish dialects into one literary language, Lallans. His endeavours to vanquish the Kailyard culture from Scotland were subverted by the unrivalled success of the *Sunday Post*, founded in 1914. Its mixture of cartoons, football, fashion, homespun homilies and social deference achieved almost saturation coverage of Scotland by the later twentieth century.

The nationalist perspective of the Literary Renaissance had a more pronounced impact than the foundation of the Scottish National Party (SNP) in 1934. The SNP was actually an amalgam of several disparate nationalist movements. The rejection of another home rule bill in 1928 spurred on the formation of the Scottish Party presided over by the international socialist Cunninghame-Graham. Differences with the more conservative National Party over the pursuit of home rule rather than a free state compromised their merger. The advocates of a free state included the former diplomat and author Sir Compton Mackenzie. The home rulers had a dynamic organiser, John McCormack, a lawyer. The SNP was an inclusive party in marked contrast to other political creations of the 1930s – the British Union of Fascists and the Protestant Association which were rigidly exclusive for their respective anti-Semitism and sectarianism. They took politics on to the streets of the major towns and cities. The Protestant Association, particularly strong in Edinburgh where there were considerably less Catholics to intimidate than in Glasgow, had some success in local government.

Although electoral success in the 1930s eluded the SNP, it helped revitalise civic patriotism to conserve and develop cultural heritage. The National Trust for Scotland was founded in 1931 and the Saltire Society in 1936. Civic patriotism in relation to the Scottish economy was less straightforward. The Scottish Office was particularly condescending in dismissing calls for special assistance in the Highlands and Islands. It initially backed the authoritarian if visionary endeavours of the English soap tycoon William Lever, Viscount Leverhulme, to transform the fishing industry in Lewis and Harris in the aftermath of World War I by working a fleet of trawlers, introducing fish canning and building an ice factory to service a chain of fish shops on the British mainland. The Scottish Office withdrew support by 1923 after land raids on two dairy farms near Stornoway exposed Leverhulme's opposition to crofting. The Scottish Office was far more sympathetic to the evacuation of the inhabitants of remote St Kilda in August 1930. Communications to the Western and Northern Isles were improved by private air services through Glasgow and Aberdeen from 1933. The Highlands were not without industrial development. The British Aluminium Company opened a new factory at Fort William in 1929 that consolidated its presence at Foyers on Loch Ness and Kinlochleven in Argyll since 1895 and 1909 respectively. Hard won supplies of Highland water powered these outposts. The Scottish Office did encourage in the Highlands, as in Galloway, the building of dams to generate hydro-electricity under private enterprise and the rapid expansion of woodland by the Forestry Commission, the biggest landowner in Scotland by 1939.

From 1931, the Scottish Office worked in tandem with the Scottish Economic Committee, which offered a platform for Sir James Lithgow to argue for the concentration of heavy industries in the most productive units, for the trade unions to adapt to more flexible working conditions at lower wages and for the growing pool of surplus labour to be re-engaged through industrial diversification. Lithgow was rather dismissive of new outlets in lighter industries, 'associated with articles of domestic consumption, ranging from tinned tomatoes to electric fires'.[3] The Scottish Office promoted regional assistance in 1934 and 1936 through commissioners who sought to ameliorate distress in urban areas of high unemployment rather than foster growth elsewhere. The first industrial estate in Scotland was created in Glasgow, at Hillington in 1937. Its major manufacturer was Rolls-Royce, who produced aircraft engines integral to the British drive for rearmament.

THE COMMAND ECONOMY

World War II lasted almost two years longer than World War I. In September 1939, Britain and France declared war on Germany which was joined in June 1940 by Italy, another fascist dictatorship. The British fight against the German–Italian axis was reinforced by troops from the Empire and greatly aided by Germany's decision to invade the Soviet Union in June 1941. Six months later, the Japanese attack on Pearl Harbor in Hawaii brought the United States into the War. World War II was a truly global affair fought by land, sea and air in Europe, Africa and Asia until Britain, the Soviet Union and the United States secured victory over Germany in May and Japan in August 1945.

Warfare was considerably more mechanised. Engagements were less attritional, more numerous and speedier. Conscription was introduced within months rather than after two years as in World War I. Scottish troops were heavily engaged in Northern Europe, across the Mediterranean, in the Balkans and in the Far East. Casualties among the armed services were roughly along the lines that two were killed in 1939–45 for every five in 1914–18. Scottish losses were not disproportionate as had been the case in World War I. Civilian casualties, mainly from air attacks, were four times greater in World War II. Although Aberdeen and other east coast ports were vulnerable to air raids from occupied Norway, only Clydebank in March and Greenock in May 1941 were blitz bombed.

Throughout the six years of war, merchant ships conveying supplies across the Atlantic remained vulnerable to submarines as well as to battleships. Wester Ross to Murmansk was the most punitive sea route for the convoys that ran regularly from 1941 to 1945 in Arctic waters carrying tanks, other armed vehicles, aircraft, munitions and food to sustain the Russian war effort. The British government introduced emergency measures for national service in industry, particularly munitions works, shipyards and coal mines; the latter remained the preserve of male workers. In addition to a Home Guard made up of volunteers otherwise ineligible for military service, civilians were conscripted to act as air-raid wardens, fire fighters and ambulance drivers. As in World War I, women played key supporting roles, from manning anti-aircraft guns to ferrying planes across the Atlantic. Women worked on farms and in forests. Numbers of civilian conscripts more than matched those recruited into the armed services. War involved nightly blackouts, the supply of gas-masks, the rationing of food, fuel and clothing, and the evacuation of children from major towns and cities.

Railways and transport services came under renewed government direction. Steamers returned to service as minesweepers as well as troop carriers. Much more than in World War I, Scotland was host to naval bases, airfields and army camps. Fishing boats were redeployed to sweep mines and entrap U-boats in their nets. Serving as the Shetland bus, fishing boats carried resistance fighters to and from Norway. Fighter aircraft and support planes for transatlantic convoys operated from coastal fields and seaplanes from protected beaches. The Highland and Islands were used to practise combined operations, train for mountain warfare and develop Commandos as elite and adaptable fighting units by land, sea and air. State funding duly consolidated the Highlands and Islands Medical Services, which had provided health care at minimal prices since 1913.

Wartime opportunities for economic and social development were harnessed by Scotland's outstanding Secretary of State, Tom Johnston. Appointed in February 1941, Johnston sought and was granted from Prime Minister Winston Churchill wide-ranging administrative powers that effectively created a devolved national government. Notwithstanding his radical background as a journalist and socialist who edited *Forward* for Labour from 1906 to 1933, Johnston sought to build non-partisan, consensual politics through two key agencies – a Council of State that included all living former Scottish Secretaries, regardless of party, and a Scottish Council for Industry that mobilised civic patriotism across class lines. The Council of State commissioned the Clyde Basin Scheme that made hospitals freely available to workers engaged in the war effort. The North of Scotland Hydro Board generated electricity as a public utility from the copious water supplies in the Highlands from 1943. The Council for Industry countered the excessive concentration of industry in the English Midlands by attracting over 700 businesses and 90,000 new jobs to Scotland. Johnston insisted that the Forestry Commission in Scotland was a national not a regional body. He established a separate Tourist Board for Scotland in 1945. Johnston convinced Churchill that maximum administrative devolution would head off political challenges from the SNP, who were making its presence felt in by-elections. Although it won Motherwell and Wishaw in April 1945; Dr Robert McIntyre held this seat for just three months. He lost out to Labour in its landslide victory at the general election: 40 seats won with just under 50% of the votes cast in Scotland.

Johnston had persuaded Scots across the political spectrum that the state should promote and finance economic and social development. However, the incoming Labour government, in their desire to continue the command economy, were intent on wide-ranging reforms that centralised power. Johnston left the Scottish Office, which was effectively reduced to a distinctive regional administration. Secretaries of State lobbied subsequently for higher public expenditure on areas within their administrative remit determined politically in Westminster with funding allocated from Whitehall. After Johnston, Secretaries tended to be the British government's voice in Scotland.

Britain lacked the political and financial muscle to sustain its Empire after World War II. On becoming independent in 1947, India was violently partitioned, with East and West Pakistan (later Bangladesh) hived off and vast numbers displaced. Decolonisation over the next two decades spread quickly to the Far East and more gradually through Arabia to Africa and the Caribbean. Colonial disturbances prolonged national service of two years for all men aged between 17 and 21 years from 1948 until 1963. Withdrawal from Empire had its biggest impact on Scotland in the rapid expansion of communities from India, Pakistan and Bangladesh following partition in 1947. Migrants from the subcontinent became particularly prominent in Glasgow, Edinburgh and Dundee where initial jobs in public transport and textiles became stepping stones, to the running of shops, retail and wholesale, and restaurants which spiced up the Scottish palate. Permanent settlement from elsewhere in Empire was largely confined to the Chinese from South East Asia who constituted small, but tightly knit communities of caterers. The phasing-out of Empire was anticipated by the creation of the Commonwealth in 1949, when the imperial dimension to British identity was being replaced through welfare and economic programmes designed to transform the United Kingdom.

The basis for the British welfare state was laid down in a series of enactments from 1946 to 1948. A comprehensive system of social security was backed up by supplementary benefits for the homeless, the physically handicapped and unmarried mothers. Means-tested benefits were administered centrally through the National Assistance Board. The National Health Service (NHS) offered free treatment for all at surgeries for general practice or at hospitals for remedial and palliative treatments. Funded from central taxation, the NHS led to immediate and lasting improvements in health care. Penicillin, which was not fully recognised as a lifesaving antibiotic until 1942, was now available to all because of the endeavours of Sir Alexander Fleming from Ayrshire, who had actually discovered its medical properties in 1928, when working as a bacteriologist in London. The NHS was on the defensive when food standards lapsed, such as the typhoid outbreak in Aberdeen in 1964 and later with the e-coli outbreak in South Lanarkshire in 1996 or when contaminated produce entered the food chain. The NHS has always competed with other pressing calls on funding.

The command economy in peacetime was signposted by the nationalisation of the Bank of England (1946), coal mines (1947), transport as covered by railways, shipping, bus services and long-distance road haulage (1948) and iron and steel (1949). Each nationalised agency was run by a board of governors, answerable to but independent of the British government. Only the railways had a specific Scottish division. Road haulage along with iron and steel were returned to private ownership when the Conservatives regained power in 1951. As a means to retain jobs rather than make the industry more competitive, steel was again nationalised by Labour in 1967. Initially the mines thrived under the National Coal Board, with significant investment in new pits and mechanisation making British coal the cheapest in Europe by 1957. However, the growth in cheap oil imports led to an ongoing contraction in the coal industry, despite a major strike by miners in 1972.

Public ownership and central planning did not lead to a more integrated transport system. The British Transport Company was the executive body for designated boards for means of communication. By far the most significant was that for the railway, which retained the ferry services connecting the United Kingdom to the continent as well as linking the British mainland to the offshore islands and Ireland. Ferries to the Northern Isles were not nationalised. By 1963, air transport was competing effectively on London–Scottish routes and the rise in private car ownership was affecting bus as well as rail services. Investment in track, rolling stock and signalling was no more than adequate for public safety. Reshaping British Railways concentrated on selected routes and stations to improve services and permit substantial economies. Rail services were axed in rural districts.

Shipbuilding was the only heavy industry not nationalised initially. The wartime boom in construction and refitting had continued, with an abundance of orders to revitalise trade worldwide. However, shipyards were slow to re-equip and modernise or invest in market research. Overseas competitors eroded the British share of transoceanic shipping, notwithstanding the launching of the luxury liner *Queen Elizabeth II* on the Clyde in 1967. Amalgamation reduced the Clyde yards to two divisions, upper and lower. Government failure to write off inherited debts led to the collapse of Upper Clyde Shipbuilders in 1971 despite shop stewards organising a celebrated work-in, fronted by the splendidly oratorical Jimmy Reid. Nationalisation in 1977 left only three shipyards on the river.

Rather than replicate interwar endeavours that focused on areas of industrial decline, post-war planning promoted industrial innovation on green belt sites freed up by the contraction of agriculture. Notwithstanding the ending of rationing by 1953, land under the plough retreated from wartime use as did the demand for agricultural labour. Productivity was increased by mechanisation, particularly the universal use of tractors, mainly from the United States, which worked more fertile soils intensively with hill farms given over to livestock. Inward investment from the United States funded a factory for tractors, giant bulldozers and other earth-moving machinery at Uddingston in Lanarkshire by 1956. Increased road haulage and a marked growth in private motoring led central government to encourage the respective relocation of truck and car manufacturers from the English Midlands to Bathgate in West Lothian and Linwood in Renfrewshire in 1959–60. Fuel for motor transport was an important consideration in the establishment of a petrochemical plant at Grangemouth on the Firth of Forth, the largest in Europe when it became operational in 1951. The demands of mechanisation and motor transport were less convincing reasons for the establishment in 1962 of a steel strip mill at Ravenscraig in Motherwell. Enhancing employment opportunities away from the Central Belt led to an integrated pulp and paper making facility at Corpach in Lochaber by 1966 and an aluminium works at Invergordon in Easter Ross in 1971.

Initially these developments created thousands of jobs. Ravenscraig excepted, they were dependent on inward investment, had limited facilities for research and development and managerial control was exercised externally. Only Grangemouth proved sustainable. The car and truck industries at Bathgate and Linwood were not supported locally by component suppliers as in the Midlands. Colvilles, who dominated the Scottish steel industry, were reluctant to take on Ravenscraig as there was insufficient demand from Scottish light industries and inadequate local supplies of coal. Ravenscraig was not on a coastal site to cut the costs of imported fuel. Although Corpach and Invergordon were coastal locations, they suffered from higher than antici- pated costs of raw materials. Technological investment at Corpach was ques- tionable. Without an immediate supply of hydro-power, Invergordon invested heavily in the nuclear reactor planned for Hunterston in Ayrshire, which did not become operational until 1976. Corpach and Invergordon, like the nuclear reactor built in 1962 at Dounreay in Caithness, did not come within the remit of the Highlands and Islands Development Board (HIDB), part of the regional outreach of the command economy from 1965. The HIDB facilitated mod- est repopulation by focusing on inshore fishing, fish-farming and tourism, offsetting its focus on Aviemore in Inverness-shire as a centre for seasonal skiing and year-round recreation by selective support for craft industries in dispersed locations.

The planned economy created new towns that drew labour away from the cities and areas of heavy industry. Notwithstanding the boom in construc- tion of council estates for more housing in the wake of World War II, the schemes established by city corporations in Glasgow, Edinburgh and Dundee were noted for their lack of shops, social centres and recreational facili- ties. In marked contrast, the new towns established at East Kilbride (1947), Glenrothes (1948), Cumbernauld (1956), Livingston (1962) and Irvine (1964) were complete urban entities, with centres for business and industry, educa- tion and leisure. Managed by development corporations, new towns initially prospered through light industries, such as electronics, chemicals and food processing. The Scottish Development Agency, an adjunct of the Scottish Office from 1975, marketed the new towns from Ayrshire to Fife as a Silicon Glen for the development of information technology. Heavily dependent on inward investment, Silicon Glen was primarily concerned with the manufac- ture of basic microchips and never matched the advanced research and devel- opment carried out in California's Silicon Valley. American companies making typewriters in Greenock from 1951 and cash machines and watches in Dundee from 1947 switched to produce sophisticated computers. The first auto- matic telling machine for dispensing cash from banks was created in Dundee in 1967.

New industries dependent on inward investment required workers to adapt to assembly lines for mass production. Despite higher wages and the increas- ing engagement of women in the labour force, repetitive tasks did not foster better industrial relations with American companies in particular resistant to collective bargaining by trade unions. UK access to the European Economic Community (EEC) in 1973, confirmed by a referendum in 1975, allowed Scotland to be marketed as a gateway to the continent. Despite inward investment from Japan and the Far East as well as North America, sterling was not a stable currency. Labour's decision in 1947 to let the pound sterling float against the US dollar for international exchange was reaffirmed by the Conservative government in 1958. Vulnerability to international speculation led Labour to devalue the pound in 1967. Hopes of boosting exports and cutting the cost of imports and international borrowing were unfulfilled.

British identity was revitalised by the welfare state, full employment, raised living standards, new and expanded schools and hospitals, and the building of reasonable council houses at controlled rents. Civic initiatives, parliamentary legislation and technological innovation combined to effect profound social change for the immediate post-war generation. Overcrowded tenements and cramped miners' rows were replaced by spacious council housing in most towns and villages which, like the cities, were connected to sewage mains and supplied with electricity. Hot and cold running water was further complemented by inside toilets. Children were afforded more privacy and space for personal development which led to the questioning, if not the overturning, of social conventions that had guided their parents. Council estates, other than the large sprawls devoid of facilities and services in the cities, integrated manual workers and clerical workers, shopkeepers and professionals into resilient communities. Technology, such as vacuum cleaners, washing machines and fridges, had a liberating impact on home life, freeing up time for women to secure gainful employment. The most notable domestic impact of biological sciences, the pill, enabled women to enjoy greater sexual freedom. Women's control over their own bodies and lifestyles was also facilitated by a raft of social legislation marked by the Abortion Act (1967), the Equal Pay Act (1970) and the Sex Discrimination Act (1975).[4] Protestant evangelicals and Roman Catholics remained implacably opposed to abortion on demand. The application of equal pay rarely worked to the advantage of women other than MPs or those in the professions for law, medicine and teaching and even for the Church after the Kirk of Scotland began to ordain women in 1968. Discriminating against women, especially those with families, was checked but not eradicated in the workplace. Glass ceilings for promotion were rarely shattered for women executives and managing directors.

The one specifically Scottish piece of social legislation, the Licensing Act of 1976, contributed hugely to the civilising of drinking practices in public bars, hotels and clubs. The drinking dens, which Hugh MacDiarmid had eulogised with respect to Glasgow in 1952, were dark and dingy places primarily designed for the heavy consumption of fortified wines and spirits by men. Apart from expanding opening hours to limit binge drinking, the Act sought to make pubs, not just lounge bars, attractive to women and men as places for social conviviality and leisure. Families were also attracted by the provision of wholesome food in the form of pub lunches or set dinners.

Changing social patterns did not immediately lead to altered political habits. General elections were dominated by the Labour and Conservative parties. The Scottish Unionists won 50% of the vote and half the seats in 1955. Labour dominance of Scottish electoral politics commenced in 1959 and was consolidated in 1964 when the *Daily Record* and its more reflective stablemate the *Sunday Mail*, both of which had been Conservative-inclined newspapers since the Boer War, switched sides. Labour never captured half the vote, but the party consistently won a clear majority of seats regardless of its performance elsewhere in the United Kingdom. Split between supporters of home rule and of a free state, the SNP remained on the fringes. In 1949, John McCormack launched a Covenant for a Scottish constitutional convention which gained 2 million signatures. Labour no more than the Unionists were prepared to countenance home rule. In 1950, SNP activists stirred popular sympathies with a covert mission to Westminster Abbey to liberate the Stone of Destiny, reputedly captured by Edward I at the outset of the thirteenth century. Gesture politics did not secure parliamentary seats. The SNP did not win a by-election from 1945 until 1967.

TOWARDS DEVOLUTION

Declining opportunities for gainful employment in Empire were more than compensated by public service openings for males and females in government agencies, higher education and broadcasting, which actually strengthened Scottish identification with Britain. The command economy as well as the welfare state required increased numbers of administrators. Employment in public service was on the rise, especially for men and women with a university education. The number of Scottish universities was doubled in 1967: only Stirling was an entirely new institution; Dundee, Strathclyde and Heriot-Watt were former degree-awarding colleges. Broadcasting diversified into television, which in the 1950s was no longer the monopoly of the BBC, with independent television companies conforming to a regional model funded by advertising rather than a licence fee. Nevertheless, despite the creation of Scottish, Grampian and Border television companies, the airwaves were dominated by British and American productions. The BBC developed a second television channel in 1976 without adding substantially to the quality of broadcasting from Scotland. Output on all Scottish channels switched from black and white to colour from 1978. Documentaries and current affairs were revitalised from 1979. BBC Scotland's development of Gaelic television was far more constructive than mainstream channels in exploring Scotland's engagement with Europe.

Winnie Ewing's stunning victory at the Hamilton by-election in 1967, a symptom of the profound post-war social change, instigated a lasting but not substantive presence of the SNP in the British Parliament. Notwithstanding sustained artistic support, the SNP has benefited less from cultural initiatives than from British global posturing. The international festival launched in Edinburgh in 1947 has a momentous record of achievement with respect to opera, music, dance and drama. Spin-offs range from a Fringe strong on comedy and cultural happenings to film, jazz and book festivals. Yet the Edinburgh Festival has done more to attract international performances to Scotland than to promote Scottish culture on the international stage. The determination of successive governments that Britain remained in a 'special relationship' with the United States placed Scotland, especially the Firth of Clyde, in the front line of the Cold War with the Soviet Union. The Holy Loch hosted American Polaris missiles from 1961. Fastlane naval base has been home to Britain's own intercontinental Trident weapons since 1982. The largest stock of nuclear weapons in Western Europe is stored underground in Glen Douglas, in close proximity to the main centre of the Scottish population.

In 1979, Winnie Ewing won and retained for over two decades the Highlands and Islands seat for the European Parliament, which regalvanised Scotland's connections to Europe and gave voice to the growing concerns about the marginalisation of Scottish decision making and entrepreneurship in the command economy. In the north-east especially the SNP benefited from unrest over the trading-away of fishing interests in the British negotiations for accession to the EEC in 1973. Nevertheless, the common fisheries policy did act in the interests of conservation by checking overfishing, especially of cod and white fish in the North Sea and Northern Atlantic. Fishing was forced to undergo the same process of retrenchment that had faced agriculture in the aftermath of World War II. Both industries resorted to larger working units, respectively farms and fishing boats, with a reduced workforce. The EEC revitalised farming by subsidies for food production through its common agricultural policy, albeit subsidies based on amounts of productive land favoured large grain producers over hill farmers of livestock on more marginal holdings. Despite the contraction in catches, Peterhead, Fraserburgh and Aberdeen steadily outperformed English fishing ports. Scottish fish processors benefited immensely from tariff-free access to markets in the EEC.

The discovery of oil and gas in the North Sea in 1966 that came on stream from 1972 yielded vast profits to the British government. Successive British governments initially minimised the economic benefits of oil extraction as insufficient to guarantee the prosperity of an independent Scotland and then, as more and more oil fields were opened up, exaggerated returns to drive home the case that an independent Scotland was too small to cope with the financial windfall. Oil presented a major problem for the command economy, a problem of resource management with which successive governments struggled. Priority was accorded to rapid development to counteract adverse balance of payments in international trade. Unlike Norway, which also benefited from the oil boom, efforts to create a nationalised exploration company were not sustained. Again unlike Norway, the United Kingdom did not create an investment fund to secure economic development and welfare services. By way of compensation for resource mismanagement, formulas on public expenditure were overhauled in 1978. Increased expenditure in England led to a proportionate increase in Scotland, which has kept Scottish public expenditure higher per capita than the rest of the United Kingdom.

The direct benefits from extraction of oil and gas have tended to be regional, with the Northern Isles and Aberdeenshire well placed to benefit from storage, refining and supply services. Aberdeen became the largest Scottish service port for the oil rigs and the largest helicopter base in Europe. The majority of the rigs were not built in Scotland. While many yards were constructed speculatively on coastal sites, only those at Methil in Fife and at Nigg in the Cromarty Firth have lasted. Oil and gas refining at Grangemouth became an important component of the petrochemical industry. Sophisticated plant for gas transmission, separation and refining developed at St Fergus in Aberdeenshire from 1977 was linked up with Mossmorran in Fife by 1985. That extraction was a highly dangerous process was borne out on 6 July 1988. The Piper Alpha platform, remuneratively operational since 1976, caught fire and exploded; 167 workers died.

North Sea oil and gas transformed the electoral prospects of the SNP which advanced from one MP in 1970 to seven then eleven in successive general elections in 1974. Home rule in the form of political devolution was back in vogue. With Scottish Unionists rebranded as Conservatives in 1965, their commitment did not survive their double defeat in 1974. The Labour government was prepared to countenance modest devolution to protect their electoral dominance in Scotland. However, rampant inflation was aggravating an adverse balance of trade as imports outstripped exports. With wages failing to keep pace, the government faced a winter of discontent in 1978 with pro-longed strikes among public sector workers. The fraught process of legislating for a Scottish Assembly in 1979 was effectively scuppered when the government accepted an amendment from its own benches that required 40% of all registered electors to vote yes in the forthcoming referendum.

The vote in favour of devolution was 52% to 48%. But when abstainers, the recently dead and those not registered on electoral rolls at their current address were brought into play, the 40% threshold was not met. Devolution fell, as did the Labour government. The ensuing general election impacted adversely on the SNP who were reduced to two seats. Governance passed to the Conservatives under Margaret Thatcher who, for 11 years, was relentlessly committed to a policy of reducing inflation, rolling back nationalisation, privatising public utilities, curbing the power of trade unions and breaking the post-war consensus in favour of the command economy. Deindustrialisation was accelerated and largely paid for by the revenues accruing from the North Sea. Britain was to become more competitive through market forces. Full employment was no longer a priority.

The first impact of this ideological shift was felt in the Highlands. The pulp mill at Corpach was closed in 1981, soon to be followed by the aluminium smelter at Invergordon. That same year, the car plant at Linwood shut; the truck assembly at Bathgate followed in 1983. The privatisation of shipbuilding in 1985 further reduced capacity on the Clyde and underscored dependence on naval orders. Although the workers, both men at women, staged a sit-in that lasted three months, the Caterpillar factory at Uddingston closed in 1987. The privatisation of the British Steel Corporation in 1988 paved the way for the shutting of Ravenscraig in 1992. The assault on trade unionism was initiated by a studied policy to close loss-making mines, the profitability of the coal industry in Scotland especially being undercut by cheaper imports and by oil and gas as alternative sources of energy. A poorly timed strike in 1984–5, when supplies were high and the weather clement, was crushed with conspicuous brutality on the part of the police and auxiliary troops. The BBC reprised its role in the General Strike of 1926 operating like a state broadcaster. Only two Scottish pits were still active in 1989, albeit privatisation of the coal industry was not implemented fully until 1994.

Thatcher's government privatised around 50 companies. To reduce public service borrowing and improve revenues, profitable enterprises in utilities and transport were privatised first. Shares were sold not just to private sector investors but to the public in an effort to stimulate popular capitalism, which was further promoted by sales of council houses at discount prices to their tenants. The real cost of this policy was a marked decline in social housing, the mushrooming of housing estates built by the private sector for the aspiring middle and skilled working classes and the loss of community focus and leadership in what was left of council estates. Successive victories in 1979, 1983 and 1987 testify to Thatcher's electoral appeal in the United Kingdom, but not in Scotland. Conservative seats fell from 22 to 10, while Labour remained dominant, if largely ineffectual even with 50 MPs. The SNP, riven by tensions over home rule and European engagement, never accrued more than three MPs. Alliance with the Social Democrats who had defected from Labour restored the fortunes of the Liberals as Scotland's third parliamentary party.

Thatcher's belligerence towards the miners was earlier manifest in her removal of Argentinian forces occupying the Falkland Islands in the South Atlantic. The Falklands War of 1982 reinvigorated British pretensions to be a world power, pretensions that were again evident when the prime minister enthusiastically joined the United States in the first Gulf War of 1990–1 to reclaim Kuwait from the clutches of Iraq. However, Thatcher was removed from office in the course of the war, her reputation having been tarnished severely by the introduction of the poll tax on all households, which was first tried out in 1989 in Scotland. Mass protests and non-payments were compounded by rioting after the poll tax was extended to England in 1990.

Despite a legacy of deindustrialisation and social despair, and an exponential spread of illicit drug dealing in towns and cities throughout Scotland, the Thatcher era witnessed the growth of financial services, aided by the privatisation and share selling which continued until 1997. After the deregulation of British financial markets in 1986, Edinburgh became the fourth financial centre in Europe after London, Frankfurt and Paris. Companies with global portfolios in insurance, asset management and unit trusts also operated from Perth, Aberdeen and Dundee. The 18 years of Conservative government between 1979 and 1997 witnessed a massive switch away from manufacturing industry in favour of services not just in finance, but in transport, wholesale and retail shopping, hospitality, leisure and tourism. Such a switch also indicates growing prosperity, with less of people's income being taken up by spending on food and more on consumer goods. But this was by no means an increase in living standards across the social spectrum.

In 1992, the number of Scottish universities was more than doubled, largely by upgrading technical colleges and art schools, albeit a new university for the Highlands and Islands was centred on Inverness. This huge expansion in student places complemented the move from selectivity in favour of comprehensive secondary schooling that was being accomplished as the minimum

age for leaving school was raised to 16 years in 1972 which, in tandem, led
to greater emphasis on attaining leaving certificates and progressing to higher
education for the many not the few. The new universities, which confirmed
that women were outperforming men in higher education, built on well-
established traditions of complementing studies in science with industrial
placements, of servicing North Sea oil and gas, of promoting hospitality and
tourism, and developing textile and lifestyle design. The new universities
took the lead in social media studies and digital gaming. They also offered less
credible courses in journalism with popular music and risk management for
beginners. However, graduates in all Scottish universities were not necessarily
equipped with the skills appropriate for an economy driven by technological
knowledge and financial management.

Nor was local government, which the Conservatives re-organised twice,
in 1973 and again in 1996. On both occasions, bureaucracy increased without enhancing local accountability. The regions and districts created from
the counties and burghs in 1973 were replaced 23 years later by single-tier
authorities. Only the three island authorities for Shetland, Orkney and the
Western Isles were retained. Civic authorities running local government
variously raised revenue from households through rates, poll taxes and
then community charges. However, the bulk of their funding came increasingly from central government. Accordingly, they were far more responsive
to the Scottish Office than to their electorates. Although accountable to the
British Parliament, the Scottish Office was staffed by members of the party
of government who did not necessarily hold the majority of parliamentary
seats in Scotland, as was the case with the Conservatives between 1979
and 1997. This democratic deficit became a driving force for devolution as
Conservatives disagreed on closer integration after the EEC was restructured
as the EU in 1993.

Despite the technical knockout of 1979, a campaign for a Scottish
Assembly, mounted from within the Labour Movement, attracted support from Liberal Democrats and even the SNP. This campaign was helped
subliminally by the papal visit to Scotland in 1982. John Paul II recognised
Scotland as a distinct nation, not as a British region. Eight years after its
launch, the campaign in 1988 published a Claim of Right attesting that
sovereignty lay with the Scottish people rather than the Westminster
Parliament. Historic precedents from the Declaration of Arbroath in
1320 to the original Claim of Right in 1689 glossed over the nature of
these documents in which the political elite upheld Scottish independence, not political devolution that would allow sovereignty to be retained
at Westminster. Nevertheless, the Claim laid the basis for a Scottish

Constitutional Convention that became an expression of civic patriotism, attended by politicians, trade unionists and representatives of the leading churches between 1989 and 1995. The SNP, which had been intellectually revitalised and radicalised under the vigorous leadership of Alex Salmond from 1990, withdrew its support when it became clear that independence was not on the agenda. Despite being unelected, the Convention laid the blueprint for a Scottish Parliament that was implemented by a New Labour government that swept to power in 1997, after an overwhelming victory in a general election that temporarily wiped out the Scottish Unionists as a parliamentary party.

Legislation for a Scottish Parliament was dependent on a referendum in which there were pronounced differences from that in 1979. No threshold was imposed on the number of registered electors that voted. Electors were required to vote not only for a Scottish Parliament but also for it having tax varying powers. In 1997, there was willing if not always enthusiastic collaboration between the SNP and the Labour and Liberal Democratic parties. The umbrella campaign for Yes–Yes was significantly better organised and more confident than their No–No opponents, mainly Conservatives who could draw only muted support from a business community that had been stridently hostile to devolution in 1979. The polls on 11 September were firmly in favour of Yes–Yes: almost three-quarters of electors voted for a Scottish Parliament and almost two-thirds for tax varying powers. As enacted in December, the composition of the Scottish Parliament was 129 members, 73 of which were to be elected by first past the post in constituencies and the remainder by proportional representation on regional lists, a system designed to prevent outright majorities and facilitate coalitions. In the first election for Members of the Scottish Parliament (MSPs) on 6 May 1999, Labour was returned as the largest party with 56 MSPs, the SNP were in clear second with 35. The Conservatives granted a political lifeline with 18, just outperforming the Liberal Democrats with 17. The Green Party gained one seat, their first in any representative assembly in the UK. On 12 May, Winnie Ewing recalled the Scottish Parliament. Donald Dewar, who had run the Labour campaign, was installed as First Minister of a Scottish Executive. The perceptive Scottish journalist Ian Bell commemorated the occasion's historical significance:

History is memory. The moment was memory retained, a right restated, a truth reaffirmed. The nation of Scotland, with all its thrawn suspicions, numberless confusions, apathy, clumsy rivalries and desperate hopes, had remembered.[5]

Notes

1. *A Source Book of Scottish Economic and Social History*, pp. 208–10.
2. *Scottish Population Statistics*, pp. 84–89. The Scottish population recovered from 4.8 million in 1931 to just under 5.1 million by 1951 and despite fluctuations every decade stood at almost 5.3 million in 2011.
3. *A Source Book of Scottish Economic and Social History*, pp. 101–02.
4. This legislation, which included a Race Relations Act (1967), had been subject to periodic amendment and amplification until replaced by a comprehensive Equality Act in 2010.
5. *Scotland: The Autobiography. 2,000 Years of Scottish History by Those That Saw It Happen*. Rosemary Goring, ed. (London, 2007), pp. 421–24.

7 1999–2018: The Road to Independence?

The creation of a Scottish Parliament in 1999 instigated a process of devolution that has provided an innovative measure of home rule. Devolution remains a process that is shaped as much by forces beyond as within Scotland. Labour under Prime Minister Tony Blair, educated privately in Edinburgh, established a cross-party consensus in favour of the privatisation policies initiated by Margaret Thatcher. He and his Chancellor of Exchequer, Gordon Brown from Fife, vastly extended the public finance initiative begun under the Conservatives, to construct schools, hospitals and other public buildings. Rather than charge these buildings to the public accounts, they were built and maintained by private contractors at rates of interest extortable for up to 40 years from local authorities. Unlike Thatcher, Blair and Brown made serious efforts to improve welfare services, particularly to lift children out of poverty. But like Thatcher, Blair was given to foreign adventuring. Ever in thrall to the United States, Blair committed British forces to military engagements in Kosovo (1999), in Afghanistan (2001–14) and in Iraq (2003–09), where regime change put him on the margins of international law.

Scottish financial services continued to thrive under Labour, but they became vulnerable to take-overs, especially in Edinburgh and Perth. The global financial crash of 2008 led to the subordination of Scotland's two largest banks. The Bank of Scotland, which had merged with the former Halifax Building Society in 2001, was taken over by Lloyds TSB, itself a product of a merger in 1996. The Royal Bank of Scotland, overextended by American and Dutch acquisitions, was effectively nationalised as the price of its survival. Brown, the architect of light-touch economic regulation and the running down of British gold reserves as chancellor, took prompt action as prime minister to mitigate recession and maintain a measure of global security by printing money. The Conservative–Liberal Democrat coalition that came to power in 2010 enthusiastically promoted austerity.

Devolution accorded only limited economic levers to the Scottish Executive. Yet the Scottish Parliament has been proactive in legislating to improve lifestyles. Under successive Labour–Liberal Democratic coalitions until 2007, the Parliament abolished feudalism, opened up access in the countryside and instigated land reform to benefit crofters and tenant-farmers. Parliament promoted the Gaelic language and revitalised the Tourist Board as Visit Scotland. It commenced free home care for the elderly, banned smoking other than as an outdoor activity and liberalised the licensing laws. However, successive coalitions under Donald Dewar, Henry McLeish and Jack McConnell were viewed increasingly as too deferential to direction from London.

Although Scottish seats were reduced from 72 to 59 in 2003, Labour had continued as the dominant party during British general elections until 2010. The growing impression that Labour voters were prepared to switch in elections to the Scottish Parliament was proved in May 2007. The SNP gained 47 seats, a narrow majority of one over Labour. Alex Salmond formed a minority government. The Scottish Executive was renamed the Scottish Government. St Andrew's Day on 30 November became an optional public holiday. A dramatic break with British and American interests was marked in 2009 by the compassionate release from prison of the Lockerbie bomber, Abdelbaset al-Megrahi from Libya, the only man convicted for blowing up a transatlantic aeroplane over Dumfriesshire in 1988. The legislative programme until 2014 was also more radical, especially in setting ambitious targets for climate change. Flood risk management was stepped up. Prescription charges on medicines were removed. Free bus passes were introduced for the elderly and disabled. Fees for students in higher education were scrapped as were all tolls on bridges. Major infrastructure projects were implemented – the Queensferry Crossing bridging the Firth of Forth, the Borders Railway and the Aberdeen Western Peripheral Route.

Salmond and his fellow members of government had extensive work experience outside of the public sector as economists, entrepreneurs, film producers, lawyers and financiers. They were not designer politicians as full-time party activists, researchers or local councillors since leaving higher education. When the SNP won the election to the Scottish Parliament in May 2011, with an outright majority with 69 seats, the course was set for a referendum on whether or not Scotland should be an independent country. Salmond had built up SNP support by appealing directly to Catholics of Irish extraction, to migrant communities from the Indian subcontinent, to business people and to women, groups hitherto distrustful of a free state. Enabling legislation passed in both the British and Scottish Parliaments prevented the result being contested in the courts. The age for voting, determined by residence not nationality, was reduced from 18 to 16 years.

The SNP were at the forefront of the Yes campaign which galvanised support through community hall meetings usually in association with groups such as socialists, women, business, academics, lawyers, nuclear disarmers and New Scots (migrants) for Independence. The British and Scottish press was uniformly hostile to Independence until the *Sunday Herald*, launched in anticipation of devolution in February 1999, declared its support in May 2014. The BBC reverted to operating like a state broadcaster. The Yes case was promoted energetically through social media, digital newspapers and magazines – *Wings over Scotland* being among the more statistically sound. The economic case for Independence rested as much on renewable energy from wind and waves as on North Sea oil and gas, on the food and drink industry including whisky, and on tourism, the creative arts, financial services, life sciences and digital technology. The political case advocated a better governed Scotland with communities regenerated through the pursuit of social justice, the removal of huge disparities in wealth and the eradication of weapons of mass destruction. The Yes cause attracted the young and the middle-aged and many established migrants from England to East Asia.

The No cause, a cross-party alliance which subsequently damaged Labour for its willing association with the austerity-driven Conservatives, competed on social media, but preferred individual canvassing and private phone calls to spread its self-confessed project fear. Scotland was too poor, too small and insufficiently adept to accomplish Independence. This negative message, endorsed by company directors, financial managers and leading trade unionists, found a ready reception from pensioners, former members of the armed services, migrant communities from Eastern Europe and from right-wing factions from the Orange Order to the Scottish Defence League. The more lavishly funded No campaign was able to exploit significant questions about Scotland's economic prospects, the extent of its dependence on oil revenues, its future constitutional status in the EU, the security of its pensions and welfare services and its currency arrangements.

On 18 September 2014, the No campaign won by 55% to 45%. This decisive result was aided by a late intervention from Gordon Brown, headlined in the *Daily Record* with a much trumpeted but nebulous vow, subscribed by the British leaders of the three unionist parties, to grant further tax and welfare powers to Scotland if Independence was rejected. With the vote lost, Alex Salmond stood down as first minister. By taking his country to the brink of Independence, he stands with Tom Johnston as the most able Scottish politician of the modern era. Salmond was replaced by Nicola Sturgeon, under whom the SNP regained its political momentum in the British general election in 2015, winning not so much by a landslide as a tsunami, returning 56 MPs with over 50% of the vote, leaving the three unionist parties with one seat apiece. Momentum was retained at the Scottish Parliamentary elections in May 2016. The SNP remained the largest party, although it lost its over-all majority by two seats. However, the Conservatives, who were freed from coalition shackles by the general election of 2015, were committed to another referendum on British engagement with the EU. In 2016, in a campaign long in assertion and short in accuracy, issues of immigration, Britain's place in the world and redirected funding for the NHS dominated. The United Kingdom voted to exit from the EU. The narrow victory for Brexit, 52% for leave to 48% for remain, was not replicated in Scotland where all 32 electoral districts voted to remain, which won decisively by 62% to 38%. Manifestly, a less densely populated Scotland was more appreciative of migrant contributions to eco-nomic vitality as to health and welfare services. Scotland also had centuries' more experience than England of not being the dominant partner in a political union and had grasped broader opportunities for scientific, cultural and voca-tional collaboration within the EU.

Neither the British government that had promoted remain nor those mem-bers who advocated leave were actually prepared for Brexit. Following the inevitable resignations and reshuffle, the Conservative government served notice in March 2017 that the United Kingdom would quit the EU in two years, albeit a transition period was subsequently negotiated for Brexit to be implemented by December 2020. Conservative attempts to secure a strong and stable hand in negotiations with the EU backfired when they lost their overall majority at the general election in June. Propped up by the Democratic Unionists of Northern Ireland, the most socially regressive and politically intransigent party in the United Kingdom, the Conservatives have made no attempt to negotiate Brexit by parliamentary consensus. Nor have negotia-tions with the EU at Brussels been marked by British coherence. Agreement in principle has been reached on harmonising citizens' rights in the United Kingdom and the EU, on a frictionless border between Northern Ireland and the Irish Republic, which remains in the EU, and on the United Kingdom initi-ating separate trade deals elsewhere in the world during the transition period.

However, the determination of Brexit supporters and the Conservative government to bring back controls over laws, finances and borders from the EU has a domestic resonance not particularly favourable for Scotland. Conservative determination to strengthen the internal British common market has led to a claw back of powers over agriculture, fisheries, environ-mental policy, public procurements and food standards which would normally be the preserve of devolved administrations in Cardiff and Belfast as well as Edinburgh. While these powers are expected to be retained temporarily, they are integral to the renegotiation of trade deals elsewhere in the world, deals in which current EU standards for work and welfare can be compromised.

In taking back these powers, the Conservatives have promised to consult with the devolved administrations. But they have not their consent. Figures released by the Scottish government and confirmed by the British government demonstrate convincingly that even if the United Kingdom were to remain in the EU as an associate member, the economic consequences of staying in the single market would be damaging, of staying in the customs union more damaging and of leaving with or without a negotiated deal most damaging. Even if the United Kingdom negotiated a bespoke deal, the EU will not consent to this being better than existing arrangements. The real prospect now opens up for supporters of Independence to argue that autonomous membership of the EU would make Scotland more prosperous.

Nevertheless, there is no ready correlation between remain voters in 2016 and Yes voters in 2014. This was borne out in the general election of 2017 when the SNP remained Scotland's largest party in the British Parliament with 35 seats, but lost 21 seats to the unionists with the Conservatives the principal gainers from a public reluctant to rush into another referendum. The SNP face further challenges to its plans to rerun a second Independence referendum, for which consent will almost certainly be withheld by the British government especially as prospects for a No vote are less assured than in 2014. The next elections to the Scottish Parliament in 2021 do not guarantee that the SNP and the Greens can retain their majority for Independence.

The SNP domestic record is open to challenge. New powers conceded in the wake of the 2014 referendum, which have come into play in 2018, have been used progressively with respect to income tax and compassionately with regards to welfare. The SNP record on social justice remains impressive for the promotion of gender equality, the mitigation of austerity for the disadvantaged and closing the attainment gap in education between children from poor and affluent families. But the SNP in government has been markedly timid in terms of land reform, especially on secure leases for tenant-farmers and community buy-outs of underused resources in urban areas. Its economic record is far from impressive, with the abandonment of Salmond's single unified approach to the economy, designed to ensure that Scotland eventually outperformed the rest of the United Kingdom. There is a proliferation of competing strategies, advisory boards, statutory bodies and discussion forums. This lack of scientific and commercial co-ordination is particularly lamentable in relation to maritime developments, from extracting seaweed for industrial lubricants to constructing windmills and other devices for renewable energy and to containing destructive dredging for shellfish.

The positive appeal of the EU, already tarnished for radicals by its imposition of austerity measures on Greece in the wake of the financial crash of

2008, has been further compromised for nationalists by its failure to condemn the excesses of the Spanish government in opposing the drive for Catalan independence in 2017, when voting stations were stormed, voters brutalised and punitive jail sentences imposed on leaders of the Catalan government.

Yet the Yes campaign remains resurgent. Grass-roots activists are creating hubs for debate and discussion, for producing pamphlets and posters and for planning demonstrations not just to bolster the cause of Independence, but to win over former No voters. To this end, the Common Weal, the foremost pro-Independence think tank, formulates policies not only to address the perceived weaknesses of the 2014 campaign, but to lay pathways for a progressive, prosperous and inclusive Scotland. *The National*, launched in November 2014 as a daily complement to the *Sunday Herald*, encourages Scots to consider themselves as living purposefully and constructively in an independent country, a necessary prerequisite to becoming independent. Nevertheless, opposition from unionists remains formidable across the mainstream media, from opaque campaign funding by affluent British diehards and on the streets from racists and sectarian bigots. The road to Independence is by no means a foregone conclusion.

Select Bibliography

GENERAL

Acts of the Parliament of Scotland, Thomas Thomson & Cosmo C. Innes (eds). 12 vols (Edinburgh, 1814–72); electronically as www.rps.ac.uk *RPS: Records of the Parliaments of Scotland to 1707*, Keith M. Brown, Alastair J. Mann & Roland J. Tanner (eds).

A Source Book of Scottish History, William C. Dickinson, Gordon Donaldson & Isobel A. Millne (eds). 3 vols (Edinburgh, 1952–61).

Broun, Dauvit., Richard Finlay & Michael Lynch (eds). *Image and Identity: The Making and Remaking of Scotland through the Ages* (Edinburgh, 1998).

Devine, Thomas M. *The Scottish Nation, 1700–2000* (London, 1999).

Early Sources of Scottish History, AD 500 to 1286, Alan O. Anderson (ed.). 2 vols (Edinburgh, 1922).

Edinburgh History of Scotland:

Duncan, Archibald A.A.M. *Scotland: The Making of the Kingdom* (Edinburgh, 1978).

Nicholson, Ranald. *Scotland: The Later Middle Ages* (Edinburgh, 1978).

Donaldson, Gordon. *Scotland: James V – James VII* (Edinburgh, 1978).

Ferguson, William. *Scotland: 1689 to the Present* (Edinburgh, 1978).

Foster, Sally, Allan I. Macinnes & Ranald MacInnes (eds). *Scottish Power Centres from the Early Middle Ages to the Twentieth Century* (Glasgow, 1998).

Glendinning, Miles, Ranald MacInnes & Aonghus Mackechnie (eds). *A History of Scottish Architecture from the Renaissance to the Present Day* (Edinburgh, 1996).

Goring, Rosemary (ed.). *Scotland: The Autobiography. 2,000 Years of Scottish History by Those Who Saw It Happen* (London, 2007).

Smout, T. C.:

A History of the Scottish People, 1560–1830 (Edinburgh, 1969).

A Century of the Scottish People, 1830–1950 (London, 1986).

Source Book of Scottish Economic and Social History, R.H. Campbell & J.B.A. Dow (eds). (Oxford, 1968).

CHAPTER 1

Broun, Dauvit. *Scottish Independence and the Idea of Britain: From the Picts to Alexander III* (Edinburgh, 2007).

Crawford, Barbara E. (ed.). *Scandinavian Settlement in Northern Britain* (London, 1995).

Forte, Angelo, Richard Oram & Frederik Pedersen. *Viking Empires* (Cambridge, 2005).
Foster, Sally. *Picts, Gaels and Scots* (Edinburgh, 2014).
Fraser, James E. *From Caledonia to Pictland: Scotland to 795* (Edinburgh, 2009).
Oram, Richard. *Domination and Lordship in Scotland 1070–1230* (Edinburgh, 2011).
Reynolds, Susan. *Fiefs and Vassals: The Medieval Evidence Reinterpreted* (Oxford, 1994).
Ross, Alasdair. *The Kings of Alba c.1000–c.1130* (Edinburgh, 2011).
Taylor, Alice. *The Shape of the State in Medieval Scotland, 1124–1290* (Oxford, 2016).
Taylor, Simon (ed.). *Kings, Clerics and Chronicles in Scotland, 500–1297* (Dublin, 2000).
Woolf, Alex. *From Pictland to Alba (789–1070)* (Edinburgh, 2007).

CHAPTER 2

Barrell, Andrew D.M. *Medieval Scotland* (Cambridge, 2000).
Barrow, Geoffrey W.S.:
   Kingship and Unity: Scotland 1000–1306 (London, 1981, revised 2003).
   Robert the Bruce and the Community of the Realm of Scotland (Edinburgh, 1988).
Boardman, Stephen. *The Early Stewart Kings: Robert II and Robert III, 1371–1406* (East Linton, 1996).
Boardman, Steve & Andrew Ross (eds). *The Exercise of Power in Medieval Scotland* (Dublin, 2003).
Broun, Dauvit. *The Irish Identity of the Kingdom of the Scots in the Twelfth and Thirteenth Centuries* (Woodbridge, 1999).
Brown, Michael. *The Wars of Scotland 1214–1371* (Edinburgh, 2004).
Cowan, Edward J. *'For Freedom Alone': The declaration of Arbroath, 1320* (East Linton, 2000).
MacDonald, Alastair J. *Border Bloodshed: Scotland, England and France at War 1369–1405* (East Linton, 2000).
Macdougall, Norman. *An Antidote to the English: The Auld Alliance, 1295–1560* (East Linton, 2001).
Penman, Michael. *The Scottish Civil War: The Bruces and the Balliols and the war for control of Scotland* (Stroud, 2002).
Stevenson, Katie. *Power and Propaganda: Scotland 1306–1488* (Edinburgh, 2014).

CHAPTER 3

Boardman, Steve & Julian Goodare (eds). *Kings, Lords and Men in Scotland and Britain 1300–1625* (Edinburgh, 2014).
Brown, Keith M.

Noble Society in Scotland: Wealth, Family and Culture, from Reformation to Revolution (Edinburgh, 2004).

Noble Power in Scotland from the Reformation to the Revolution (Edinburgh, 2011).

Cathcart, Alison. *Kinship and Clientage: Highland Clanship 1451–1609* (Leiden & Boston, 2006).

Dawson, Jane E. *Scotland Re-formed 1488–1587* (Edinburgh, 2007).

Ditchburn, David. *Scotland and Europe: The Medieval Kingdom and its Contacts with Christendom, c.1215–1545* (East Linton, 2000).

Dodgshon, Robert A. *Land and Society in Early Scotland* (Oxford, 1981).

Fitch, Audrey-Beth. *The Search for Salvation: Lay Faith in Scotland, 1480–1560* (Edinburgh, 2009).

Kirk, James (ed.), *Humanism and Reform: The Church in Europe, England and Scotland 1400–1642* (Oxford, 1991).

Mason, Roger A. *Kingship and the Commonweal: Political Thought in Renaissance and Reformation Scotland* (East Linton, 1998).

Murdoch, Steve. *The Terror of the Seas: Scottish Maritime Warfare, 1513–1713* (Leiden & Boston, 2010).

Wormald, Jenny. *Court, Kirk and Community: Scotland 1470–1625* (London, 1981).

CHAPTER 4

Devine, Thomas M. & John R. Young (eds). *Eighteenth Century Scotland: New Perspectives* (East Linton, 1999).

Harris, Tim. *Rebellion, Charles II and His Kingdoms* (London, 2005).

Livesey, James. *Civil Society and Empire: Ireland and Scotland in the Eighteen-Century Atlantic World* (New Haven, CT & London, 2009).

Macinnes, Allan I.:
  Clanship, Commerce and the House of Stuart, 1603–1788 (East Linton, 1996).
  Union and Empire: The Making of the United Kingdom in 1707 (Cambridge, 2007).

Mijers, Esther. *'News from the Republick of Letters'. Scottish Students, Charles Mackie and the United Provinces, 1650–1750* (Leiden & Boston, 2012).

Murdoch, Steve. *Network North: Scottish Kin, Commercial and Covert Associations in Northern Europe, 1603–1746* (Leiden & Boston, 2006).

Pincus, Steve. *1688: The First Modern Revolution* (New Haven, CT & London, 2009).

Stephen, Jeffrey. *Defending the Revolution: The Church of Scotland 1689–1716* (Farnham, 2013).

Szechi, Daniel. *1715: The Great Jacobite Rebellion* (New Haven, CT & London, 2006).

Whatley, Christopher A. *The Scots and the Union* (Edinburgh, 2007).

Young, John R. *The Scottish Parliament 1639–1661: A Political and Constitutional Analysis* (Edinburgh, 1996).

CHAPTER 5

Barclay, Katie. *Love, Intimacy and Power: Marriage and Patriarchy in Scotland, 1650–1850* (Manchester, 2011).

Brown, Callum G. *Religion and Society in Scotland since 1707* (Edinburgh, 1997).

Checkland, S.G. *Scottish Banking: A History 1695–1973* (Glasgow & London, 1975).

Devine, Thomas M. (ed.). *Recovering Scotland's Slavery Past: The Caribbean Connection* (Edinburgh, 2015).

Dunyach, Jean-François & Ann Thomson (eds). *The Enlightenment in Scotland: National and International Perspectives* (Oxford, 2015).

Macinnes, Allan I. & Douglas J. Hamilton (eds). *Jacobitism, Enlightenment and Empire, 1680–1720* (London, 2014).

McCaffrey, John F. *Scotland in the Nineteenth Century* (Basingstoke, 1998).

McIllvanney, Liam. *Burns the Radical: Poetry and Politics in Late Eighteenth-Century Scotland* (East Linton, 2002).

Pentland, Gordon N. *Radicalism, Reform and National Identity in Scotland, 1820–1833* (Woodbridge, 2008).

People and Society in Scotland

Devine, Thomas M. & Rosalind Mitchison (eds). *Volume I, 1760–1830* (Edinburgh, 1988).

Fraser, Hamish & R.J. Morris (eds). *Volume II, 1830–1914* (Edinburgh, 1990).

Whatley, Christopher A. *Scottish Society 1701–1830: Beyond Jacobitism, towards Industrialisation* (Manchester & New York, 2000).

CHAPTER 6

Cameron, Ewen A. *Impaled upon a Thistle: Scotland since 1880* (Edinburgh, 2010).

Devine, Thomas M., Clive Lee & George Peden (eds). *The Transformation of Scotland: The Economy since 1700* (Edinburgh, 2005).

Durie, Alastair. *Scotland for the Holidays: Tourism in Scotland c.1780–1939* (East Linton, 2003).

Finlay, Richard J. *Modern Scotland: 1914–2000* (London, 2004).

Harvie, Christopher, *No Gods and Precious Few Heroes: Twentieth-Century Scotland* (Edinburgh, 1998).

Knox, William. *Industrial Nation: Work, Culture and Society in Scotland, 1800–Present* (Edinburgh, 1999).

Lee, Clive. *Scotland and the United Kingdom: The Economy and the Union in the Twentieth Century* (Manchester, 1995).

Macdonald, Catriona M.M. *Whaur Extremes Meet: Scotland's Twentieth Century* (Edinburgh, 2009).

MacPhail, I.M.M. *The Crofters' War* (Stornoway, 1989).

Payne, Peter. *Growth and Contraction: Scottish Industry c.1860–1990* (Dundee, 1992).

Phillips, Jim. *The Industrial Politics of Devolution: Scotland in the 1960s* and 1970s (Manchester, 2008).

CHAPTER 7

Evans, Geoffrey & Anand Menon. *Brexit and British Politics* (Cambridge, 2017).

Keating, Michael. *The Independence of Scotland* (Oxford, 1999).

Mitchell, James. *Devolution in the UK* (Manchester, 2009).

Appendix: Scottish Kindreds

Clan/Family Name	Origins	Locations
Armstrong	Celtic	Angus & Borders
Balliol	Anglo-Norman	Galloway, Ayr & Lothians
Barclay	Anglo-Norman	Kirkcudbright, Aberdeen & Fife
Bruce	Anglo-Norman	Annandale & Carrick
Buchanan	Celtic	Lennox & Trossachs
Burnett	Anglo-Norman	Roxburgh & Deeside
Cameron	Anglo-Norman	Fife, Perth & Lochaber
Campbell	Britons	Lennox, Argyll & Ayr
Chattan/Cattenach	Celtic	Caithness, Inverness, Banff, Aberdeen
Chisholms	Anglian	Borders, Perth & Strathglass
Colquhoun	Anglo-Norman	Lennox
Colville	Anglo-Norman	Roxburgh, Ayr & Stirling
Cumming/Comyn	Anglo-Norman	Buchan, Inverness, Perth & Galloway
Cunningham	Anglo-Norman	Ayr
Dempster	Celtic	Perth & Angus
Douglas	Flemish	Lanark, Lothians, Borders & Angus
Drummond	Britons	Lennox, Menteith & Strathearn
Duff/MacDuff	Celtic	Fife
Elphinstone	Celtic	Garioch, Stirling & Lothians
Forbes	Celtic	Strathdon & Buchan
Fraser	Anglo-Norman	Borders, Lothians, Aberdeen & Stratherrick
Gordon	Anglian	Borders, Galloway, Aberdeen & Sutherland
Graham	Anglo-Norman	Lothians, Borders & Strathearn
Grant	Anglo-Norman	Strathspey, Glenurquhart & Glenmoriston

Gunn	Norse	Caithness
Hamilton	Anglians	Lothians, Lanark & Renfrew
Hay	Anglo-Norman	Perth, Aberdeen, Lothians & Borders
Keith	Celtic	Banff & Lothians
Kennedy	Gaelic	Carrick & Galloway
Kerr	Ayr	Borders
Lamont	Norse-Gael	Cowal
Leslie	Celtic	Garioch, Perth & Fife
Lindsay	Anglo-Norman	Borders, Ayr, Lanark & Lothians
Lockhart	Flemish	Ayr & Lanark
Lumsden	Anglo-Norman	Berwick, Fife & Aberdeen
MacArthur	Britons	Lennox, Argyll
MacBrayne	Norse-Gaels	Outer Hebrides
MacDonald	Norse-Gaels	Kintyre, Lochaber, Skye & Western Isles
MacDougall	Norse-Gael	Argyll & Inner Hebrides
MacEwen	Gaelic	Argyll
MacFarlane	Britons	Lennox
MacGregor	Gaelic	Breadalbane
MacInnes	Gaelic	Argyll
Mackay	Norse-Gael	Kintyre & Islay
Mackay	Celtic	Moray & Sutherland
MacKenzie	Celtic	Ross
Mackinnon	Gaelic	Mull & Skye
Mackintosh	Celtic	Fife & Badenoch
Maclachlan	Norse-Gael	Cowal
Maclean	Celtic	Perth, Morvern, & Mull
Maclellan	Celtic	Easter Ross
Maclennan	Celtic	Galloway
MacLeod	Norse-Gael	Skye, Raasay, Lewis & Harris
MacLey (Livingstone)	Gaelic	Cowal
Macmillan	Celtic	Moray & Argyll
MacNab	Gaelic	Lochtayside
MacNaughton	Celtic	Moray & Argyll
MacNeill	Norse-Gael	Knapdale & Barra
Macpherson	Celtic	Badenoch & Lochaber
MacSween	Norse-Gael	Knapdale
Mactaggart	Gaelic	Ross

MacTavish	Britons	Lennox, Argyll
Maxwell	Anglian	Borders, Nithsdale & Galloway
Menzies	Anglo-Norman	Borders, Dumfries, Breadalbane & Aberdeen
Moncrieff	Celtic	Tayside
Montgomerie	Anglo-Norman	Renfrew & Ayr
Morrison	Norse-Gaels	Lewis
Munro	Celtic	Easter Ross
Murray	Flemish	Lanark, Moray, Strathnaver & Strathearn
Ogilvie	Celtic	Angus, Aberdeen & Banff
Ramsay	Anglo-Norman	Lothians, Angus and Banff
Robertson	Celtic	Atholl, Inverness & Aberdeen
Ross	Celtic	Easter Ross
Ross	Anglo-Norman	Inverness, Renfrew & Ayr
Sinclair	Anglo-Norman	Lothians, Orkney & Caithness
Stewart	Anglo-Norman/Breton	Renfrew, Ayr, Bute & Argyll
Wallace	Britons	Ayr & Renfrew
Wauchope	Anglo-Norman	Dumfries, Aberdeen & Lothians

Index